# THE BOOK OF LIFE

# Madonna and Child

By Murillo, Bartolomé Estéban (1617-1682)
In the Prado Gallery, Madrid, Spain

MURILLO, known as Spain's greatest religious painter, could rise to heights of mystical religious feeling, of high imaginative power, when he wished to present Mary in full consciousness of the grandeur of her destiny. At other times, as in the present picture, he excelled in presenting her as a living everyday person, just as she may have lived and worked in the modest home of Joseph, the carpenter.

Perhaps these simple scenes of mother and child filled with the warmth and comfort of maternal affection and security may have had a special beauty and meaning to Murillo. As an orphaned boy he had known hardship and poverty. He had eked out an existence doing menial tasks in the art studio. He had "hawked" his paintings in the noisy, squalid street-fairs of Seville. Alone and on foot he had made a 250 mile journey over the mountains to Madrid, to find the painter Velasquez and fame. During such a life he must often have dreamed of a haven of maternal peace and loving protection, such as he pictures here.

Here we see Mary painted as a comely, dark-haired matron. The beautiful dark eyes, the finely modelled nose and mouth, give her a pensive, shy expression, as of one whose thoughts are turned inward on her own reflections. The Child has alertness and vitality. His eyes look directly at us, and he shows curiosity about the outside world. By this skilfull variety of expression and rich coloring Murillo gives life to the repose of the composition.

More of Murillo's pictures are in this volume on pages 242 and 254 and in Volume I.

# THE
# BOOK OF LIFE

ARRANGED AND EDITED BY

## NEWTON MARSHALL HALL, A.M., D.D.

PASTOR AND CHRISTIAN EDUCATOR
AUTHOR OF CIVIC RIGHTEOUSNESS AND CIVIC PRIDE

AND

## IRVING FRANCIS WOOD, PH.D., D.D.

PROFESSOR OF RELIGION AND BIBLE
AUTHOR OF THE SPIRIT OF GOD IN BIBLICAL LITERATURE

JOINT AUTHORS OF THE BIBLE STORY,
EARLY DAYS OF ISRAEL, DAYS OF THE KINGS OF ISRAEL,
ADULT BIBLE CLASSES AND HOW TO TEACH THEM

---

VOLUME SIX

## LIFE OF THE MASTER

---

## JOHN RUDIN & COMPANY INC.

CHICAGO

TWENTY-FIRST EDITION
Copyright 1953

PRINTED IN THE U.S.A.

THE ENTRANCE OF THY WORD GIVETH LIGHT

This edition of THE BOOK OF LIFE is presented to:

_____

From: _____

Date: _____

# PREFACE

HE Old Testament is of profound value, but the life of the Saviour of Men is the culmination of prophecy, the flower of God's long preparation of his people, through their failures and repentance. Every part of the Bible is inspired; the life of Jesus is the supreme inspiration. "In him was life and the life was the light of men." And Isaiah of old prophesied, "they that dwell in the land of the shadow of death, upon them hath the light shined." In this volume, the life of Jesus is given in a continuous narrative in which the Gospels of Matthew, Mark, and Luke are combined—a life of Jesus without repetitions and as far as possible in chronological order. The Book of John which contains so much material not found in the other three—a beautiful poem in itself, is given entire.

The Gospel of John is not only distinctive in the fact that it contains much material not found in the other three Gospel narratives, but also in the manner in which it sets forth the deity of Christ. Throughout the Gospels of Matthew, Mark, and Luke, Jesus is presented as the unique personality of history—as the divine Son of God, as well as the man of Galilee. The fuller and more comprehensive revelations concerning the deity of Christ and of his eternal unity with the Father are found in the Gospel of John.

The beginnings of the Christian Church recorded in the earlier chapters of the Book of Acts are naturally included in this volume.

PRIMITIVE PLOWING

*Photograph by Publishers Photo Service*

"Hearken! Behold, there went out a sower to sow: . . . And some fell on stony ground, where it had not much earth; . . . because it had no root, it withered away." See Mark 4, pages 102-4. Sixty parables of Jesus are listed in Volume VIII, page 468.

# CONTENTS

# HYMNS AND POEMS

# Madonna and Child

By Carlo Dolci (1616-1686)
In the Vatican Gallery of Ancient Art, Rome, Italy
Color Photograph by Alinari Brothers, Florence

IN this picture a sweet Madonna looks upon the sleeping child Jesus. The delicate refinement of the mother is shown in her face and hands. She is clothed in the traditional red robe and blue mantle. Do you remember what these colors signify? (See Volume VIII page 117.) A halo of golden light, symbol of divinity, encircles each head. The whole picture expresses soft and tranquil devotion.

The work of the artist, Carlo Dolci, was characterized by the delicacy and tenderness which we notice here. Dolci was particularly noted for the painstaking, highly-polished finish he gave to his paintings. He always painted devout subjects, generally in small size, and was a prolific artist. He was born in Florence in 1616 and died there in 1686. Hence he belongs to the late Florentine school, and was the last of that school in style and taste as well as in point of time. In Italian art he is a minor painter, as are most Italian artists who come after the sixteenth century.

If we compare Dolci with High Renaissance painters such as Andrea del Sarto (page 89), Titian (page 190), or Raphael (page 246), we will see that artistic tastes had changed radically by Dolci's time. Instead of del Sarto's balanced dignity, Titian's refined gravity or Raphael's elevated grandeur, we have here a less remote art characterized by attractive grace of form and display of emotion. This tendency toward the popular and sentimental in painting appeared also in the sculpture and architecture of the seventeenth century and in the social and religious attitudes. We see by our picture that Dolci was a true son of his time and place.

Paintings by other artists of this period are on pages 22, 44, 238 and 328. Do you find similarities in their work?

# The Story of the Master

## From the Gospels of Matthew, Mark, and Luke

THIS is the story of the greatest One who ever lived, the gentlest, the most self-sacrificing—the world's Saviour. He was born in a manger in the little town of Bethlehem in the hills of Judea. All the Christian world celebrates his birthday.

More books, many times over, have been written about Jesus than about any of the world's greatest heroes. People never tire of hearing the story told—

"Tell me the old, old story,
    Of unseen things above,
    Of Jesus and His glory
    Of Jesus and His love."

The world is realizing more and more that life is at its best when it is lived most closely in accordance with his teachings and spirit. Human life fails when it fails to look unto Him.

FOUR BIBLE NAMES

*Photograph by Frances Jenkins Olcott*

This lovely lake, shaped like a harp, is mentioned in the Bible under four names—in Moses' time it was called the Sea of Chinnereth; in Jesus' day, the Sea of Tiberias, the Lake of Gennesaret, and the Sea of Galilee, which we Christians love, because we think of him living on its shores.

The Sea of Galilee is 682 feet below sea level in the Jordan gorge. It is 13½ miles long and 7½ miles wide. At its deepest it is 160 feet. In row boats and small ships with sail, the Galilee fishermen net its fish, as did the disciples long ago.

# The Nazarene

Painted in 1932 by Henry Stanley Todd (1871-1941)
In The Boulevard Christian Church, Miami, Florida

"We ought to form the habit of looking
at a good picture every day."—Goethe

IN our appreciation of a great painting, we sooner or
later turn from the study of the canvas to the personality and background of the artist, to his ideals and
motives, and the story behind the creation of his
masterpiece.

Henry Stanley Todd, a distinguished American portrait painter who conceived and painted The Nazarene,
was born in St. Louis, Missouri. He studied painting
under leading masters in the United States and Europe.
His artistic genius and skill as a portrait painter were
soon recognized and won for him fame and success
both at home and abroad. Among some of his best
known portraits of Americans are Frances Willard,
President William McKinley and President Theodore
Roosevelt.

In his moving story, "Why I Painted Christ"
Mr. Todd tells us that the memory of a mother's
prayer filled his mind from his early youth with the
deep desire to "paint for all to see, a symbol of the
living God who gave His all for me . . . ."

The Nazarene has been acclaimed both in the United
States and Europe as a veritable masterpiece. This
beloved picture of Jesus came into national prominence
in 1933 at the Century of Progress, World's Fair,
Chicago, where the original was exhibited for several
months in the Hall of Religion.

"A Face of wondrous loveliness
With speaking eyes of sky-touched blue
Sweetness and light are in that Face."

For the privilege of sharing this Triumphant Christ
with the readers of *The Book of Life* we are deeply
indebted to the gracious generosity of the owner,
Mr. William P. Thurston of Richmond, Virginia.

# The Story of the Master

### From the Gospels of Matthew, Mark and Luke

## The Good Tidings

THE most precious books in the world are the four accounts of the life of Jesus which we call the Gospels. At first, it would not occur to any of the disciples, probably, to write a "Life of Jesus." Thousands of people had seen him. They remembered what he said. They remembered how he looked. In those days of few books, the memory was wonderfully cultivated. In the schools of that time the pupils must remember every word of the teacher. There were many, doubtless, who could repeat accurately, not only much of the Old Testament, but much also of the Rabbinic comments upon it, known as "The Talmud."

The disciples were busy, at first, in the absorbing task of winning converts to the new faith, "The Way," as it was called, by personal persuasion, by word of mouth. It is quite certain that there began to be little written collections of the sayings of Jesus before the Gospels were actually written. It was the general belief, also, in the early years of the church that the second coming of Christ would take place in that age, so that there would be no need of written documents.

As time went on, as those who had seen Jesus passed on, as the gospel spread to more distant lands, among an ever widening circle of people who had not only not seen Jesus, but who had only the vaguest idea of the land in which he lived, the demand for an authentic record of the life of the Master became insistent. To meet this need of the churches, of men and women and little children who longed to know about Jesus and to know what he said, the four beautiful stories of his life came into existence.

We may imagine the joy with which these accounts were received by the Christians of Ephesus, of Corinth, of Rome, in latter days by the people in Gaul and Spain and the far away island of Britain. We will suppose that one of these churches has met in secret to welcome a Christian brother from Philippi. He rises and says, "I have here a papyrus roll which contains an account of the life of our Master written by Brother Luke, the good physician, who was here with Paul in the days before the persecution, when Peter and Paul were yet with us." We may imagine the joy, the eagerness, with which the wonderful story would be received. How the children would love the story of the little child who was born in the manger of Bethlehem, and of sweet Mary, his mother! How glad they would be to know that Jesus loved the little children and took them, for so the Greek word means, "in the crook of his arm"! For the first time, those matchless stories of Jesus' love for lost humanity, for the sinner and the suffering, the parable of the Good Samaritan and the parable of the Prodigal Son could be read and treasured. Think what these stories would mean to the poor Christians of Rome,—laborers, slaves, hunted now and persecuted by the Roman government.

This precious manuscript would be copied and passed on from hand to hand, from church to church, throughout the empire. These books are familiar now. They have been copied millions of times by pen and by the printing-press, but they are just as precious as they were on the day when Luke and the other evangelists took their pens

# The Child John the Baptist

By Bernardino Luini (c.1475-c.1533)
In the Gallery Ambrosiana, Milan, Italy
Photograph by Anderson, Rome

THIS exquisite picture shows the infant John the Baptist embracing a lamb. The lamb is a symbolic allusion to the fact that John hailed Jesus as the Lamb of God. It is interesting to compare this with Murillo's painting on page 242.

We glimpse here the ideal character of the boy set apart from all others by his constant association with the Divine Child. We love him because he was the playmate of the infant Saviour, the constant friend of the Redeemer, and the divinely-appointed instrument of the inauguration of Christ's work on earth. John was beheaded at the age of thirty-three by order of Herod Antipas, the same Herod before whom Jesus was brought some six months later.

Scarcely a painter or sculptor of religious subjects, of whatever nationality, has failed to produce one or more renderings of the fascinating themes suggested by the life of John the Baptist. Among those who have been most successful in portraying the young child John, Bernardino Luini stands high as we may see by this sweet picture. Is not this curly-headed boy most exquisitely childlike as he presses his head against the lamb's and, in his baby way, almost strangles it with too much affection?

This is a fresco, which means a picture painted on freshly-spread wet plaster, a method of painting which Luini mastered and preferred to either tempera or oil. This picture is now very much damaged and faded, but it is still full of beautiful meaning and splendid genius.

You will find other paintings by Luini on pages 12 and 268, and in Volume VIII, page 338.

and wrote on papyrus the story of Jesus. They are still the words of life; they still have power to inform and redeem the world. They ought to fill the Christians of to-day with the same joy which was felt by the first readers in the far-off beginnings of Christian faith.

The Gospel of Matthew was written on the basis of the recollections of Matthew, the publican. The other Gospels were written by Luke, the good physician, John, the fisherman, and Mark, that young man whose mother, a friend of Jesus, lived at Jerusalem. It has been conjectured that the last supper was held at her house and that she sent the young man, Mark, to warn Jesus of the coming betrayal. The Gospel of Mark says that a "certain young man followed with him," and that he too fled with the rest, when Jesus was left alone in the garden. This young man was Mark himself. All the writers probably knew of early collections of the sayings of Jesus.

The Gospels agree in all essential particulars. Each contains material not given by the others in a remarkable way. Each has its own characteristic style and emphasis. "Matthew" contains the remembrances of the publican who was called by Jesus from the custom-house at Capernaum. It emphasizes, perhaps, the Jewish side of Jesus' ministry, the fulfillment of the long hope of the nation for a Messiah. It is businesslike, straightforward in its treatment. The Gospel of Mark, it is believed, is based upon the testimony of Peter. It is brief, vivid, direct in its treatment. It might almost be called the Gospel of Peter. We feel that the modest author is effacing himself in order to get perfectly into the spirit of the great apostle who saw and heard the things which he relates. The Gospel of Luke was addressed specifically to a friend, Theophilus, a Greek. Luke, the physician, was a man of education and culture, who writes in a charming style and tells many of the most beautiful parables which the other Gospels omit,—the parable of the Good Samaritan (How that would interest a doctor like Luke!), the parable of the Prodigal Son, the lost coin, and others. John, the fisherman-poet, one of the supreme geniuses of any age, tells in a narrative which is like a great poem, or a superb piece of music, his impressions of Jesus. It is written, some believe, near the close of his long life of nearly a century. His majestic theme is the living Christ for the world,—"Lo! I am with you always even unto the end of the world." He tells us of Jesus, the Good Shepherd, who gives his life for the sheep,—of the truth which makes us free; and he gives in great detail that dramatic scene at the last supper and the words which the Master spoke.

In this volume the three Gospels of Matthew, Mark, and Luke are woven together in one consecutive narrative. The story marches on without any halt or repetition or omission. You may read here in a continuous and consecutive narrative the life of Jesus as written by these three great authors. Because the Gospel of John is so different, because it is such a marvelous interpretation of the spirit of the Master, the recollections and experiences of the disciple "whom Jesus loved," it is given by itself.

Each of the gospel writers of the character, life, ministry, death, resurrection and ascension of our Lord Jesus, in which they incorporated much of His teachings, was moved by the Holy Spirit. Christ himself assured His followers that the Holy Spirit would "bring all things to your remembrance, whatsoever I have said unto you." What Matthew, Mark, Luke and John wrote is, therefore, "the power of God unto salvation to every one that believeth."

# Mary and Jesus With Elizabeth and John

Attributed to Bernardino Luini (c.1475-c.1533)
In the Galleria Colonna, Rome, Italy
Photograph by Anderson, Rome

WE have here another lovely representation of the Holy Family. The Madonna holds the infant Jesus who bends forward to embrace the kneeling child John. Behind John is his mother Elizabeth.

Do you feel the sadness of the two mothers, as if they could not keep from their thoughts the knowledge of the suffering which is to come? Yet they appear sustained and comforted by an inner strength. A quietness of devotion pervades the scene.

The artist Luini worked in Milan when the influence of the great master, Leonardo da Vinci, was uppermost. Leonardo had seen that the painting of his times lacked expressiveness, especially significant human expression. His instinctive understanding and penetrating observation of people taught him that the quality of the human mind and spirit was often revealed in the features and movements of a person. He then demonstrated by his own paintings, particularly The Last Supper and the Mona Lisa, that character could be caught by the painter's brush. Through this discovery of Leonardo's an immense fund of completely new expression was added to art. All serious artists then living in Milan were influenced. Luini's work reflects this especially in his facial types.

Very little exact information is known about the life of Bernardino Luini. It is supposed that he was born in Luino, Italy, on Lake Maggiore, because of the way he signed his pictures. ("Of Luino" becomes, "Luini" in Italian.) He worked in and around Milan and is believed to have died at Lugano. Judging from the numerous paintings which have come down to us he must have been a very busy and popular artist. Luini's pictures show that he was an original and sincere artist and a man of deep religious feeling. For other of his works see pages 8 and 268.

# The Story of the Master
From the Gospels of Matthew, Mark and Luke

## The Child of Bethlehem

Forasmuch as many have taken in hand to set forth in order a declaration of those things which are most surely believed among us, even as they delivered them unto us, which from the beginning were eyewitnesses, and ministers of the word; it seemed good to me also, having had perfect understanding of all things from the very first, to write unto thee, in order, most excellent Theophilus, that thou mightest know the certainty of those things, wherein thou hast been instructed.  — Luke 1:1-4

### THE ANGEL OF THE LORD APPEARS TO HIS SERVANT IN THE TEMPLE

#### WAITING IN THE SILENCE OF THE HILLS

The coming of the child who is to be the forerunner of Jesus, the great prophet of repentance and righteousness, John the Baptist, is announced to Zacharias and Elisabeth.

THERE was in the days of Herod, the King of Judæa, a certain priest named Zacharias, of the course of Abia: and his wife was of the daughters of Aaron, and her name was Elisabeth. And they were both righteous before God, walking in all the commandments and ordinances of the Lord blameless. And they had no child, and they both were now well stricken in years.

13

And it came to pass, that while he executed the priest's office before God in the order of his course, according to the custom of the priest's office, his lot was to burn incense when he went into the temple of the Lord. And the whole multitude of the people were praying without at the time of incense. And there appeared unto him an angel of the Lord standing on the right side of the altar of incense. And when Zacharias saw him, he was troubled, and fear fell upon him.

But the angel said unto him, "Fear not, Zacharias: for thy prayer is heard; and thy wife Elisabeth shall bear thee a son, and thou shalt call his name John. And thou shalt have joy and gladness; and many shall rejoice at his birth. For he shall be great in the sight of the Lord, and shall drink neither wine nor strong drink; and he shall be filled with the Holy Ghost, and many of the children of Israel shall he turn to the Lord their God.

And he shall go before him in the spirit and power of Elias, to turn the hearts of the fathers to the children, and the disobedient to the wisdom of the just; to make ready a people prepared for the Lord."

And Zacharias said unto the angel, "Whereby shall I know this; for I am an old man, and my wife well stricken in years?"

And the angel answering said unto him, "I am Gabriel, that stand in the presence of God; and am sent to speak unto thee, and to shew thee these glad tidings. And, behold, thou shalt be dumb, and not able to speak, until the day that these things shall be performed, because thou believest not my words, which shall be fulfilled in their season."

And the people waited for Zacharias, and marveled that he tarried so long in the temple. And when he came out, he could not speak unto them: and they perceived

# The Annunciation, Dated 1486

By Carlo Crivelli (c.1440-c.1493)
In the National Gallery, London, England

THIS very elaborate picture was painted for the Church of The Annunciation in Ascoli, Italy. Mary, a very sweet and girlish figure, is reading at a desk. A celestial beam passes through the little window and descends in the form of a dove upon her head. In the street are two kneeling figures. The one carrying the lily is the announcing angel. He is accompanied by the youthful Bishop Emidius of Ascoli who carries a model of the Italian hill town with its tall towers.

Mary's surroundings are those of a richly decorated Italian house of the Renaissance. In the well-ordered room household furnishings are seen and on the shelf are candlesticks, plates and books. On the balcony above stands a gorgeous peacock and an oriental rug hangs over the parapet. Notice also the bird-cage, the parrot and the potted plant, as well as the beautiful carved ornamentation everywhere.

The street scene is that of an Italian city in the fifteenth century. Various figures are to be seen in the street and neighboring houses. A little child looks around the corner of a balustrade. Only one figure seems to see anything unusual. He shades his eyes as he catches a glimpse of the light which streams down from the sky.

The artist has signed and dated this picture on the columns of the door. "Opus Caroli Crivelli, Veneti" means "The work of Carlo Crivelli of Venice." The date is 1486. The words at the bottom of the picture, "Libertas Ecclesiastica," mean "Independence under the Church." This refers to the charter given the town of Ascoli by the Pope in 1482.

Carlo Crivelli almost always introduces fruit into his pictures. Here we see an apple and a cucumber lying in the foreground.

# The Annunciation

By Sandro Botticelli, Alessandro Filipepi (c. 1444-1510)
In the Uffizi Gallery, Florence, Italy
Color Photograph by Alinari Brothers, Florence

THIS beautiful representation of the Annunciation
shows the angel Gabriel bringing to Mary God's
message that she, "blessed among women," is to be
the mother of the Saviour. With what mingled awe
and humility the Virgin perceives the heavenly visitor,
and with what eagerness the angel comes bearing the
lily of purity. This lovely Bible story begins on page 17.

In the painting Mary is represented as not yet quite
risen from the desk at which she has been kneeling, as
she turns towards the angel. An open book lies upon
the lectern which is partially seen on the extreme right.
The angel has just alighted, his raiment still caught
by the air as he kneels to the Virgin and stretches forth
his hand in a gesture of greeting and reassurance.
Behind the figure of the angel a doorway opens upon a
delicate landscape. Is not this picture a beautiful conception of the scene, both in feeling and in treatment?

This picture, dating from about 1490, is an altarpiece painted originally for the chapel of the Guardi
family in the Church of the Cestello at Florence.
Alessandro Filipepi, called Sandro Botticelli, was a
Florentine who worked during the lifetime of Lorenzo
de'Medici, scholarly ruler, and Savonarola, Dominican
preacher and reformer of Florence. Botticelli's art shows
a sensitive fusion of these two influences, the literary
and the religious, resulting in an exquisite poetry of
feeling. More about this unusual artist is given in
Volume I, page 275.

Compare this Annunciation with those by Botticelli's
contemporaries, Carlo Crivelli, the Venetian painter
(page 16), Melozzo da Forli (page 283), and Verrocchio
and Leonardo (Volume VIII, page 1).

that he had seen a vision in the temple; for he beckoned unto them, and remained speechless.

And it came to pass, that, as soon as the days of his ministration were accomplished, he departed to his own house. And after those days his wife Elisabeth hid herself five months, saying,

"Thus hath the Lord dealt with me in the days wherein he looked on me, to take away my reproach among men." — Luke 1:5-25.

## THE ANNUNCIATION TO MARY

The coming of Jesus who is to be the Messiah, the Saviour of the world, is foretold to Mary. The announcement to Mary, the sweet maiden of Bethlehem, has been made the subject of some of the most beautiful pictures of Christian art.

And in the sixth month the angel Gabriel was sent from God unto a city of Galilee, named Nazareth, to a virgin espoused to a man whose name was Joseph, of the house of David; and the virgin's name was Mary.

And the angel came in unto her, and said, "Hail, thou that art highly favoured, the Lord is with thee: blessed art thou among women."

And when she saw him, she was troubled at his saying, and cast in her mind what manner of salutation this should be.

And the angel said unto her, "Fear not, Mary: for thou hast found favour with God. And, behold, thou shalt bring forth a son, and shalt call his name JESUS. He shall be great, and shall be called the Son of the Highest: and the LORD God shall give unto him the throne of his father David: and he shall reign over the house of Jacob forever; and of his kingdom there shall be no end."

Then said Mary unto the angel, "How shall this be, seeing I know not a man?

And the angel answered and said unto her, "The Holy Ghost shall come upon thee, and the power of the Highest shall overshadow thee: therefore also that holy thing which shall be born of thee shall be called the Son of God. And, behold, thy cousin Elisabeth, shall have a son in her old age. For with God nothing shall be impossible."

And Mary said, "Behold the handmaid of the LORD; be it unto me according to thy word." And the angel departed from her. — Luke 1:26–38.

## MARY'S VISIT TO HER COUSIN ELISABETH IN THE HILL COUNTRY OF JUDA

The inspired words uttered by Mary resemble one of the great Psalms. This song has always been called "The Magnificat."

And Mary arose in those days, and went into the hill country with haste, into a city of Juda; and entered into the house of Zacharias, and saluted Elisabeth.

And it came to pass, that, when Elisabeth heard the salutation of Mary, Elisabeth was filled with the Holy Ghost.

And she spake out with a loud voice, and said, "Blessed art thou among women. And whence is this to me, that the mother of my Lord should come to me? For, lo, as soon as the voice of thy salutation sounded in mine ears, the babe leaped in my womb for joy. And blessed is she that believed: for there shall be a performance of those things which were told her from the LORD. — Luke 1:39–45.

## THE MAGNIFICAT

And Mary said, "My soul doth magnify the LORD, And my spirit hath rejoiced in God my Saviour. For he hath regarded the low estate of his handmaiden:

CHURCH OF THE NATIVITY
*Photograph by W. A. Pottenger
expressly for The Book of Life*

The altar is over the star which is said to mark the exact spot where Jesus was born.

INTERIOR OF THE CHURCH OF THE NATIVITY
*Photograph by Professor Lewis Bayles Paton*

This fine church is built over the spot where it is believed Jesus was born. It is one of the oldest Christian churches in the world, having been built by the Empress Helena in 330 A.D.

For, behold, from henceforth all generations shall call
   me blessed.
For he that is mighty hath done to me great things;
And holy is his name.
And his mercy is on them that fear him
From generation to generation.
He hath showed strength with his arm;
He hath scattered the proud in the imagination of their
   hearts.
He hath put down the mighty from their seats,
And exalted them of low degree.
He hath filled the hungry with good things;
And the rich he hath sent empty away.
He hath holpen his servant Israel,
In remembrance of his mercy;
As he spake to our fathers,
To Abraham, and to his seed forever.''

And Mary abode with her about three months, and
returned to her own house.            — Luke 1:46–56.

### "His Name Shall Be Called John"

Now Elisabeth brought forth a son.  And her neighbours and her cousins heard how the LORD had showed
great mercy upon her; and they rejoiced with her.

And it came to pass, that on the eighth day they came
to circumcise the child; and they called him Zacharias,
after the name of his father.   And his mother answered
and said, "Not so; but he shall be called John."

And they said unto her, "There is none of thy kindred
that is called by this name."

And they made signs to his father, how he would have
him called.  And he asked for a writing table, and wrote,
saying, "His name is John."  And they marveled all.

# Adoration of the Shepherds

By Charles LeBrun (1619-1690)
In the Louvre, Paris, France

THIS painting is based on Luke's beautiful account of the birth of Jesus which begins on page 27. The painter has taken the artistic liberty of having many others besides the "multitude of the heavenly host" assist the shepherds in their adoration of the Holy Child. In the center, Mary sits with the Infant cradled on her knee, looking upward in reverent exaltation, while, in the shadows behind her, Joseph stands adoring.

The light of the central fire reveals the encircling worshipers, human and celestial. The boldest of the shepherds, awed yet irresistibly attracted, crawls forward on hands and knees. The others are content to gaze reverently upon mother and Child. Angels, some represented merely by baby heads with wings, some carrying musical instruments, others bearing a long, ribbon-like streamer, add a joyous activity and a suggestion of music as they float in on wing and cloud.

Do you find it difficult to reconcile the beautiful simplicity of the Bible story with the studied grandeur of this scene? Compare the quieter, simpler paintings by Murillo, LeBrun's Spanish contemporary, and those by Couse, an American of our own times (See Volume I, pages 254, 184). Still, don't you think that the feeling of joyful exuberance expressed here is appropriate to the sacred occasion of Jesus' birth?

Charles LeBrun, son of a sculptor, began his artistic training before he was eleven and at fifteen painted several remarkable pictures for Richelieu. In 1662 he became "premier Peintre" to art-loving Louis XIV, and from then until his death, LeBrun's—and the King's—taste for extreme grandeur dominated all artistic productions in France. LeBrun is best known for his immense decorations, particularly those in the Palace of Versailles depicting the life of the "Grand Monarch."

And his mouth was opened immediately, and his tongue loosed, and he spake, and praised God. And fear came on all that dwelt round about them: and all these sayings were noised abroad throughout all the hill country of Judæa. And all they that heard them laid them up in their hearts, saying, "What manner of child shall this be!" And the hand of the LORD was with him.

And his father Zacharias was filled with the Holy Ghost, and prophesied, saying,

"Blessed be the LORD God of Israel;
  For he hath visited and redeemed his people,
  And hath raised up an horn of salvation for us
  In the house of his servant David;
  As he spake by the mouth of his holy prophets, which
    have been since the world began:
  That we should be saved from our enemies, and from
    the hand of all that hate us;
  To perform the mercy promised to our fathers, and to
    remember his holy covenant;
  The oath which he sware to our father Abraham
  That he would grant unto us, that we being delivered
    out of the hand of our enemies
  Might serve him without fear,
  In holiness and righteousness before him, all the days
    of our life.
  And thou, child, shalt be called the prophet of the
    Highest:
  For thou shalt go before the face of the LORD to prepare
    his ways;
  To give knowledge of salvation unto his people by the
    remission of their sins,
  Through the tender mercy of our God;
  Whereby the dayspring from on high hath visited us,

To give light to them that sit in darkness and in the
  shadow of death,
To guide our feet into the way of peace."

And the child grew, and waxed strong in spirit, and
was in the deserts till the day of his showing unto Israel.
— Luke 1:57–80.

## MARY AND JOSEPH GO UP TO BETHLEHEM

### THERE IS NO ROOM FOR THEM IN THE INN
### JESUS IS BORN IN THE MANGER

The sweetest story of all the ages is told simply and beautifully
in the Gospels. No other subject has been so often treated in literature and art. Christmas Day is the day of the little child, of innocence,
of affection; and all the world loves it.

"O little town of Bethlehem!
  How still we see thee lie,
Above thy deep and dreamless sleep,
  The silent stars go by;
Yet in thy dark streets shineth
  The everlasting Light;
The hopes and fears of all the years,
  Are met in thee to-night.

For Christ is born of Mary,
  And gathered all above,
While mortals sleep the angels keep
  Their watch of wondering love.
O morning stars together
  Proclaim the holy birth!
And praises sing to God the King,
  And peace to men on earth.

How silently, how silently,
  The wondrous gift is given;
So God imparts to human hearts
  The blessings of His heaven,

# Madonna and Child

By Borgognone (Ambrogio Fassano, c.1450-1523)
In the Brera Gallery, Milan, Italy
Photograph by Anderson, Rome

OF all the many themes suggested to artists by the pages of our Bible, that of the Mother and Child is loved best by all the world. A glance through these volumes will reveal how the skill and artistry of many generations were drawn to this appealing subject again and again.

In this delightful painting the gentle Mary and the sleeping baby Jesus win our sympathies at once. With what tenderness the young mother pauses to adore the chubby, sleeping Infant before covering him with a veil! The quiet intimacy of the whole representation and the sweet but real pathos of the Madonna add much to the charm and spirituality of the picture.

Here the Madonna, with the Child pillowed on her knee, is seated in a curtained room before a bench on which are placed a book and an apple. The book symbolizes the Gospel and the apple the redemption of man from his fall. Mary's robe is edged with a rich brocade and a similar decoration appears on the curtain. Jesus is lying on her lap, his head resting on a delicately embroidered pillow. Through an open window we see two monks seated under a tree by a lake. In the distance are boats and an island with a castle or monastery on it. How well this quiet scene emphasizes the mood of the young Mother and Child!

This picture is from the hand of a North Italy painter of the Renaissance named Ambrogio Fassano and called Borgognone. This master worked in Milan and was one of the chief artists of the local school there prior to the arrival of Leonardo da Vinci from Florence in 1482. Borgognone's work is characterized by a charming intimacy and idealism, a wonderful gift for color, and beautiful execution.

No ear may hear His coming,
But in this world of sin,
Where meek souls will receive Him still,
The dear Christ enters in.

O holy Child of Bethlehem!
Descend to us, we pray,
Cast out our sin and enter in,
Be born in us to-day.
We hear the Christmas angels,
The great glad tidings tell,
O, come to us, abide with us,
Our Lord Immanuel!"

— *Phillips Brooks.*

And it came to pass in those days, that there went out a decree from Cæsar Augustus that all the world should be taxed. (And this taxing was first made when Cyrenius was governor of Syria.) And all went to be taxed, every one into his own city. And Joseph also went up from Galilee, out of the city of Nazareth, into Judæa, unto the city of David, which is called Bethlehem; (because he was of the house and lineage of David:) to be taxed with Mary his espoused wife, and so it was, that, while they were there, the days were accomplished that she should be delivered. And she brought forth her first-born son, and wrapped him in swaddling clothes, and laid him in a manger; because there was no room for them in the inn.

And there were in the same country shepherds abiding in the field, keeping watch over their flock by night. And, lo, the angel of the LORD came upon them, and the glory of the LORD shone round about them: and they were sore afraid.

And the angel said unto them, "Fear not: for, behold, I bring you good tidings of great joy, which shall be to all people. For unto you is born this day in the city of David a Saviour, which is Christ the Lord. And this shall be a sign unto you; ye shall find the babe wrapped in swaddling clothes, lying in a manger."

And suddenly there was with the angel a multitude of the heavenly host praising God, and saying,

"Glory to God in the highest,
And on earth peace, good will toward men."

And it came to pass, as the angels were gone away from them into heaven, the shepherds said one to another, "Let us now go even unto Bethlehem, and see this thing which is come to pass, which the LORD hath made known unto us."

And they came with haste, and found Mary, and Joseph, and the babe lying in a manger. And when they had seen it, they made known abroad the saying which was told them concerning this child. And all they that heard it wondered at those things which were told them by the shepherds. But Mary kept all these things, and pondered them in her heart. And the shepherds returned, glorifying and praising God for all the things that they had heard and seen, as it was told unto them. — Luke 2:1-20.

THE WELL OF THE STAR

*Photograph by W. A. Pottenger expressly for The Book of Life*

In the foreground is the Well of the Star, as it is some times called. There is a tradition that the Wise Men on the way to Bethlehem saw the star reflected in the water of this well. The picture might also be called "The Old and New in Palestine." The man on the donkey and his companion might belong to Jacob's day while in the middle of the road stands a young soldier of the present time.

## His Name Was Called Jesus

And when eight days were accomplished for the circumcising of the child, his name was called JESUS, which was so named of the angel before he was conceived in the womb. And when the days of her purification according to the law of Moses were accomplished, they brought him to Jerusalem, to present him to the Lord; and to offer a sacrifice according to that which is said in the law of the Lord, a pair of turtledoves, or two young pigeons.

—Luke 2:21, 22, 24.

## Simeon and Anna Prophesy

And, behold, there was a man in Jerusalem, whose name was Simeon; and the same man was just and devout, waiting for the consolation of Israel: and the Holy Ghost was upon him. And it was revealed unto him by the Holy Ghost, that he should not see death, before he had seen the Lord's Christ. And he came by the Spirit into the temple: and when the parents brought in the child Jesus, to do for him after the custom of the law, then took he him up in his arms, and blessed God, and said, "Lord, now lettest thou thy servant depart in peace, according to thy word: for mine eyes have seen thy salvation, which thou hast prepared before the face of all people; a light to lighten the Gentiles, and the glory of thy people Israel."

And Joseph and his mother marvelled at those things which were spoken of him. And Simeon blessed them, and said unto Mary his mother, "Behold, this child is set for the fall and rising again of many in Israel; and for a sign which shall be spoken against; (yea, a sword shall pierce through thy own soul also,) that the thoughts of many hearts may be revealed."

And there was one Anna, a prophetess, the daughter of Phanuel, of the tribe of Aser: she was of a great age, and had lived with an husband seven years from her virginity; and she was a widow of about fourscore and four years, which departed not from the temple, but served God with fastings and prayers night and day. And she coming in that instant gave thanks likewise unto the Lord, and spake of him to all them that looked for redemption in Jerusalem.

And when they had performed all things according to the law of the Lord, they returned into Galilee, to their own city Nazareth.                    —Luke 2:25–39.

ARABS ON THE WAY
TO BETHLEHEM

*Photograph by W. A. Pottenger expressly for The Book of Life*

These are the Arabs of the better class, "dressed up" for the Christmas Eve celebration at Bethlehem. The woman wears the peculiar head dress of the women of Nazareth. She carries her shoes in her hand until she reaches the town. An elderly woman who lived in New England used to tell her children how she carried her precious shoes in her hand to save the wear as she walked down the mountain road, to church. Just before she reached the church she put her shoes on.

## The Coming of the Wise Men

The Wise Men from the East with their stately camels, following the star, bringing gifts to the infant Jesus, have always made their strong appeal to the imagination. Tradition has given their names as Balthasar, Gaspar and Melchior.

Now when Jesus was born in Bethlehem of Judæa in the days of Herod, the king, behold, there came wise men from the east to Jerusalem, saying, "Where is he that is born King of the Jews? For we have seen his star in the east, and are come to worship him."

When Herod, the king, had heard these things, he was troubled, and all Jerusalem with him. And when he had gathered all the chief priests and scribes of the people together, he demanded of them where Christ should be born.

And they said unto him, "In Bethlehem of Judæa: for thus it is written by the prophet, 'And thou Bethlehem, in the land of Juda, art not the least among the princes of Juda: for out of thee shall come a Governor, that shall rule my people Israel.'"

Then Herod, when he had privily called the wise men, enquired of them diligently what time the star appeared. And he sent them to Bethlehem, and said, "Go and search diligently for the young child; and when ye have found him, bring me word again, that I may come and worship him also."

When they had heard the king, they departed; and, lo, the star, which they saw in the east, went before them, till it came and stood over where the young child was. When they saw the star, they rejoiced with exceeding great joy. And when they were come into the house, they saw the young child with Mary, his mother, and fell down, and worshiped him: and when they had opened their treasures, they presented unto him gifts; gold, and frankincense, and myrrh. And being warned of God in a dream that they should not return to Herod, they departed into their own country another way.

—Matthew 2:1–12.

### The Flight into Egypt

And when they were departed, behold, the angel of the LORD appeareth to Joseph in a dream, saying, "Arise, and take the young child and his mother, and flee into Egypt, and be thou there until I bring thee word: for Herod will seek the young child to destroy him."

When he arose, he took the young child and his mother by night, and departed into Egypt: and was there until the death of Herod: that it might be fulfilled which was spoken of the LORD by the prophet, saying, "Out of Egypt have I called my son."

— Matthew 2:13–15.

### The Slaughter of the Children at Bethlehem

Then Herod, when he saw that he was mocked of the wise men, was exceeding wroth, and sent forth, and slew all the children that were in Bethlehem, and in all the coasts thereof, from two years old and under, according to the time which he had diligently enquired of the wise men. Then was fulfilled that which was spoken by Jeremy the prophet, saying,

"In Rama was there a voice heard,
Lamentation, and weeping, and great mourning,
Rachel weeping for her children
And would not be comforted, because they are not."

But when Herod was dead, behold, an angel of the LORD appeareth in a dream to Joseph in Egypt, saying, "Arise, and take the young child and his mother, and go into the land of Israel: for they are dead which sought the young child's life."

## The Three Wise Men

"Now when Jesus was born in Bethlehem of Judea in the days of Herod the king, behold, there came wise men from the east to Jerusalem,

"Saying, 'Where is he that is born King of the Jews? For we have seen his star in the east, and are come to worship him.'" —

Matthew 2:1, 2.

BETHLEHEM  AT  SUNSET

*Photograph by W. A. Pottenger expressly for The Book of Life*

This beautiful picture of the little hill town of Bethlehem shows the country as it must have looked when Mary and Joseph came wearily up the road only to find that there was "no room for them at the inn."

CHRISTMAS  EVE  AT  BETHLEHEM

*Photograph by W. A. Pottenger expressly for The Book of Life*

Pilgrims flock to Bethlehem on Christmas eve for the service in the Church of the Nativity. The picture shows a religious procession coming down the street.

And he arose, and took the young child and his mother, and came into the land of Israel. But when he heard that Archelaus did reign in Judæa in the room of his father Herod, he was afraid to go thither: notwithstanding, being warned of God in a dream, he turned aside into the parts of Galilee. —Matthew 2:16–22.

### The Home at Nazareth

And he came and dwelt in a city called Nazareth: that it might be fulfilled which was spoken by the prophets, "He shall be called a Nazarene."

And the child grew, and waxed strong in spirit, filled with wisdom: and the grace of God was upon him.
— Matthew 2:23; Luke 2:40.

### The First Visit to Jerusalem

Now his parents went to Jerusalem every year at the feast of the passover. And when he was twelve years old, they went up to Jerusalem after the custom of the feast. And when they had fulfilled the days, as they returned, the child Jesus tarried behind in Jerusalem; and Joseph and his mother knew not of it. But they, supposing him to have been in the company, went a day's journey; and they sought him among their kinsfolk and acquaintance. And when they found him not, they turned back again to Jerusalem, seeking him.

And it came to pass, that after three days they found him in the temple, sitting in the midst of the doctors, both hearing them, and asking them questions. And all that heard him were astonished at his understanding and answers. And when they saw him, they were amazed: and his mother said unto him, "Son, why hast thou thus dealt with us? Behold, thy father and I have sought thee sorrowing."

# The Flight Into Egypt

By Giotto di Bondone (1266-1336)
In the Chapel of the Arena, Padua, Italy
Photograph by Alinari Brothers, Florence

THIS picture by Giotto shows the flight into Egypt. The Bible story may be found on page 32 in this Volume.

Here we see Mary and the Infant Jesus mounted on an ass being urged and pushed along by Joseph and attendants. An angel directs them. Note the sense of strain and hurry.

To us Giotto's painting may seem crude, the figures too stiff. But to the people of Giotto's day here was the first convincingly real portrayal of actual living things that they had seen in painting. To understand this we should remember that before Giotto, most trained Italian artists worked in the Byzantine style. A good example of this style is the twelfth century mosaic artist's version of Joseph's Dream and the flight into Egypt in Volume VIII, on page 116. Notice how flat and conventionalized the figures are and how unemotional. This Byzantine art had great decorative refinement but little human feeling. It was Giotto who saw that an entirely new way of painting things was needed if Italian art was to live in the minds and hearts of men. He decided to go directly to nature and paint from what he saw about him, and thus in his pictures of sacred history and of legend he taught himself how to render living things and human emotion.

When we remember that in those days the great mass of the people had no books and could not read, and that these mural paintings in the churches were their Bibles, we can better realize how much this new, living representation of their favorite stories must have meant to them. Here was an art full of noble persons they could both revere and love. No wonder the people of Giotto's time thought there was magic in his brush.

NEARER VIEW OF NAZARETH

*Photograph by W. A. Pottenger expressly for The Book of Life*

Jesus was familiar with every aspect of the village. During all his life up to the days of his ministry he knew no other home.

"Is not this the carpenter, the son of Mary, the brother of James, and Joses, and of Juda, and Simon? and are not his sisters here with us?" And they were offended at him."—*Mark 6:3.*

NAZARETH LOOKING NORTHEAST

Nazareth has a beautiful situation in a hollow of the hill which Jesus must often have climbed for the glorious views. From the references in the gospel we may be sure that Jesus loved the hills and the fields, the birds and the beasts.

He must have known every person in the little town, and the children must have come to see him in the old carpenter shop.

And he said unto them, "How is it that ye sought me? Wist ye not that I must be about my Father's business?"

And they understood not the saying which he spake unto them. —Luke 2:41–50.

### How the Boy Jesus Grew at Nazareth

And he went down with them, and came to Nazareth, and was subject unto them: but his mother kept all these sayings in her heart.

And Jesus increased in wisdom and stature, and in favour with God and man. —Luke 2:51, 52.

CHILDREN OF NAZARETH
*Photograph by C. H. Crathern, Jr.*

These two little boys and the girl, who seems to be a mother to the baby who is so bundled up that you can hardly see it, seem poor, and yet not unhappy. If you look closely you will see that some child has been drawing pictures on the old wooden door.

## THE CARPENTER SHOP AT NAZARETH

By Sir John Everett Millais (1829–1896)
In the National (Tate) Gallery, London

IN THIS beautiful symbolic picture the boy Jesus has hurt his hand, a nail has pierced it. Notice how tender is the interest of the father and the mother and the others. An older boy, a little apprentice perhaps, is bringing a bowl of water. Notice all the details: the tools, the planks in the outer room, the half finished basket, the dove on the ladder, the sheep in the fold outside, the shavings on the floor. Perhaps Jesus remembered how tender was his mother's kiss, when he came to heal the hurts of the people in other days, and perhaps Mary remembered it when the hands of Jesus were pierced at the crucifixion.

# The Story of the Master
## From the Gospels of Matthew, Mark and Luke

## Jesus, the Carpenter of Nazareth

From the time Jesus returned with his parents after the visit to the Temple to the beginning of his active ministry, there is nothing told of his life in the New Testament. This was a period of eighteen years, the most important and formative of a young man's life. The Gospel says that "he increased in wisdom and stature and in favor with God and man." We may suppose that after a few years Joseph died and Jesus was left to support the family. Perhaps he succeeded Joseph as the village carpenter.

People would have come to him to make tables and stools, ox-yokes, wooden plows, and all articles of wood such as are even now used in Eastern villages. They must have loved to come, to linger for a while, to talk with the strong, young carpenter with the grave, pleasant face. We may be sure that the children loved to come, to play with blocks on the floor. When work was done, he would take them in his arms and tell them stories. He always loved children and they always loved him. When, later, he blessed them in his ministry, the Greek word which is used really means, "He took them in the crook of his arm." What a pleasant picture we may draw of Jesus in the old carpenter-shop at Nazareth, a little child in the "crook of his arm," others at his knee and about his feet, as he tells them perhaps of the boy Moses, or Samuel whom God called, or the little captive-maiden who sent the great captain, Naaman, to be healed in Jordan!

The teaching of Jesus, every word of it, the world holds precious beyond price. It is persuasive, luminous, authoritative. "Whither shall we go?" said his disciples, "Thou hast the words of eternal life." Where did he get such knowledge? Not from books. Aside from the Old Testament he perhaps never read a book. The town of Nazareth was his university; the people were his books. He took that life and so filled it with his own personality and so related it to

41

God that it became precious not only to the people of his own time but to those of all times. This is a miracle as great as any of those of healing which he later performed. Other people saw the things which he saw, but to them such things were dull and commonplace. Jesus lifted them up and made them shine like jewels. He made immortal poetry of the daily round of life.

This is shown especially in that matchless series of little stories we call his parables. He may have seen that dramatic story of the prodigal son enacted. Perhaps the rich boy who left home for the far country had been a playmate. Perhaps he had seen him returning home, ragged, forsaken, hungry. Perhaps he had gone by the house that evening and had heard the sounds of music and feasting, and rejoiced with the old father that his son had come back. He knew about the woman, she was perhaps a neighbor, who lost the coin. So precious to her was a single coin! Perhaps he joined the other neighbors in rejoicing when it was found. He knew the man who found the treasure which somebody in the old days of war had hidden in a field, the merchant who bought the pearl of great price. He was acquainted with the shepherds on the hills; perhaps he helped them look for the lost lamb in the mountain pastures where he had roamed as a boy. The shepherd separating the sheep and the goats; the sheep among wolves; the good fruit and the thorns; the lilies of the field; the grass that is cast into the oven; the hen and her brood; the carcase on the hill and the eagles gathered about it; the village dogs,— all these he knew through his experience in the fields and among the hills and in the village streets. He had seen that house swept away by the flood and the other dwelling securely founded on a rock. He knew what good building was like. The sower in the fields, the stealthy enemy who sowed tares, the rich man who planned to pull down his barns to build greater,—Jesus may have known them all. Perhaps that foolish rich man came to Jesus to talk about building the new barn, and died that very night.

The city set on a hill; the light which must be placed on a candle-stick if it is to give light to all the house; yeast; salt; meal; bread-making; the children playing in the market-place, pretending to pipe or to mourn; the strait gate; the narrow way; the fishermen with their nets; the debtor going to prison; the wedding; the wise and the foolish maidens; the pigs of the village; the blind leading the blind into the ditch; the birds' nest; the sparrow fallen out of it to the ground, not

# Madonna and Child
# with St. Anthony of Padua

By Sir Anthony Van Dyck (1599-1641)
In the Brera Gallery, Milan, Italy
Photograph by Anderson, Rome

ST. ANTHONY of Padua (1195-1231) was a Franciscan friar, celebrated for his piety and eloquence. It is related that one day, as he was explaining to his hearers the mystery of the Incarnation (the union of Deity with humanity in the person of Jesus), the Christ Child appeared to him in a vision. This legend Van Dyck probably had in mind when he painted his lovely picture showing St. Anthony, clothed in monk's tunic, kneeling before the Madonna and Child in an ecstasy of devotion. An open book lies on the ground, suggesting that St. Anthony was reading out-of-doors when the vision broke upon him. The gentle, poetic refinement of his nature shows in his face which the joyous Infant reaches out to caress, while the gracious, queenly Madonna quietly assists.

Van Dyck, the great Flemish painter, was born at Antwerp into a home of wealth and refinement. At ten he began his artistic apprenticeship and, when nineteen, became an assistant in the studio of the celebrated Rubens. In 1619 he was admitted a member of the painters' Guild of St. Luke, an unusual honor for one so young.

In 1628 when, after five years' study and work in Italy, Van Dyck established himself in Antwerp, he already ranked with the greatest artists of his age. Compare Van Dyck with: Dolci, page 1; LeBrun, page 22; Rembrandt, page 238; Murillo, page 254; Rubens, page 328; and Teniers, Volume VIII, page 326.

So great was Van Dyck's influence, particularly in portraiture, that English painters were to imitate his work for one hundred years, until the arrival of Reynolds (see Volume I, page 126).

without God's notice; the water from the well, springing up into everlasting life; the reed shaken by the wind; the wind itself blowing mysteriously about the houses; the people who live in kings' houses; the coin with the image and superscription of Caesar,—all these things had been a part of his daily life in the town of Nazareth.

There were imagination and humor, too, sometimes in his remembrance. The empty house! Perhaps the children had passed it fearful, afraid of spirits. To that empty house, all swept and garnished come seven spirits worse than the first. You can almost see one of these spirits coming back, looking and listening, and then the whole crew trooping in. The dead burying the dead! How sombre and ghostly is that thought! The hearers of Jesus must have been amused at his description of the Pharisee who carefully wiped the outside of the cup and forgot to wash the inside,—and still more at the picture of the Pharisee who strained his water so that not even a gnat should pollute it and then swallowed a camel! "How many of us," says Dr. Glover, the famous English Baptist of Cambridge University, "have ever pictured the process and the series of sensations, as the long, hairy neck slid down the throat of the Pharisee—all that amplitude of loose hung anatomy—the hump—two humps—both of them slid down and he never noticed—and the legs—all of them— with the whole outfit of knees and big, padded feet! The Pharisee swallowed a camel and never noticed it! Did no one see the picture with his own mind's eye—no one grasp the humor and the irony with delight? Could any one on the other hand forget it?" A modern teacher would have said that the Pharisee had no sense of proportion— and no one would have thought the remark worth remembering.

Then there is the man who detects the mote in his brother's eye, and does not realize that he is going about with a great beam in his own eye;—one of the beams which Jesus hewed with his carpenter's adze. Another picture is that of the astonished government official who has required a citizen to go with him a mile and finds the cheerful man going two! There are pictures of feasts at rich men's houses, and little stories of business; the man hiring laborers for his vineyard in the market and paying generously the same price at the last hour as at the first; the merchant who went away to a far country and what his servants did with the talents entrusted to them; the Samaritan merchant who picked up the wounded man on the Jericho road, after priest and Levite had passed him by, and paid for his care at an inn. All these people Jesus knew or else he had heard about them. Jesus saw all these things. He pondered them as he worked in the carpenter's shop or in his walks over the hills. The other people of the village thought of these things merely as incidents and the most ordinary incidents of a monotonous life. Jesus saw them in relation to the life and destiny of man, and he lifted up the common things and exalted them until they had a universal application.

Then, at the age of thirty, he closed the door of the shop at Nazareth and went out upon his great mission to men.

There are two aspects of the life of Jesus of this period which are too commonly neglected. He was a carpenter. He did not exalt himself above his friends. When he came back to Nazareth, the village people looked at him in astonishment because he spoke now with authority and they said, "Is this not the carpenter?"

When Millais painted a picture of Jesus in the carpenter shop and it was exhibited in the great cities of England, hundreds of workingmen came flocking to see it, because, they said, "This is our Comrade. He is one of us!" There is ample warrant for this feeling of comradeship, of brotherhood. It is possible to exaggerate it, to try to prove that Jesus was never anything but a workman, but we must remember that Jesus, like many of the truly great characters of history, bore the marks of toil in his youth and carried the insignia of his craft.

Jesus is unique in all history. He is the ideal man, the Hero of humanity. He is also true God, the Creator of the universe. All his life reflects this two-fold nature of his Person. If he worked in a carpenter's shop, he was also crucified for man's sin and rose again from the dead. He was meek and lowly, the servant of all; yet he was the King of Kings, the Redeemer of the world. He faced an opposition, a hostility, which finally crushed him, but out of that hostility came his supreme triumph. Other men conquered by force. He took the wood of the cross, a symbol of shame, and fashioned it into an emblem of universal power and victory. He transformed the apparent defeat of the cross into triumph by his death thereon as an atonement for the sins of the world, and the certainty of redemption certified in his resurrection three days later. "Thanks be to God who giveth us the victory."

# Madonna and Child with Saints

By Girolamo dai Libri (1474-1556)
In the Civic Museum, Verona, Italy
Photograph by Alinari Brothers, Florence

THIS beautiful and elaborate painting shows the
Madonna and Child enthroned, attended by a saint
and by the angel Raphael, leading the youthful Tobias.
Mary is seated on a richly decorated throne over the
step of which is laid a beautiful oriental rug. The
Christ Child stands on Mary's lap holding a globe,
symbol of dominion, and gazing toward Tobias. From
beneath an ornate canopy a joyous cherub looks down
adoringly. Behind the throne a beautiful olive-tree lifts
its branches. In the background stretches a grand and
harmonious expanse of rugged hills crowned with
castles, perhaps a distant view of the painter's native
city of Verona.

Raphael, whose name means, medicine of God, was
believed to be the heavenly messenger of God whose
particular vocation was that of guardian angel of all
humanity. His attributes and deeds are gathered from
the Jewish story of the Book of Tobit in the APOCRYPHA.
In this picture, Raphael is represented in his character
of guardian angel wearing his spirit-wings and leading
the child Tobias, son of Tobit. Tobias, with his fish
and dog, represents the christian, the believer, guarded
and guided through his life-pilgrimage by the angelic
monitor and minister of divine mercy. The words on
Raphael's breast are "Ecce Mater Gratie" and mean
"Behold the Mother of Grace."

The painter, Girolamo dai Libri, was born in Verona,
Italy. He was educated for a miniaturist and was con-
sequently known as "dai Libri" from the choral books
which he illuminated. His fondness of detail and his
feeling for the poetic beauty of landscape show clearly
in this picture. Girolamo was one of the most talented
artists in the local school of Verona, but only a minor
artist in Italian painting. Another of Libri's pictures is
given in Volume VIII, page 128.

# The Story of the Master

From the Gospels of Matthew, Mark and Luke

## The Master Goes Forth to the Service of Men

### JOHN THE BAPTIST

#### A VOICE CRYING IN THE WILDERNESS

John the Baptist is one of the splendid, austere, heroic figures of history. His fearless preaching of repentance swept Judea like a flame. His humility was equal to his greatness of soul. He recognized Jesus at once as the Son of God, the Saviour of men, the latchet of whose shoes he was not worthy to unloose. "He must increase, but I must decrease." Short was the time of John's ministry.

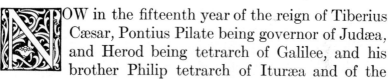NOW in the fifteenth year of the reign of Tiberius Cæsar, Pontius Pilate being governor of Judæa, and Herod being tetrarch of Galilee, and his brother Philip tetrarch of Ituræa and of the region of Trachonitis, and Lysanias the tetrarch of Abilene, Annas and Caiaphas being the high priests, the word of God came unto John, the son of Zacharias, in the wilderness. And he came into all the country about Jordan, preaching the baptism of repentance for the remission of sins; as it is written in the book of the words of Esaias, the prophet, saying,

"The voice of one crying in the wilderness,
'Prepare ye the way of the LORD,
Make his paths straight.
Every valley shall be filled,
And every mountain and hill shall be brought low;

49

And the crooked shall be made straight,
And the rough ways shall be made smooth;
And all flesh shall see the salvation of God.'"

Then said he to the multitude that came forth to be baptized of him, "O generation of vipers, who hath warned you to flee from the wrath to come? Bring forth therefore fruits worthy of repentance, and begin not to say within yourselves, 'We have Abraham to our father:' for I say unto you, that God is able of these stones to raise up children unto Abraham. And now also the axe is laid unto the root of the trees: every tree therefore which bringeth not forth good fruit is hewn down, and cast into the fire."

And the people asked him, saying, "What shall we do then?"

He answereth and saith unto them, "He that hath two coats, let him impart to him that hath none; and he that hath meat, let him do likewise."

Then came also publicans to be baptized, and said unto him, "Master, what shall we do?"

And he said unto them, "Exact no more than that which is appointed you."

And the soldiers likewise demanded of him, saying, "And what shall we do?"

And he said unto them, "Do violence to no man, neither accuse any falsely; and be content with your wages."

And as the people were in expectation, and all men mused in their hearts of John, whether he were the Christ, or not; John answered, saying unto them all, "I indeed baptize you with water; but one mightier than I cometh, the latchet of whose shoes I am not worthy to unloose: he shall baptize you with the Holy Ghost and with fire

FORD OF THE JORDAN WHERE JESUS
WAS BAPTIZED

Photographed by W. A. Pottenger expressly for The
Book of Life

AND straightway coming up out of the
water, he saw the heavens opened, and the
spirit like a dove descending upon him.
— Mark 1:10.

whose fan is in his hand, and he will thoroughly purge his floor, and will gather the wheat into his garner; but the chaff he will burn with fire unquenchable."

And many other things in his exhortation preached he unto the people. But Herod the tetrarch, being reproved by him for Herodias, his brother Philip's wife, and for all the evils which Herod had done, added yet this above all, that he shut up John in prison.

—Luke 3:1–20.

### THE BAPTISM OF JESUS

And it came to pass in those days, that Jesus came from Nazareth of Galilee, and was baptized of John in Jordan. But John forbade him, saying, I have need to be baptized of thee, and comest thou to me? And Jesus answering said unto him, Suffer it to be so now: for thus it becometh us to fulfill all righteousness. Then he suffered him. And straightway coming up out of the water, he saw the heavens opened, and the Spirit like a dove descending upon him: and there came a voice from heaven, saying, "Thou art my beloved Son, in whom I am well pleased."

—Mark 1:9–11; Matthew 3:14–15.

### MY DEAR REDEEMER AND MY LORD

My dear Redeemer and my Lord,
I read my duty in Thy word;
But in Thy life the law appears,
Drawn out in living characters.

Such was Thy truth, and such Thy zeal,
Such deference to Thy Father's will,
Such love, and meekness so divine,
I would transcribe and make them mine.

Be Thou my pattern; make me bear
More of Thy gracious image here;
Then God, the Judge, shall own my name
Among the followers of the Lamb

—Isaac Watts.

## The Temptation in the Wilderness

The temptation was a crucial experience in Jesus' life. Through it he was commissioned and empowered by the Holy Spirit for his mission to man. He had put on his armour of light. He was ready to stand against all the wiles of the devil. This was his first great victory, though not the last struggle. The final struggle was the crucifixion; the final victory, the resurrection.

And Jesus being full of the Holy Ghost returned from Jordan, and was led by the Spirit into the wilderness, being forty days tempted of the devil. And in those days he did eat nothing: and when they were ended, he afterward hungered.

And the devil said unto him, "If thou be the Son of God, command this stone that it be made bread."

And Jesus answered him, saying, "It is written that man shall not live by bread alone, but by every word of God."

And the devil, taking him up into an high mountain, showed unto him all the kingdoms of the world in a moment of time. And the devil said unto him, "All this power will I give thee, and the glory of them: for that is delivered unto me; and to whomsoever I will I give it. If thou therefore wilt worship me, all shall be thine."

And Jesus answered and said unto him, "Get thee behind me, Satan: for it is written, 'Thou shalt worship the Lord thy God, and him only shalt thou serve.'"

And he brought him to Jerusalem, and set him on a pinnacle of the temple, and said unto him, "If thou be the Son of God, cast thyself down from hence: for it is written, 'He shall give his angels charge over thee, to keep thee:' and 'In their hands they shall bear thee up, lest at any time thou dash thy foot against a stone.'"

And Jesus answering said unto him, "It is said, 'Thou shalt not tempt the Lord thy God.'"

# Christ and the Fishermen

Ernst Zimmermann (1852-1901)
National Gallery, Berlin, Germany

THIS picture shows Jesus seated earnestly talking with three men. One of these, much older than the others, holds a net in his lap. In the background a man, with oar on shoulder, balances himself in a boat. Thus we know that the scene is a lake and these rough-hewn listeners, so full of self-reliant strength and simple dignity, are fishermen.

The key to the story here portrayed is given in Mark 1: 19-20: "And when he had gone a little further thence, he saw James the son of Zebedee and John his brother, who were also in the ship mending their nets. And straightway he called them, and they left their father Zebedee in the ship with the hired servants and went after him."

Here we see Jesus as he was; not taking, but winning men to Him. Patiently, lovingly he explains his plans tor James and John to their father Zebedee. The Lord already recognizes in John the qualities which will make him the "Beloved Disciple," and in both brothers, the dynamic traits of "Sons of Thunder." Jesus is calling them to an entirely new venture of faith in which they will be "fishers of men."

All work has stopped while the three listen. Their searching, reverent concentration reflects the power and inspiration of Jesus and his message. The toil-worn father, won by the vibrant persuasiveness and gentle touch of the Master, slowly turns from the worry of carrying on alone to the vision of "The gospel of the Kingdom of God." Already we read in his face the decision which Jesus longs for.

The artist, Ernst Zimmermann, was born and died in Munich, Germany. We are grateful to him for this beautiful painting, a gift embodying his skill and reverence.

And when the devil had ended all the temptation, he departed from him for a season.

For Herod himself had sent forth and laid hold upon John, and bound him in prison for Herodias' sake, his brother Philip's wife: for he had married her. For John had said unto Herod, "It is not lawful for thee to have thy brother's wife."

Now after that John was put in prison, Jesus came into Galilee, preaching the gospel of the kingdom of God, and saying, "The time is fulfilled, and the kingdom of God is at hand: repent ye, and believe the gospel."

— Luke 4:1–13; Mark 6:17–18; 1:14–15.

### JESUS CALLS HIS FIRST DISCIPLES

Walking beside the sea, Jesus calls his first disciples, the four fishermen of Galilee.

Jesus calls us; o'er the tumult
  Of our life's wild restless sea,
Day by day His sweet voice soundeth,
  Saying, "Christian, follow Me."

Jesus calls us from the worship
  Of the vain world's golden store,
From each idol that would keep us,
  Saying, "Christian, love Me more."

In our joys and in our sorrows,
  Days of toil and hours of ease,
Still He calls, in cares and pleasures,
  That we love Him more than these.

Jesus calls us: by Thy mercies,
  Saviour, make us hear Thy call,
Give our hearts to Thine obedience,
  Serve and love Thee best of all.
          —*Cecil Frances Alexander.*

And it came to pass, that, as the people pressed upon him to hear the word of God, he stood by the lake of Gennesaret, and saw two ships standing by the lake: but the fishermen were gone out of them, and were washing their nets. And he entered into one of the ships, which was Simon's, and prayed him that he would thrust out a little from the land. And he sat down, and taught the people out of the ship.

Now when he had left speaking, he said unto Simon, "Launch out into the deep, and let down your nets for a draught."

And Simon answering said unto him, "Master, we have toiled all the night, and have taken nothing: nevertheless at thy word I will let down the net."

And when they had this done, they inclosed a great multitude of fishes: and their net brake. And they beckoned unto their partners, which were in the other ship, that they should come and help them. And they came, and filled both the ships, so that they began to sink.

When Simon Peter saw it, he fell down at Jesus' knees, saying, "Depart from me; for I am a sinful man, O Lord." For he was astonished, and all that were with him, at the draught of the fishes which they had taken: and so was also James, and John, the sons of Zebedee, which were partners with Simon.

And Jesus said unto Simon,

"Fear not; from henceforth thou shalt catch men."

And when they had brought their ships to land, they forsook all, and followed him. — Luke 5:1-11.

## A Prophet Without Honor

Many of the people who gathered in the synagogue at Nazareth must have known Jesus. They knew him well. This was "Joseph's son." They wondered at his words of grace and truth, but they, nevertheless, cast him out of the city, and tried to send him to his death from the brow of a steep hill.

And he came to Nazareth, where he had been brought up: and, as his custom was, he went into the synagogue on the sabbath day, and stood up for to read. And there was delivered unto him the book of the prophet Esaias. And when he had opened the book, he found the place where it was written,

"The Spirit of the LORD is upon me,
Because he hath anointed me to preach the gospel to the poor;
He hath sent me to heal the broken-hearted, to preach deliverance to the captives,
And recovering of sight to the blind,
To set at liberty them that are bruised,
To preach the acceptable year of the LORD."

And he closed the book, and he gave it again to the minister, and sat down. And the eyes of all them that were in the synagogue were fastened on him. And he began to say unto them, "This day is this scripture fulfilled in your ears."

And all bare him witness, and wondered at the gracious words which proceeded out of his mouth. And they said, "Is not this Joseph's son?"

And he said unto them, "Ye will surely say unto me this proverb, 'Physician, heal thyself: whatsoever we have heard done in Capernaum, do also here in thy country.'"

And he said, "Verily I say unto you, No prophet is accepted in his own country. But I tell you of a truth, many widows were in Israel in the days of Elias, when the heaven was shut up three years and six months, when great famine was throughout all the land; but unto none of them was Elias sent, save unto Sarepta, a city of Sidon, unto a woman that was a widow. And many lepers were in Israel in the time of Eliseus the prophet: and none of them was cleansed, saving Naaman, the Syrian."

And all they in the synagogue, when they heard these things, were filled with wrath, and rose up, and thrust him out of the city, and led him unto the brow of the hill whereon their city was built, that they might cast him down headlong. But he passing through the midst of them went his way.                  — Luke 4:16–30.

SYNAGOGUE

*Photograph by Professor Lewis Bayles Paton*

This is the interior of a Jewish Synagogue in Palestine very similar to those which were familiar to Jesus.

TIBERIAS

*Photograph by W. A. Pottenger expressly for The Book of Life*

Tiberias was the capital of Galilee. In the days of the Old Testament, Galilee was the home of the tribes of Asher, Zebulon, and Issachar. After the captivity, it was re-populated with a mixed population.

NEAR CAPERNAUM ON THE SEA OF GALILEE

*Photograph by W. A. Pottenger expressly for The Book of Life*

The Sea of Galilee, which was once crowded with boats, is now very silent, but it is still lovely as it was in Jesus' time, now calm and now swept by the fierce storms which sweep down from the hills to lash the waters to foam—the storms which are mentioned in the Gospels. In the time of Jesus, Tiberias was a large and rich city.

RUINS OF THE JEWISH SYNAGOGUE AT CAPERNAUM
*Photograph by Professor Lewis Bayles Paton*

Jesus always attended the synagogue services on the Sabbath.
"And when he was departed thence, he went into their synagogue."

NEAR NAZARETH
*Photograph by W. A. Pottenger expressly for The Book of Life*

This picture shows the old city of Nazareth, the home of Jesus, as it looks as one approaches along the road in the foreground. There is still a considerable town here where in the old days was the carpenter shop of Jesus and Joseph.

## Jesus Leaves Nazareth to Dwell in Capernaum

And leaving Nazareth, he came and dwelt in Capernaum, which is upon the sea coast, in the borders of Zabulon and Nephthalim: that it might be fulfilled which was spoken by Esaias the prophet, saying,

"The land of Zabulon, and the land of Nephthalim,
By the way of the sea, beyond Jordan,
Galilee of the Gentiles;
The people which sat in darkness
Saw great light; and to them which sat in the region
and shadow of death
Light is sprung up." — Matthew 4:13-16.

## A Day of Miracles at Capernaum

As Jesus went about his ministry of mercy and healing, his popularity increased. Everywhere the news spread in the villages and thousands flocked to the new teacher.

But warm, sweet, tender, even yet
A present help is He;
And faith has still its Olivet,
And love its Galilee.

The healing of His seamless dress
Is by our beds of pain;
We touch Him in life's throng and press,
And we are whole again.
—J. G. Whittier.

And they went into Capernaum; and straightway on the sabbath day he entered into the synagogue, and taught. And they were astonished at his doctrine: for he taught them as one that had authority, and not as the scribes.

And there was in their synagogue a man with an unclean spirit; and he cried out, saying, "Let us alone;

what have we to do with thee, thou Jesus of Nazareth? art thou come to destroy us? I know thee who thou art, the Holy One of God."

And Jesus rebuked him, saying, "Hold thy peace, and come out of him."

And when the unclean spirit had torn him, and cried with a loud voice, he came out of him.

And they were all amazed, insomuch that they questioned among themselves, saying, "What thing is this? What new doctrine is this? for with authority commandeth he even the unclean spirits, and they do obey him."

And immediately his fame spread abroad throughout all the region round about Galilee. And forthwith, when they were come out of the synagogue, they entered into the house of Simon and Andrew, with James and John. But Simon's wife's mother lay sick of a fever, and anon they tell him of her. And he came and took her by the hand, and lifted her up; and immediately the fever left her, and she ministered unto them.

And at even, when the sun did set, they brought unto him all that were diseased, and them that were possessed with devils. And all the city was gathered together at the door. And he healed many that were sick of divers diseases, and cast out many devils; and suffered not the devils to speak, because they knew him.  — Mark 1:21–34.

### Jesus Heals a Leper

And in the morning, rising up a great while before day, he went out, and departed into a solitary place, and there prayed. And Simon and they that were with him followed after him. And when they had found him, they said unto him, "All men seek for thee."

And he said unto them, "Let us go into the next towns, that I may preach there also: for therefore came I forth."

# Healing the Sick Man Let Down Through the Roof

By Alexandré Bida (1813-1895)
Lithograph Illustration for the Bossuet
Translation of The Four Gospels

THE people throughout all the country had heard
of Jesus' preaching and of the many sick people
He had made well. Wherever He went He was sur-
rounded by throngs of eager people. Now, when Jesus
returned to Capernaum, after an absence of several
days in the country and smaller towns, it was only a
little while until everyone knew it and began to gather
to see and to hear him. Among those who came to the
place where Jesus was staying were four men who were
bringing a sick friend for Jesus to heal. But the crowd
was so great that they could not reach even the door.
So they went up to the house top, uncovered the roof,
and let the man down on his bed at Jesus' feet. Pages
67-68 tell us how Jesus rewarded the splendid faith of
these men.

Alexandré Bida, a nineteenth century French artist,
was well-known for his illustrations of the Gospels of
which this is one. He traveled and worked in the
Orient, especially in Palestine, and depicted the life of
those countries with great feeling and understanding.
He was born in Toulouse, France in 1813 and died at
his home near there in 1895. Another of his scriptural
illustrations is given in Volume I, page 344.

And he preached in their synagogues throughout all Galilee, and cast out devils.

And there came a leper to him, beseeching him, and kneeling down to him, and saying unto him, "If thou wilt, thou canst make me clean."

And Jesus, moved with compassion, put forth his hand, and touched him, and saith unto him, "I will; be thou clean."

And as soon as he had spoken, immediately the leprosy departed from him, and he was cleansed. And he straitly charged him, and forthwith sent him away; and saith unto him, "See thou say nothing to any man: but go thy way, show thyself to the priest, and offer for thy cleansing those things which Moses commanded, for a testimony unto them."

But he went out, and began to publish it much, and to blaze abroad the matter, insomuch that Jesus could no more openly enter into the city, but was without in desert places: and they came to him from every quarter.

— Mark 1:35–45.

### THE MAN WHO WAS LET DOWN THROUGH THE ROOF

And again he entered into Capernaum after some days; and it was noised that he was in the house. And straightway many were gathered together, insomuch that there was no room to receive them, no, not so much as about the door: and he preached the word unto them. And they come unto him, bringing one sick of the palsy, which was borne of four. And when they could not come nigh unto him for the press, they uncovered the roof where he was: and when they had broken it up, they let down the bed wherein the sick of the palsy lay.

When Jesus saw their faith, he said unto the sick of the palsy, "Son, thy sins be forgiven thee."

But there were certain of the scribes sitting there, and reasoning in their hearts, "Why doth this man thus speak blasphemies? Who can forgive sins but God only?"

And immediately when Jesus perceived in his spirit that they so reasoned within themselves, he said unto them, "Why reason ye these things in your hearts? Whether is it easier to say to the sick of the palsy, 'Thy sins be forgiven thee;' or to say, 'Arise, and take up thy bed, and walk?' But that ye may know that the Son of man hath power on earth to forgive sins," (he saith to the sick of the palsy,) "I say unto thee, Arise, and take up thy bed, and go thy way into thine house.'"

And immediately he arose, took up the bed, and went forth before them all; insomuch that they were all amazed, and glorified God, saying, "We never saw it on this fashion."  — Mark 2:1-12.

### The Call of Matthew the Tax-Gatherer

The taxes imposed by the Roman government upon subject peoples were very burdensome. Taxes were imposed with the greatest ingenuity upon every conceivable object. There were import and export taxes, bridge-money, road-money, harbor dues, town dues, taxes on axles, wheels, pack animals, pedestrians, carriers, bridges, ships, quays. Payment was necessary before one could be admitted to towns, markets, highways, and before one could cross rivers. At every collecting station, pack animals must be unloaded and every article examined. At every port, ships must be unloaded, and the cargo taxed. This system was particularly distasteful to the proud Jew. The tax-gatherers were especially hated and despised. A Jew who would accept such an office was beneath the contempt of his countrymen. It is very significant, then, that Jesus, rising above this prejudice, should see the worth of the soul of this hated publican, Matthew, and admit him to the intimate fellowship of the apostles.

And as Jesus passed forth from thence, he saw a man, named Matthew, sitting at the receipt of custom: and he saith unto him, "Follow me."

And he arose, and followed him.

And it came to pass, as Jesus sat at meat in the house, behold, many publicans and sinners came and sat down with him and his disciples.

And when the Pharisees saw it, they said unto his disciples, "Why eateth your Master with publicans and sinners?"

But when Jesus heard that, he said unto them, "They that be whole need not a physician, but they that are sick. But go ye and learn what that meaneth, 'I will have mercy, and not sacrifice': for I am not come to call the righteous, but sinners to repentance." —Matthew 9:9–13.

## "New Cloth on an Old Garment"

And the disciples of John and of the Pharisees used to fast: and they come and say unto him, "Why do the disciples of John and of the Pharisees fast, but thy disciples fast not?"

And Jesus said unto them, "Can the children of the bridechamber fast, while the bridegroom is with them? as long as they have the bridegroom with them, they cannot fast. But the days will come, when the bridegroom shall be taken away from them, and then shall they fast in those days.

No man also seweth a piece of new cloth on an old garment: else the new piece that filled it up taketh away from the old, and the rent is made worse. And no man putteth new wine into old bottles; else the new wine doth burst the bottles, and the wine is spilled, and the bottles will be marred: but new wine must be put into new bottles." — Mark 2:18–22.

## "THE SON OF MAN IS LORD EVEN OF THE SABBATH DAY"

At that time Jesus went on the sabbath day through the corn; and his disciples were an hungred, and began to pluck the ears of corn, and to eat.

But when the Pharisees saw it, they said unto him, "Behold, thy disciples do that which is not lawful to do upon the sabbath day."

But he said unto them, "Have ye not read what David did, when he was an hungred, and they that were with him; how he entered into the house of God, and did eat the shewbread, which was not lawful for him to eat, neither for them which were with him, but only for the priests? Or have ye not read in the law, how that on the sabbath days the priests in the temple profane the sabbath, and are blameless? But I say unto you, that in this place is one greater than the temple. But if ye had known what this meaneth, 'I will have mercy, and not sacrifice,' ye would not have condemned the guiltless. For the Son of man is Lord even of the sabbath day."

— Matthew 12:1–8.

## "IT IS LAWFUL TO DO WELL ON THE SABBATH"

And when he was departed thence, he went into their synagogue. And, behold, there was a man which had his hand withered. And they asked him, saying, "Is it lawful to heal on the sabbath days?" that they might accuse him.

And he said unto them, "What man shall there be among you, that shall have one sheep, and if it fall into a pit on the sabbath day, will he not lay hold on it, and lift it out? How much then is a man better than a sheep? Wherefore it is lawful to do well on the sabbath days."

Then saith he to the man, "Stretch forth thine hand."

And he stretched it forth; and it was restored whole, like as the other.

Then the Pharisees went out, and held a council against him, how they might destroy him.
— Matthew 12:9–14.

BURDEN BEARERS IN JERUSALEM
*Photograph by the Reverend Frederick J. Moore*

"Come unto me all ye that labour and are heavy laden, and I will give you rest." (See pages 95 and 96.)

# The Story of the Master

## From the Gospels of Matthew, Mark, and Luke

## Days of Popular Favor

### Jesus Heals the Multitude

ND Jesus went about all Galilee, teaching in their synagogues, and preaching the gospel of the kingdom, and healing all manner of sickness and all manner of disease among the people. And his fame went throughout all Syria: and they brought unto him all sick people that were taken with divers diseases and torments, and those which were possessed with devils, and those which were lunatic, and those that had the palsy; and he healed them. And there followed him great multitudes of people from Galilee, and from Decapolis, and from Jerusalem, and from Judæa, and from beyond Jordan.

But when Jesus knew it, he withdrew himself from thence: and great multitudes followed him, and he healed them all; and charged them that they should not make him known: that it might be fulfilled which was spoken by Esaias the prophet, saying,

"Behold my servant, whom I have chosen;
My beloved, in whom my soul is well pleased:
I will put my spirit upon him,
And he shall show judgment to the Gentiles.
He shall not strive, nor cry;
Neither shall any man hear his voice in the streets.
A bruised reed shall he not break,

# Jesus Healing the Sick

By Karl Gottlieb Schönherr (1824-1906)
Location of original painting unknown

THIS painting shows one of the many occasions when Jesus stopped along the way to comfort and heal the sick. We see him here in a path leading away from the village. Some of the people can be seen still pouring out from the town gate. Others have kept so close to the Master that He has paused to speak with them and to help them. What reverence in the faces of these poor people who surround him! See the woman bent to the ground at Jesus' feet; the poor man with his crutches kneeling behind him; the man in chains, bowing his head against the knee of the Saviour; and the aged woman leaning on her staff and the shoulder of a child. The love shown in these faces tells us something of the blessings that have been bestowed upon them by Jesus through their faith in him.

Carl Gottlieb Schönherr was a German artist born in the village of Lengefeld in the Erz Mountains, Germany. He studied first in the Dresden Academy and then for two years, from 1852 to 1854, in Rome. In 1857 he returned to the Dresden Academy to teach where he continued until 1900. He died in Dresden in 1906.

This realistic portrayal of Jesus' healing ministry is one of Schönherr's best religious paintings. It is interesting to compare Schönherr's work with that of contemporary European artists such as the Frenchman, Alexandré Bida, page 66; the Italian, Nicolo Barabino, page 107; the German, Gustav Richter, page 112, and others. Do you see any important differences in the way each handles his subject?

And smoking flax shall he not quench,
Till he send forth judgment unto victory.
And in his name shall the Gentiles trust. "

And he goeth up into a mountain and calleth unto him whom he would: and they came unto him. And he ordained twelve, that they should be with him, and that he might send them forth to preach, and to have power to heal sicknesses, and to cast out devils: and Simon he surnamed Peter: and James the son of Zebedee, and John the brother of James: and he surnamed them "Boanerges," which is, "The Sons of Thunder": and Andrew, and Philip, and Bartholomew, and Matthew, and Thomas, and James the son of Alphaeus, and Thaddaeus, and Simon the Canaanite, and Judas Iscariot, which also betrayed him.  —Matthew 4:23-25; 12:15-21; Mark 3:13-19a.

## "THE GLORIOUS COMPANY OF THE APOSTLES"

We have to depend upon the traditions of the early Church for the meager accounts of the lives of the apostles after the narrative of the Book of Acts. These traditions contained in the works of the "Fathers" of the Church in the first two or three centuries are for the main facts entitled to acceptance.

By "tradition" we do not necessarily mean something doubtful or untrue, but simply the reports or accounts which have come down to us from early periods. They are often confused and sometimes contradictory but they are all we have for this period.

SIMON PETER—A brother of Andrew; a fisherman of Bethsaida; married and the owner of a home in Capernaum. One of the leaders of the early Church. Possibly martyred in Rome by Nero.

ANDREW—Brother of Peter. Occupation: fisherman. Home: Bethsaida. Tradition says he preached in Scythia, Bithynia, Parthia, as well as in Greece. One tradition says he was stoned and crucified in Scythia; another that he was crucified by the Proconsul Aegeas in Achaia.

JAMES—Brother of John. Occupation: fisherman. Home: Bethsaida. James was the first of the Apostles to be martyred. He was beheaded by Herod about 44 A.D.

JOHN—Brother of James. Occupation: fisherman. Home: Bethsaida. There are many traditions concerning the later life of John. According to some, he was an exile on the Island of Patmos, he lived to an extreme old age and died at Ephesus. See "A Death in the Desert," by Browning.

PHILIP—Resident of Bethsaida. Said to have preached in Gaul and in Phrygia. Crucified in Phrygia.

BARTHOLOMEW—Home: Cana of Galilee. Said to have preached in India and to have been martyred by being tied in a sack and thrown into the sea.

THOMAS—Occupation and residence unknown. Tradition says that he preached in India with great success. Some stories say that he died a natural death, others that he was martyred by "Mesdae, King of India."

MATTHEW—Customs officer. Residence: Capernaum. Tradition says that he preached in many places—Ethiopia, Macedonia, Syria, Persia, and died a natural death.

JAMES, "THE LESS"—Said to have been stoned by the Jews.

SIMON, "THE ZEALOT"—Probably a Galilean. Nothing is known of his career.

JUDAS (not Iscariot)—Nothing known of his life.

JUDAS ISCARIOT—Home: Kerioth in Judea. Committed suicide.

## THE SERMON ON THE MOUNT

This great discourse is universally recognized as the most complete explanation of the true meaning of the holy law of God, set forth in a most attractive and persuasive way. It is also a masterpiece of literature, full of beautiful imagery and poetic feeling.

### THE BEATITUDES

And seeing the multitudes, he went up into a mountain: and when he was set, his disciples came unto him: And he opened his mouth, and taught them, saying,

"Blessed are the poor in spirit: for theirs is the kingdom of heaven.

"Blessed are they that mourn: for they shall be comforted.

"Blessed are the meek: for they shall inherit the earth.

"Blessed are they which do hunger and thirst after righteousness: for they shall be filled.

"Blessed are the merciful: for they shall obtain mercy.

"Blessed are the pure in heart: for they shall see God.

"Blessed are the peacemakers: for they shall be called the children of God.

"Blessed are they which are persecuted for righteousness' sake: for theirs is the kingdom of heaven.

"Blessed are ye, when men shall revile you, and persecute you, and shall say all manner of evil against you falsely, for my sake.

"Rejoice, and be exceeding glad: for great is your reward in heaven: for so persecuted they the prophets which were before you.

"Ye are the salt of the earth: but if the salt have lost his savour, wherewith shall it be salted? It is thenceforth good for nothing, but to be cast out, and to be trodden under foot of men. Ye are the light of the world. A city that is set on an hill cannot be hid. Neither do men light a candle, and put it under a bushel, but on a candlestick; and it giveth light unto all that are in the house. Let your light so shine before men, that they may see your good works, and glorify your Father which is in heaven."

—Matthew 5:1–16.

## "I AM NOT COME TO DESTROY BUT TO FULFILL"

"Think not that I am come to destroy the law, or the prophets: I am not come to destroy, but to fulfill. For verily I say unto you, Till heaven and earth pass, one jot or one tittle shall in no wise pass from the law, till all be fulfilled. Whosoever therefore shall break one of these least commandments, and shall teach men so, he shall be called the least in the kingdom of heaven: but whosoever shall do and teach them, the same shall be called great in the kingdom of heaven. For I say unto you, that except your righteousness shall exceed the righteousness of the scribes and Pharisees, ye shall in no case enter into the kingdom of heaven."

### THE LAW EXPLAINED

"Ye have heard that it was said by them of old time, 'Thou shalt not kill; and whosoever shall kill shall be in danger of the judgment': but I say unto you, that whosoever is angry with his brother without a cause shall be in danger of the judgment: and whosoever shall say to his brother, 'Raca,' shall be in danger of the council: but whosoever shall say, 'Thou fool,' shall be in danger of hell fire. Therefore if thou bring thy gift to the altar, and there rememberest that thy brother hath aught against thee; leave there thy gift before the altar, and go thy way; first be reconciled to thy brother, and then come and offer thy gift. Agree with thine adversary quickly, whiles thou art in the way with him; lest at any time the adversary deliver thee to the judge, and the judge deliver thee to the officer, and thou be cast into prison. Verily I say unto thee, 'Thou shalt by no means come out thence, till thou hast paid the uttermost farthing.'

"Ye have heard that it was said by them of old time, 'Thou shalt not commit adultery': but I say unto you, that whosoever looketh on a woman to lust after her hath committed adultery with her already in his heart. And if thy right eye offend thee, pluck it out, and cast it from thee: for it is profitable for thee that one of thy members should perish, and not that thy whole body should be cast into hell. And if thy right hand offend thee, cut it off, and cast it from thee: for it is profitable for thee that one of thy members should perish, and not that thy whole body should be cast into hell. It hath been said, 'Whosoever shall put away his wife, let him give her a writing of divorcement': but I say unto you, that whosoever shall put away his wife, saving for the cause of fornication, causeth her to commit adultery: and whosoever shall marry her that is divorced committeth adultery.

"Again, ye have heard that it hath been said by them of old time, 'Thou shalt not forswear thyself, but shalt perform unto the LORD thine oaths': but I say unto you, 'Swear not at all; neither by heaven; for it is God's throne: nor by the earth; for it is his footstool: neither by Jerusalem; for it is the city of the great King. Neither shalt thou swear by thy head, because thou canst not make one hair white or black. But let your communication be, Yea, yea; Nay, nay: for whatsoever is more than these cometh of evil.'

"Ye have heard that it hath been said, 'An eye for an eye, and a tooth for a tooth': but I say unto you, that ye resist not evil: but whosoever shall smite thee on thy right cheek, turn to him the other also. And if any man will sue thee at the law, and take away thy coat, let him have thy cloke also. And whosoever shall compel thee to go a mile, go with him twain. Give to him that asketh thee, and from him that would borrow of thee turn not thou away." —Matthew 5:17–42.

## "LOVE YOUR ENEMIES"

"Ye have heard that it hath been said, 'Thou shalt love thy neighbour, and hate thine enemy.' But I say unto you, 'Love your enemies, bless them that curse you, do good to them that hate you, and pray for them which despitefully use you, and persecute you; that ye may be the children of your Father which is in heaven': for he maketh his sun to rise on the evil and on the good, and sendeth rain on the just and on the unjust. For if ye love them which love you, what reward have ye? Do not even the publicans the same? And if ye salute your brethren only, what do ye more than others? Do not even the publicans so? Be ye therefore perfect, even as your Father which is in heaven is perfect."

### DO NOT BOAST OF YOUR GOOD WORKS

"Take heed that ye do not your alms before men, to be seen of them: otherwise ye have no reward of your Father which is in heaven. Therefore when thou doest thine alms, do not sound a trumpet before thee, as the hypocrites do in the synagogues and in the streets, that they may have glory of men. Verily I say unto you, they have their reward. But when thou doest alms, let not thy left hand know what thy right hand doeth: that thine alms may be in secret: and thy Father which seeth in secret himself shall reward thee openly.

"And when thou prayest, thou shalt not be as the hypocrites are: for they love to pray standing in the synagogues and in the corners of the streets, that they may be seen of men. Verily I say unto you, they have their reward. But thou, when thou prayest, enter into thy closet, and when thou hast shut thy door, pray to thy Father which is in secret; and thy Father which seeth in secret shall reward thee openly. But when ye

# Christ Among the Lowly

By Léon Augustin Lhermitte (1844-1925)
In the Metropolitan Museum of Art, New York
From a Copley Print, Copyright by Curtis and Cameron,
Boston

JESUS comes bearing glad tidings of hope to this humble peasant family just as they are gathering to give thanks for their simple meal. The pathos of peasant life is quietly indicated in the pose of the figures. Yet more than of hardship this scene speaks of a trust and devotion too deep and too complete for words. See the wonder and expectancy on the faces of old and young alike. The children sense that something important is happening and turn upon the Visitor that completely undivided attention known only to childhood. Such intensity and expressiveness make this scene a part of one's own experience, so human and so natural is it.

The artist, Léon Augustin Lhermitte, was born in 1844 in the village of Mont-Saint-Père where his father was a schoolmaster. Léon was sickly as a child and amused himself by copying pictures from illustrated papers and drawing the things about him. He studied for a time at the Imperial School of Design under Lecoq de Boisbaudran, but soon decided to study out methods of work and technique by himself. He worked only in charcoal for some time and became a very fine draughtsman and etcher. Besides this he had the gift of seeing and interpreting the beauties of nature and the simple life in terms that were easily understood. He aimed at expressing something beyond the outward appearance of things, something of the inner beauty of character in both men and things. We are told that Lhermitte's best pictures owe their inspiration to his old home at Mont-Saint-Père. Certain it is that there is something so natural and so living about this picture and the one in Volume I, page 370, that the spirit given voice in these scenes finds an echo in the heart.

pray, use not vain repetitions, as the heathen do: for they think that they shall be heard for their much speaking. Be not ye therefore like unto them: for your Father knoweth what things ye have need of, before ye ask him."

—Matthew 5:43–6:8.

### THE LORD'S PRAYER

The universal prayer of Christian faith, the prayer of the little child and of the aged saint! The common ground of all faiths! It is used by all churches and spoken in all tongues. It is used on all occasions, at the marriage ceremony and at the funeral service. It is the prayer of the humblest individual and of the great church universal.

"After this manner therefore pray ye:

'Our Father which art in heaven, hallowed be thy name. Thy kingdom come. Thy will be done in earth, as it is in heaven. Give us this day our daily bread. And forgive us our debts, as we forgive our debtors. And lead us not into temptation, but deliver us from evil: for thine is the kingdom, and the power, and the glory, forever. Amen.'

"For if ye forgive men their trespasses, your heavenly Father will also forgive you: but if ye forgive not men their trespasses, neither will your Father forgive your trespasses.

"Moreover when ye fast, be not, as the hypocrites, of a sad countenance: for they disfigure their faces, that they may appear unto men to fast. Verily I say unto you, they have their reward. But thou, when thou fastest, anoint thine head, and wash thy face; that thou appear not unto men to fast, but unto thy Father which is in secret: and thy Father, which seeth in secret, shall reward thee openly."

—Matthew 6:9–18.

CHURCH OF THE LORD'S PRAYER ON THE MOUNT OF OLIVES
*Photograph by W. A. Pottenger expressly for The Book of Life*

This church is built on the traditional site where Jesus taught His disciples to pray.  Luke 11: 1-13.  THE BOOK OF LIFE  Volume 6, pages 143-4.

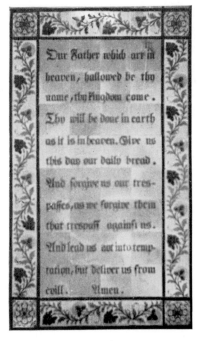

Our Father which art in heaven, hallowed be thy name, thy Kingdom come. Thy will be done in earth as it is in heaven. Give us this day our daily bread. And forgive us our trespasses, as we forgive them that trespass against us. And lead us not into temptation, but deliver us from evil. Amen.

This church stands on one of the most beautiful sites on the Mount of Olives, where one can look down across the Jehoshaphat Valley and see clearly the City of Jerusalem.

The present building was erected in 1868 by the Princess La Tour d'Auvergne.  It is built in the form of a square with a large interior court open to the sky.  On each side of the church and facing the court are eight bronze tablets, like the one in English on the left.  On each of the thirty-two tablets may be seen the Lord's Prayer in one of thirty-two different languages.

## "WHERE YOUR TREASURE IS THERE WILL YOUR HEART BE ALSO"

"Lay not up for yourselves treasures upon earth, where moth and rust doth corrupt, and where thieves break through and steal: but lay up for yourselves treasures in heaven, where neither moth nor rust doth corrupt, and where thieves do not break through nor steal: for where your treasure is, there will your heart be also. The light of the body is the eye: if therefore thine eye be single, thy whole body shall be full of light. But if thine eye be evil, thy whole body shall be full of darkness. If therefore the light that is in thee be darkness, how great is that darkness!

"No man can serve two masters: for either he will hate the one, and love the other; or else he will hold to the one, and despise the other. Ye cannot serve God and mammon. Therefore I say unto you, 'Take no thought for your life, what ye shall eat, or what ye shall drink; nor yet for your body, what ye shall put on.' Is not the life more than meat, and the body than raiment? Behold the fowls of the air: for they sow not, neither do they reap, nor gather into barns; yet your heavenly Father feedeth them. Are ye not much better than they? Which of you by taking thought can add one cubit unto his stature?"

## "THE LILIES OF THE FIELD"

"And why take ye thought for raiment? Consider the lilies of the field, how they grow; they toil not, neither do they spin: and yet I say unto you, that even Solomon in all his glory was not arrayed like one of these. Wherefore, if God so clothe the grass of the field, which to-day is, and to-morrow is cast into the oven, shall he not much more clothe you, O ye of little faith? Therefore take no thought, saying, 'What shall we eat?' or, 'What shall we drink?' or, 'Wherewithal shall we be clothed?' (for after all these things do the Gentiles seek:) for your heavenly Father knoweth that ye have need of all these things. But seek ye first the kingdom of God, and his righteousness; and all these things shall be added unto you. Take therefore no thought for the morrow: for the morrow shall take thought for the things of itself. Sufficient unto the day is the evil thereof." —Matthew 6:19-34.

## "JUDGE NOT THAT YE BE NOT JUDGED"

"Judge not, that ye be not judged. For with what judgment ye judge, ye shall be judged: and with what measure ye mete, it shall be measured to you again. And why beholdest thou the mote that is in thy brother's eye, but considerest not the beam that is in thine own eye? Or how wilt thou say to thy brother, 'Let me pull out the mote out of thine eye'; and, behold, a beam is in thine own eye? Thou hypocrite, first cast out the beam out of thine own eye; and then shalt thou see clearly to cast out the mote out of thy brother's eye.

"Give not that which is holy unto the dogs, neither cast ye your pearls before swine, lest they trample them under their feet, and turn again and rend you."

## "ASK AND IT SHALL BE GIVEN YOU"

"Ask, and it shall be given you; seek, and ye shall find; knock, and it shall be opened unto you: for every one that asketh receiveth; and he that seeketh findeth; and to him that knocketh it shall be opened. Or what man is there of you, whom if his son ask bread, will he give him a stone? Or if he ask a fish, will he give him a serpent? If ye then, being evil, know how to give good gifts unto your children, how much more shall your

Father which is in heaven give good things to them that ask him?"

—Matthew 7:1-11.

As the Lord's Prayer is the most concise and authoritative example of true prayer, so the Golden Rule is the clearest interpretation of the fundamental law of love.

### THE GOLDEN RULE

"Therefore all things whatsoever ye would that men should do to you, do ye even so to them: for this is the law and the prophets.

"Enter ye in at the strait gate: for wide is the gate, and broad is the way, that leadeth to destruction, and many there be which go in thereat: because strait is the gate, and narrow is the way, which leadeth unto life, and few there be that find it.

"Beware of false prophets, which come to you in sheep's clothing, but inwardly they are ravening wolves. Ye shall know them by their fruits. Do men gather grapes of thorns, or figs of thistles? Even so every good tree bringeth forth good fruit; but a corrupt tree bringeth forth evil fruit. A good tree cannot bring forth evil fruit, neither can a corrupt tree bring forth good fruit. Every tree that bringeth not forth good fruit is hewn down, and cast into the fire. Wherefore by their fruits ye shall know them.

"Not every one that saith unto me, 'Lord, Lord,' shall enter into the kingdom of heaven; but he that doeth the will of my Father which is in heaven. Many will say to me in that day, 'Lord, Lord, have we not prophesied in thy name? and in thy name have cast out devils? and in thy name done many wonderful works?' And then will I profess unto them, 'I never knew you: depart from me, ye that work iniquity.'"

### THE HOUSE THAT WAS FOUNDED ON A ROCK AND THE HOUSE THAT WAS BUILT ON THE SAND

"Therefore whosoever heareth these sayings of mine, and doeth them, I will liken him unto a wise man, which built his house upon a rock. And the rain descended, and the floods came, and the winds blew, and beat upon that house; and it fell not: for it was founded upon a rock. And every one that heareth these sayings of mine, and doeth them not, shall be likened unto a foolish man, which built his house upon the sand. And the rain descended, and the floods came, and the winds blew, and beat upon that house; and it fell: and great was the fall of it."

And it came to pass, when Jesus had ended these sayings, the people were astonished at his doctrine: for he taught them as one having authority, and not as the scribes.                         — Matthew 5, 6, 7.

### THE SERMON ON THE MOUNT
#### FROM THE GOSPEL OF LUKE

And he lifted up his eyes on his disciples, and said,

"Blessed be ye poor: for yours is the kingdom of God.

"Blessed are ye that hunger now: for ye shall be filled.

"Blessed are ye that weep now: for ye shall laugh.

"Blessed are ye, when men shall hate you, and when they shall separate you from their company, and shall reproach you, and cast out your name as evil, for the Son of man's sake.

"Rejoice ye in that day, and leap for joy: for, behold, your reward is great in heaven: for in the like manner did their fathers unto the prophets.

"But woe unto you that are rich! for ye have received your consolation. Woe unto you that are full! for ye shall

# Madonna of the Harpies

By Andrea del Sarto (1486-1531)
In the Uffizi Gallery, Florence, Italy
Color Photograph by Alinari Brothers, Florence

THIS illustration shows part of the central figures of del Sarto's finest altar picture. The Madonna stands on a low pedestal, one arm supporting the Holy Child, who clings to her neck with a movement of exquisite grace. Her other hand holds a book upon which the Child has placed a foot.

In the original, two child-angels playfully clasp the Madonna's feet. On the pedestal are painted small carved decorative figures called harpies, whence the name of the picture.

The dignified, harmonious, luminous beauty of the picture is beyond praise. Its misty tone, bathing and almost obliterating the outlines, shows a masterly handling of color which few painters have equalled.

There is a personal suggestion in this famous picture, for the Madonna face is plainly that of his wife, the beautiful Lucrezia.

Giorgio Vasari, one of Andrea's pupils who is remembered for his picturesque "Lives of the Most Eminent Painters, Sculptors, Etc.," recorded that del Sarto's life was "full of glory and domestic trials." Glory came as frescoes and easel pictures from his gifted hand began to adorn cloister and palace of his native Florence; domestic trials came with his marriage, in 1512, to beautiful, capricious Lucrezia del Fede, whose features he painted over and over again. Robert Browning, in his noble poem "Andrea del Sarto," has distilled into words the story of "The Faultless Painter."

Other paintings by Andrea are on page 226 and in Volume I, page 245 and Volume VIII, page 334.

hunger. Woe unto you that laugh now! for ye shall mourn and weep. Woe unto you, when all men shall speak well of you! for so did their fathers to the false prophets.

"But I say unto you which hear, 'Love your enemies, do good to them which hate you, bless them that curse you, and pray for them which despitefully use you. And unto him that smiteth thee on the one cheek offer also the other; and him that taketh away thy cloke forbid not to take thy coat also. Give to every man that asketh of thee; and of him that taketh away thy goods ask them not again. And as ye would that men should do to you, do ye also to them likewise. For if ye love them which love you, what thank have ye? for sinners also love those that love them. And if ye do good to them which do good to you, what thank have ye? for sinners also do even the same. And if ye lend to them of whom ye hope to receive, what thank have ye? for sinners also lend to sinners, to receive as much again. But love ye your enemies, and do good and lend, hoping for nothing again; and your reward shall be great, and ye shall be the children of the Highest: for he is kind unto the unthankful and to the evil. Be ye therefore merciful, as your Father also is merciful. Judge not, and ye shall not be judged: condemn not, and ye shall not be condemned: forgive, and ye shall be forgiven: give, and it shall be given unto you; good measure, pressed down, and shaken together, and running over, shall men give into your bosom. For with the same measure that ye mete withal it shall be measured to you again.'"

And he spake a parable unto them, " Can the blind lead the blind? Shall they not both fall into the ditch? The disciple is not above his master: but every one that is perfect shall be as his master. And why beholdest thou the mote that is in thy brother's eye, but perceivest not the beam that is in thine own eye? Either how canst thou say to thy brother, 'Brother, let me pull out the mote that is in thine eye,' when thou thyself beholdest not the beam that is in thine own eye? Thou hypocrite, cast out first the beam out of thine own eye, and then shalt thou see clearly to pull out the mote that is in thy brother's eye. For a good tree bringeth not forth corrupt fruit; neither doth a corrupt tree bring forth good fruit. For every tree is known by his own fruit. For of thorns men do not gather figs, nor of a bramble bush gather they grapes. A good man out of the good treasure of his heart bringeth forth that which is good; and an evil man out of the evil treasure of his heart bringeth forth that which is evil: for of the abundance of the heart his mouth speaketh.

"And why call ye me, 'Lord, Lord,' and do not the things which I say? Whosoever cometh to me, and heareth my sayings, and doeth them, I will show you to whom he is like. He is like a man which built an house, and digged deep, and laid the foundation on a rock: and when the flood arose, the stream beat vehemently upon that house, and could not shake it: for it was founded upon a rock. But he that heareth, and doeth not, is like a man that without a foundation built an house upon the earth; against which the stream did beat vehemently, and immediately it fell; and the ruin of that house was great." — Luke 6:20–49.

JESUS HEALS THE SERVANT OF THE ROMAN CAPTAIN

Now when he had ended all his sayings in the audience of the people, he entered into Capernaum. And a certain centurion's servant, who was dear unto him, was sick, and ready to die. And when he heard of Jesus, he sent unto him the elders of the Jews, beseeching him that he would come and heal his servant.

And when they came to Jesus, they besought him instantly, saying, that "he was worthy for whom he should do this: for he loveth our nation, and he hath built us a synagogue."

Then Jesus went with them. And when he was now not far from the house, the centurion sent friends to him, saying unto him, "Lord, trouble not thyself: for I am not worthy that thou shouldest enter under my roof. Wherefore neither thought I myself worthy to come unto thee: but say in a word, and my servant shall be healed. For I also am a man set under authority, having under me soldiers, and I say unto one, 'Go,' and he goeth; and to another, 'Come,' and he cometh; and to my servant, 'Do this,' and he doeth it."

When Jesus heard these things, he marveled at him, and turned him about, and said unto the people that followed him, "I say unto you, I have not found so great faith, no, not in Israel." And they that were sent, returning to the house, found the servant whole that had been sick.

And it came to pass the day after, that he went into a city called Nain; and many of his disciples went with him, and much people. Now when he came nigh to the gate of the city, behold, there was a dead man carried out, the only son of his mother, and she was a widow: and much people of the city was with her.

And when the LORD saw her, he had compassion on her, and said unto her, "Weep not."

And he came and touched the bier: and they that bare him stood still. And he said, "Young man, I say unto thee, Arise." And he that was dead sat up, and began to speak. And he delivered him to his mother. And there came a fear on all: and they glorified God, saying, "A great prophet is risen up among us"; and, "God hath visited his people." — Luke 7:1–16.

## Jesus and John

Now when John had heard in the prison the works of Christ, he sent two of his disciples, and said unto him, "Art thou he that should come, or do we look for another?"

Jesus answered and said unto them, "Go and show John again those things which ye do hear and see: the blind receive their sight, and the lame walk, the lepers are cleansed, and the deaf hear, the dead are raised up, and the poor have the gospel preached to them. And blessed is he, whosoever shall not be offended in me."

And as they departed, Jesus began to say unto the multitudes concerning John, "What went ye out into the wilderness to see? A reed shaken with the wind? But what went ye out for to see? A man clothed in soft raiment? Behold, they that wear soft clothing are in kings' houses. But what went ye out for to see? A prophet? Yea, I say unto you, and more than a prophet. For this is he, of whom it is written, 'Behold, I send my messenger before thy face, which shall prepare thy way before thee.' Verily I say unto you, Among them that are born of women there hath not risen a greater than John the Baptist: notwithstanding he that is least in the kingdom of heaven is greater than he. And from the days of John the Baptist until now the kingdom of heaven suffereth violence, and the violent take it by force. For all the prophets and the law prophesied until John. And if ye will receive it, this is Elias, which was for to come. He that hath ears to hear, let him hear.

"But whereunto shall I liken this generation? It is like unto children sitting in the markets, and calling unto their fellows, and saying, 'We have piped unto you, and ye have not danced; we have mourned unto you, and ye have not lamented.' For John came neither eating nor drinking, and they say, 'He hath a devil.'

# Madonna and Child With Saints

By Francia (Francesco Raibolini, c.1450-1517)
In the Royal Art Gallery at Bologna, Italy
Photograph by Alinari Brothers, Florence

HERE we have a fine Renaissance altarpiece showing the Madonna and Child enthroned and
attended by four saints and an angel. The Madonna,
sweet of face, is holding the infant Jesus who has a
little bird in his left hand and raises his right in benedic-
tion. On the step of the throne a worshipping angel is
seated. At the sides stand four saints in repose.

The two saints on the left represent Augustine,
robed as a bishop holding a crozier or pastoral staff
and a book; and St. George, in armor, the vanquished
dragon at his feet. On the right are John the Baptist
holding his cross and pointing heavenward, and Stephen
in a deacon's robe, holding a book on which lie three
stones, symbol of the manner in which he was martyred.
The scene is placed out-of-doors between two buildings.
A hilly landscape is seen in the distance.

We can see that the painter loved rich detail. Notice
the frieze and columns of the side buildings, the
exquisitely patterned robe of Stephen and the even
richer robe of Augustine the original of which was
evidently studded with jewels. The armor of St. George
is carefully worked out even to the chain vest, and the
robes of the Madonna and angel are finely if simply
decorated. The key color of the composition is green.

The painter, Francesco Raibolini, called Il Francia,
was a North Italy goldsmith who took up painting
in his maturity. He lived and worked in Bologna and
achieved great popularity locally as an artist and
teacher. Francia devoted his artistic talent to portraying his sincere devotion to the Christian faith. Other
pictures by him appear in Volume VIII on pages
176 and 348.

The Son of man came eating and drinking, and they say, 'Behold a man gluttonous, and a winebibber, a friend of publicans and sinners.' But wisdom is justified of her children."

— Matthew 11:2-19.

## WARNINGS TO REPENTANCE

Then began he to upbraid the cities wherein most of his mighty works were done, because they repented not: "Woe unto thee, Chorazin! Woe unto thee, Bethsaida! for if the mighty works, which were done in you, had been done in Tyre and Sidon, they would have repented long ago in sackcloth and ashes. But I say unto you, 'It shall be more tolerable for Tyre and Sidon at the day of judgment, than for you.'

"And thou, Capernaum, which art exalted unto heaven, shalt be brought down to hell: for if the mighty works, which have been done in thee, had been done in Sodom, it would have remained until this day. But I say unto you, that it shall be more tolerable for the land of Sodom in the day of judgment, than for thee."

— Matthew 11:20-24.

## "COME UNTO ME, ALL YE THAT LABOUR"

I heard the voice of Jesus say,
"Come unto Me and rest;
Lay down, thou weary one, lay down
Thy head upon My breast."
I came to Jesus as I was,
Weary, and worn, and sad;
I found in Him a resting place,
And He has made me glad.

— *Horatius Bonar.*

At that time Jesus answered and said, "I thank thee, O Father, Lord of heaven and earth, because thou hast hid these things from the wise and prudent, and hast revealed them unto babes. Even so, Father: for so it seemed good in thy sight. All things are delivered unto me of my Father: and no man knoweth the Son, but the Father; neither knoweth any man the Father, save the Son, and he to whomsoever the Son will reveal him.

"Come unto me, all ye that labour and are heavy laden, and I will give you rest. Take my yoke upon you, and learn of me; for I am meek and lowly in heart: and ye shall find rest unto your souls. For my yoke is easy, and my burden is light."          —Matthew 11:25-30.

## THE ALABASTER BOX

### THE STORY OF THE TWO DEBTORS

The beautiful story of the anointing of Jesus by the woman who was a sinner.

### MASTER, NO OFFERING

Master, no offering
Costly and sweet,
May we, like Magdalene,
Lay at Thy feet;
Yet may love's incense rise,
Sweeter than sacrifice,
Dear Lord, to Thee.

Daily our lives would show
Weakness made strong,
Toilsome and gloomy ways
Brightened with song;
Some deeds of kindness done,
Some souls by patience won,
Dear Lord, to Thee.

Some word of hope, for hearts
Burdened with fears,
Some balm of peace, for eyes
Blinded with tears,

Some dews of mercy shed,
Some wayward footsteps led,
Dear Lord, to Thee.

Thus, in Thy service, Lord,
Till eventide
Closes the day of life,
May we abide.
And when earth's labors cease,
Bid us depart in peace,
Dear Lord, to Thee.
— *Edwin Pond Parker.*

And one of the Pharisees desired him that he would eat with him. And he went into the Pharisee's house, and sat down to meat. And, behold, a woman in the city, which was a sinner, when she knew that Jesus sat at meat in the Pharisee's house, brought an alabaster box of ointment, and stood at his feet behind him weeping, and began to wash his feet with tears, and did wipe them with the hairs of her head, and kissed his feet, and anointed them with the ointment. Now when the Pharisee which had bidden him saw it, he spake within himself, saying, "This man, if he were a prophet, would have known who and what manner of woman this is that toucheth him: for she is a sinner."

And Jesus answering said unto him, "Simon, I have somewhat to say unto thee."

And he saith, "Master, say on."

"There was a certain creditor which had two debtors: the one owed five hundred pence, and the other fifty. And when they had nothing to pay, he frankly forgave them both. Tell me therefore, which of them will love him most?"

Simon answered and said, "I suppose that he, to whom he forgave most."

And he said unto him, "Thou hast rightly judged."

And he turned to the woman, and said unto Simon, "Seest thou this woman? I entered into thine house; thou gavest me no water for my feet: but she hath washed my feet with tears, and wiped them with the hairs of her head. Thou gavest me no kiss: but this woman since the time I came in hath not ceased to kiss my feet. My head with oil thou didst not anoint: but this woman hath anointed my feet with ointment. Wherefore I say unto thee, 'Her sins, which are many, are forgiven; for she loved much: but to whom little is forgiven, the same loveth little.'"

And he said unto her, "Thy sins are forgiven."

And they that sat at meat with him began to say within themselves, "Who is this that forgiveth sins also?"

And he said to the woman, "Thy faith hath saved thee; go in peace." — Luke 7:36–50.

### Preaching and Healing in the Cities and Villages

And it came to pass afterward, that he went throughout every city and village, preaching and showing the glad tidings of the kingdom of God: and the twelve were with him, and certain women, which had been healed of evil spirits and infirmities, Mary called Magdalene, out of whom went seven devils, and Joanna, the wife of Chuza, Herod's steward, and Susanna, and many others, which ministered unto him of their substance. — Luke 8:1–3.

### Jesus' Defense of His Own Mission

Then was brought unto him one possessed with a devil, blind, and dumb: and he healed him, insomuch that the blind and dumb both spake and saw. And all the people were amazed, and said, "Is not this the son of David?"

RUINS OF AN ANCIENT SYNAGOGUE AT CHORAZIN
*Photograph by the Reverend Doctor Charles W. Gilkey*

RUINS OF AN ANCIENT SYNAGOGUE AT CHORAZIN
*Photograph by the Reverend Doctor Charles W. Gilkey*

But when the Pharisees heard it, they said, "This fellow doth not cast out devils, but by Beelzebub, the prince of the devils."

And Jesus knew their thoughts, and said unto them, "Every kingdom divided against itself is brought to desolation; and every city or house divided against itself shall not stand: and if Satan cast out Satan, he is divided against himself; how shall then his kingdom stand? And if I by Beelzebub cast out devils, by whom do your children cast them out? therefore they shall be your judges. But if I cast out devils by the Spirit of God, then the kingdom of God is come unto you. Or else how can one enter into a strong man's house, and spoil his goods, except he first bind the strong man? and then he will spoil his house. He that is not with me is against me; and he that gathereth not with me scattereth abroad.

"Wherefore I say unto you, All manner of sin and blasphemy shall be forgiven unto men: but the blasphemy against the Holy Ghost shall not be forgiven unto men. And whosoever speaketh a word against the Son of man, it shall be forgiven him: but whosoever speaketh against the Holy Ghost, it shall not be forgiven him, neither in this world, neither in the world to come. Either make the tree good, and his fruit good; or else make the tree corrupt, and his fruit corrupt: for the tree is known by his fruit. O generation of vipers, how can ye, being evil, speak good things? For out of the abundance of the heart the mouth speaketh. A good man out of the good treasure of the heart bringeth forth good things: and an evil man out of the evil treasure bringeth forth evil things. But I say unto you, that every idle word that men shall speak, they shall give account thereof in the day of judgment. For by thy words thou shalt be justified, and by thy words thou shalt be condemned."

Then certain of the scribes and of the Pharisees answered, saying, "Master, we would see a sign from thee." But he answered and said unto them, "An evil and adulterous generation seeketh after a sign; and there shall no sign be given to it, but the sign of the prophet Jonas: for as Jonas was three days and three nights in the whale's belly; so shall the Son of man be three days and three nights in the heart of the earth. The men of Nineveh shall rise in judgment with this generation, and shall condemn it: because they repented at the preaching of Jonas; and, behold, a greater than Jonas is here. The queen of the south shall rise up in the judgment with this generation, and shall condemn it: for she came from the uttermost parts of the earth to hear the wisdom of Solomon; and, behold, a greater than Solomon is here. When the unclean spirit is gone out of a man, he walketh through dry places, seeking rest, and findeth none. Then he saith, 'I will return into my house from whence I came out'; and when he is come, he findeth it empty, swept, and garnished. Then goeth he, and taketh with himself seven other spirits more wicked than himself, and they enter in and dwell there: and the last state of that man is worse than the first. Even so shall it be also unto this wicked generation."

— Matthew 12:22–45.

## Who Is My Mother or My Brethren?

There came then his brethren and his mother, and, standing without, sent unto him, calling him. And the multitude sat about him, and they said unto him, "Behold, thy mother and thy brethren without seek for thee."

And he answered them, saying, "Who is my mother, or my brethren?"

And he looked round about on them which sat about him, and said, "Behold my mother and my brethren! For whosoever shall do the will of God, the same is my brother, and my sister, and mother." — Mark 3:31–35.

## STORIES BY THE SEA

And he began again to teach by the seaside: and there was gathered unto him a great multitude, so that he entered into a ship, and sat in the sea; and the whole multitude was by the sea on the land. And he taught them many things by parables, and said unto them in his doctrine,

### THE STORY OF THE SOWER

"Hearken! Behold, there went out a sower to sow: and it came to pass, as he sowed, some fell by the wayside, and the fowls of the air came and devoured it up. And some fell on stony ground, where it had not much earth; and immediately it sprang up, because it had no depth of earth: but when the sun was up, it was scorched; and because it had no root, it withered away. And some fell among thorns, and the thorns grew up, and choked it, and it yielded no fruit. And other fell on good ground, and did yield fruit that sprang up and increased; and brought forth, some thirty, and some sixty, and some an hundred."

And he said unto them, "He that hath ears to hear, let him hear."

And when he was alone, they that were about him with the twelve asked of him the parable. And he said unto them, "Unto you it is given to know the mystery of the kingdom of God: but unto them that are without, all these things are done in parables: that seeing they may see, and not perceive; and hearing they may hear, and not understand; lest at any time they should be converted, and their sins should be forgiven them."

And he said unto them, "Know ye not this parable? And how then will ye know all parables?

"The sower soweth the word. And these are they by the wayside, where the word is sown; but when they have heard, Satan cometh immediately, and taketh away the word that was sown in their hearts. And these are they likewise which are sown on stony ground; who, when they have heard the word, immediately receive it with gladness; and have no root in themselves, and so endure but for a time: afterward, when affliction or persecution ariseth for the word's sake, immediately they are offended. And these are they which are sown among thorns; such as hear the word, and the cares of this world, and the deceitfulness of riches, and the lusts of other things entering in, choke the word, and it becometh unfruitful. And these are they which are sown on good ground; such as hear the word, and receive it, and bring forth fruit, some thirtyfold, some sixty, and some an hundred."

And he said unto them, "Is a candle brought to be put under a bushel, or under a bed? and not to be set on a candlestick? For there is nothing hid, which shall not be manifested; neither was any thing kept secret, but that it should come abroad. If any man have ears to hear, let him hear."

And he said unto them, "Take heed what ye hear: with what measure ye mete, it shall be measured to you: and unto you that hear shall more be given. For he that hath, to him shall be given: and he that hath not, from him shall be taken even that which he hath."

THE KINGDOM OF GOD IS LIKE THE GROWING CORN

And he said, "So is the kingdom of God, as if a man should cast seed into the ground; and should sleep, and rise night and day, and the seed should spring and grow up, he knoweth not how. For the earth bringeth forth fruit of herself; first the blade, then the ear, after that the full corn in the ear. But when the fruit is brought forth, immediately he putteth in the sickle, because the harvest is come."

And he said, "Whereunto shall we liken the kingdom of God? Or with what comparison shall we compare it? It is like a grain of mustard seed, which, when it is sown in the earth, is less than all the seeds that be in the earth: but when it is sown, it groweth up, and becometh greater than all herbs, and shooteth out great branches; so that the fowls of the air may lodge under the shadow of it."

And with many such parables spake he the word unto them, as they were able to hear it. But without a parable spake he not unto them: and when they were alone, he expounded all things to his disciples. —Mark 4:1–34.

### THE STORY OF THE ENEMY WHO SOWED TARES

Another parable put he forth unto them, saying, "The kingdom of heaven is likened unto a man which sowed good seed in his field: but while men slept, his enemy came and sowed tares among the wheat, and went his way. But when the blade was sprung up, and brought forth fruit, then appeared the tares also. So the servants of the householder came and said unto him, 'Sir, didst not thou sow good seed in thy field? From whence then hath it tares?'

"He said unto them, 'An enemy hath done this.'

"The servants said unto him, 'Wilt thou then that we go and gather them up?'

"But he said, 'Nay; lest while ye gather up the tares, ye root up also the wheat with them. Let both grow together until the harvest: and in the time of harvest I will say to the reapers, "Gather ye together first the tares, and bind them in bundles to burn them: but gather the wheat into my barn.""""

### THE STORY OF THE WOMAN AND THE YEAST

Another parable spake he unto them: "The kingdom of heaven is like unto leaven, which a woman took, and hid in three measures of meal, till the whole was leavened."

All these things spake Jesus unto the multitude in parables; and without a parable spake he not unto them: that it might be fulfilled which was spoken by the prophet, saying,

"I will open my mouth in parables;
I will utter things which have been kept secret from the foundation of the world."

Then Jesus sent the multitude away, and went into the house: and his disciples came unto him, saying, "Declare unto us the parable of the tares of the field."

He answered and said unto them, "He that soweth the good seed is the Son of man; the field is the world; the good seed are the children of the kingdom; but the tares are the children of the wicked one: the enemy that sowed them is the devil; the harvest is the end of the world; and the reapers are the angels. As therefore the tares are gathered and burned in the fire; so shall it be in the end of this world. The Son of man shall send forth his angels, and they shall gather out of his kingdom all things that offend, and them which do iniquity; and shall cast them into a furnace of fire: there shall be wailing and gnashing of teeth. Then shall the righteous shine forth as the sun in the kingdom of their Father. Who hath ears to hear, let him hear."

### THE STORY OF THE TREASURE HID IN THE FIELD

"Again, the kingdom of heaven is like unto treasure hid in a field; the which when a man hath found, he hideth, and for joy thereof goeth and selleth all that he hath, and buyeth that field."

### THE STORY OF THE MERCHANTMAN AND THE PEARL OF GREAT PRICE

"Again, the kingdom of heaven is like unto a merchantman, seeking goodly pearls: who, when he had found one pearl of great price, went and sold all that he had, and bought it."

### THE STORY OF THE NET AND THE FISHES

"Again, the kingdom of heaven is like unto a net, that was cast into the sea, and gathered of every kind: which, when it was full, they drew to shore, and sat down, and gathered the good into vessels, but cast the bad away. So shall it be at the end of the world: the angels shall come forth, and sever the wicked from among the just, and shall cast them into the furnace of fire: there shall be wailing and gnashing of teeth."

Jesus saith unto them, "Have ye understood all these things?"

They say unto him, "Yea, Lord."

Then said he unto them, "Therefore every scribe which is instructed unto the kingdom of heaven is like unto a man that is an householder, which bringeth forth out of his treasure things new and old."

And it came to pass, that when Jesus had finished these parables, he departed thence.    —Matthew 13:24–30, 33–53.

# Madonna of the Olives

Painted by Nicolo Barabino (1832-1891)
In the Cathedral at St. Pier d'Arena, Italy
Color Photograph by Alinari Brothers, Florence

THIS exquisite painting of a modern mother and child was done near the close of the artist's life. Like other great artists who have studied closely and reverently the life of the Master, Barabino shows us by this picture that Jesus belongs to all ages and all peoples. The sweet, humble face of this beautiful young mother might well be that of the Virgin, and the figure of the infant might be that of Jesus.

Nicolo Barabino was born at St. Pier d'Arena, near Genoa, Italy. His first notable picture was a religious one painted for a hospital in Savona, and was the beginning for him of a life largely devoted to church art. In all his works he showed originality, careful drawing and strength of color. His skill and good taste place him among the first painters of his time. He died in Florence in 1891.

The Madonna of the Olives was purchased by the Queen of Italy in 1887 and now rests in the Cathedral of the little village where Barabino was born.

## "The Wind and the Sea Obey Him"

### "PEACE, BE STILL"

Jesus, Saviour, pilot me,
Over life's tempestuous sea;
Unknown waves before me roll,
Hiding rock and treacherous shoal;
Chart and compass came from Thee:
Jesus, Saviour, pilot me.

As a mother stills her child,
Thou canst hush the ocean wild;
Boisterous waves obey Thy will
When Thou say'st to them "Be still!"
Wondrous Sovereign of the sea.
Jesus, Saviour, pilot me.

When at last I near the shore,
And the fearful breakers roar
'Twixt me and the peaceful rest,
Then, while leaning on Thy breast,
May I hear Thee say to me,
"Fear not, I will pilot thee!"

— *E. Hopper.*

And the same day, when the even was come, he saith unto them, "Let us pass over unto the other side."

And when they had sent away the multitude, they took him even as he was in the ship. And there were also with him other little ships. And there arose a great storm of wind, and the waves beat into the ship, so that it was now full. And he was in the hinder part of the ship, asleep on a pillow: and they awake him, and say unto him, "Master, carest thou not that we perish?"

And he arose, and rebuked the wind, and said unto the sea, "Peace, be still." And the wind ceased, and there was a great calm.

A FAMILY WHO LIVED IN A TOMB

*Photograph by Professor Lewis Bayles Paton*

This poor family of Palestine have made a home in an empty rock-hewn tomb. In New Testament times, lepers, those mentally deranged and other outcasts, often lived in rock tombs.

"And when he went forth to land, there met him out of the city a certain man, which had devils long time, and ware no clothes, neither abode in any house, but in the tombs."—*Luke 8:27.*

And he said unto them, "Why are ye so fearful? How is it that ye have no faith?"

And they feared exceedingly, and said one to another, "What manner of man is this, that even the wind and the sea obey him?"                    — Mark 4:35-41.

## The Man with Many Demons

And they came over unto the other side of the sea, into the country of the Gadarenes. And when he was come out of the ship, immediately there met him out of the tombs a man with an unclean spirit, who had his dwelling among the tombs; and no man could bind him, no, not with chains: because that he had been often bound with fetters and chains, and the chains had been plucked asunder by him, and the fetters broken in pieces: neither could any man tame him. And always, night and day, he was in the mountains, and in the tombs, crying, and cutting himself with stones.

But when he saw Jesus afar off, he ran and worshiped him, and cried with a loud voice, and said, "What have I to do with thee, Jesus, thou Son of the most high God? I adjure thee by God, that thou torment me not."

For he said unto him, "Come out of the man, thou unclean spirit."

And he asked him, "What is thy name?"

And he answered, saying, "My name is Legion: for we are many."

And he besought him much that he would not send them away out of the country. Now there was there nigh unto the mountains a great herd of swine feeding. And all the devils besought him, saying, "Send us into the swine, that we may enter into them."

And forthwith Jesus gave them leave. And the unclean spirits went out, and entered into the swine: and the herd ran violently down a steep place into the sea, (they were about two thousand;) and were choked in the sea. And they that fed the swine fled, and told it in the city, and in the country. And they went out to see what it was that was done.

And they come to Jesus, and see him that was possessed with the devil, and had the legion, sitting, and clothed, and in his right mind: and they were afraid. And they that saw it told them how it befell to him that was possessed with the devil, and also concerning the swine. And they began to pray him to depart out of their coasts. And when he was come into the ship, he that had been possessed with the devil prayed him that he might be with him. Howbeit Jesus suffered him not, but saith unto him, "Go home to thy friends, and tell them how great things the LORD hath done for thee, and hath had compassion on thee."

And he departed, and began to publish in Decapolis how great things Jesus had done for him: and all men did marvel.                                        — Mark 5:1–20.

## THE THRONGING MULTITUDES

### HOW HE. CAME

When the golden evening gathered on the shore of Galilee,
When the fishing boats lay quiet by the sea,
Long ago the people wondered, tho' no sign was in the sky,
For the glory of the Lord was passing by.

Not in robes of purple splendor, not in silken softness shod,
But in raiment worn with travel came their God,
And the people knew His presence by the heart that ceased to sigh
When the glory of the Lord was passing by.

For He healed their sick at even, and He cured the leper's sore,
And sinful men and women sinned no more,
And the world grew mirthful-hearted, and forgot its misery
When the glory of the Lord was passing by.

Not in robes of purple splendor, but in lives that do His will,
In patient acts of kindness He comes still;
And the people cry with wonder, tho' no sign is in the sky,
That the glory of the Lord is passing by.
                                        — W. J. Dawson.

And when Jesus was passed over again by ship unto the other side, much people gathered unto him: and he was nigh unto the sea. And, behold, there cometh one of the rulers of the synagogue, Jairus by name; and when he saw him, he fell at his feet, and besought him greatly,

# Jesus Raising Jairus' Daughter

By Gustav Karl Ludwig Richter (1823-1884)
In the National Gallery, Berlin, Germany

PERHAPS you would like to read the Bible account of the raising of Jairus' daughter, beginning on page 110 in this Volume.

The scene is laid in Jairus' house. Our Lord has sent away the crowd of friends and mourners who had "laughed him to scorn" when He told them, "The damsel is not dead, but sleepeth." Jesus kept with him only the parents and three of his disciples, Peter, James and John, those whose faith made them worthy to witness the miracle He was about to perform.

It is the moment when Jesus says "unto her, 'Talitha cumi'; which being interpreted is, 'Damsel, I say unto thee, arise'." We see the young girl beginning to move, lifting her head toward the Master. Note the hope and astonishment on the faces and in the gestures of the others. As the Bible says, "They were astonished with a great astonishment." Is it not an impressive conception of this event? Note the finely wrought character of each individual. Does the picture help make the Bible story more real to you?

This painting was the first artistic success of the German artist, Gustav Richter, and started him on a long and useful career. Richter was born in Berlin, studied at the Berlin Academy, and lived and taught there most of his life. He studied also for two years in Paris and three years in Rome. In 1861 he was commissioned by the King of Bavaria to visit Egypt and make sketches of the Pyramids. During his later life he was elected member of several European academies and received other honors which indicate the high esteem in which he was held. He died in Berlin in 1884. His works were made very popular in Europe and America by color reproductions.

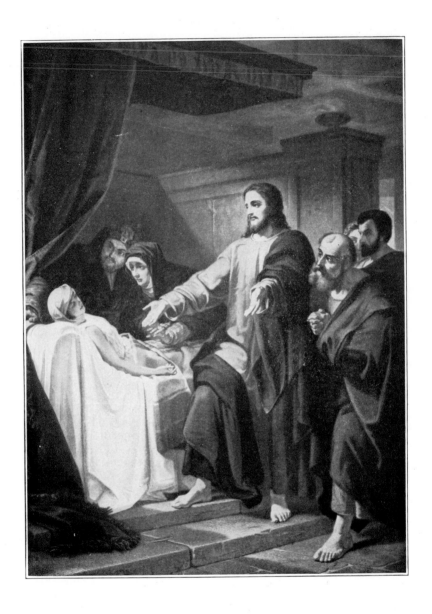

saying, "My little daughter lieth at the point of death: I pray thee, come and lay thy hands on her, that she may be healed; and she shall live."

And Jesus went with him; and much people followed him, and thronged him. And a certain woman, which had an issue of blood twelve years, and had suffered many things of many physicians, and had spent all that she had, and was nothing bettered, but rather grew worse, when she had heard of Jesus, came in the press behind, and touched his garment. For she said, "If I may touch but his clothes, I shall be whole." And straightway the fountain of her blood was dried up; and she felt in her body that she was healed of that plague.

### "WHO TOUCHED MY CLOTHES?"

And Jesus, immediately knowing in himself that virtue had gone out of him, turned him about in the press, and said, "Who touched my clothes?"

And his disciples said unto him, "Thou seest the multitude thronging thee, and sayest thou, 'Who touched me?'"

And he looked round about to see her that had done this thing. But the woman fearing and trembling, knowing what was done in her, came and fell down before him, and told him all the truth.

And he said unto her, "Daughter, thy faith hath made thee whole; go in peace, and be whole of thy plague."                    — Mark 5:21–34.

### "TALITHA CUMI"

While he yet spake, there came from the ruler of the synagogue's house certain which said, "Thy daughter is dead: why troublest thou the Master any further?"

As soon as Jesus heard the word that was spoken, he

saith unto the ruler of the synagogue, "Be not afraid, only believe."

And he suffered no man to follow him, save Peter, and James, and John the brother of James. And he cometh to the house of the ruler of the synagogue, and seeth the tumult, and them that wept and wailed greatly.

And when he was come in, he saith unto them, "Why make ye this ado, and weep? The damsel is not dead, but sleepeth."

And they laughed him to scorn. But when he had put them all out, he taketh the father and the mother of the damsel, and them that were with him, and entereth in where the damsel was lying.

And he took the damsel by the hand, and said unto her, "Talitha cumi"; which is, being interpreted, "Damsel, I say unto thee, arise."

And straightway the damsel arose, and walked; for she was of the age of twelve years. And they were astonished with a great astonishment. And he charged

OUTSIDE THE CITY OF NAZARETH
*Photograph by W. A. Pottenger expressly for The Book of Life*

The country about Nazareth looks much as it did in Jesus' day. The fields in the foreground are those in which Jesus saw the "sower go forth to sow," in which the "lilies of the field" grew when Jesus was a boy.

them straitly that no man should know it; and commanded that something should be given her to eat.

— Mark 5:35–43.

## The Two Blind Men

And when Jesus departed thence, two blind men followed him, crying, and saying, "Thou son of David, have mercy on us."

And when he was come into the house, the blind men came to him: and Jesus saith unto them, "Believe ye that I am able to do this?"

They said unto him, "Yea, Lord."

Then touched he their eyes, saying, "According to your faith be it unto you."

And their eyes were opened; and Jesus straitly charged them, saying, "See that no man know it."

But they, when they were departed, spread abroad his fame in all that country.

As they went out, behold, they brought to him a dumb man possessed with a devil. And when the devil was cast out, the dumb spake: and the multitudes marveled, saying, "It was never so seen in Israel."

But the Pharisees said, "He casteth out devils through the prince of the devils." — Matthew 9:27–34.

## Nazareth Again Rejects the Carpenter, the Son of Mary

Jesus went back to his house, but his old townsmen, though more respectful than before, refused again to believe on him, and thereby lost the blessing and his mighty works.

And he went out from thence, and came into his own country; and his disciples follow him. And when the sabbath day was come, he began to teach in the synagogue: and many hearing him were astonished, saying,

"From whence hath this man these things? And what wisdom is this which is given unto him, that even such mighty works are wrought by his hands? Is not this the carpenter, the son of Mary, the brother of James, and Joses, and of Juda, and Simon? And are not his sisters here with us?" And they were offended at him.

But Jesus said unto them, "A prophet is not without honour, but in his own country, and among his own kin, and in his own house."

And he could there do no mighty work, save that he laid his hands upon a few sick folk, and healed them. And he marveled because of their unbelief.  — Mark 6:1-6a.

### Preaching the Gospel of the Kingdom

And Jesus went about all the cities and villages, teaching in their synagogues, and preaching the gospel of the kingdom, and healing every sickness and every disease among the people.          — Matthew 9:35.

### The Twelve Apostles Are Sent Out to the Sheep Scattered Abroad Without a Shepherd

But when he saw the multitudes, he was moved with compassion on them, because they fainted, and were scattered abroad, as sheep having no shepherd. Then saith he unto his disciples, "The harvest truly is plenteous, but the labourers are few; pray ye therefore the Lord of the harvest, that he will send forth labourers into his harvest."

And when he had called unto him his twelve disciples, he gave them power against unclean spirits, to cast them out, and to heal all manner of sickness and all manner of disease. Now the names of the twelve apostles are these: The first,

**Simon,** who is called Peter,
**Andrew,** his brother;
**James,** the son of Zebedee,
**John,** his brother;
**Philip,**
**Bartholomew,**
**Thomas,**
**Matthew,** the publican;
**James,** the son of Alphaeus;
**Lebbæus,** whose surname was Thaddeus;
**Simon,** the Canaanite;
**Judas Iscariot,** who also betrayed him.

(Lebbæus is also known as Judas, not Iscariot.)

These twelve Jesus sent forth, and commanded them, saying, "Go not into the way of the Gentiles, and into any city of the Samaritans enter ye not: but go rather to the lost sheep of the house of Israel. And as ye go, preach, saying, 'The kingdom of heaven is at hand.' Heal the sick, cleanse the lepers, raise the dead, cast out devils: freely ye have received, freely give. Provide neither gold, nor silver, nor brass in your purses, nor scrip for your journey, neither two coats, neither shoes, nor yet staves: for the workman is worthy of his meat. And into whatsoever city or town ye shall enter, enquire who in it is worthy; and there abide till ye go thence. And when ye come into an house, salute it. And if the house be worthy, let your peace come upon it: but if it be not worthy, let your peace return to you. And whosoever shall not receive you, nor hear your words, when ye depart out of that house or city, shake off the dust of your feet. Verily I say unto you, It shall be more tolerable for the land of Sodom and Gomorrha in the day of judgment, than for that city."

## "AS SHEEP IN THE MIDST OF WOLVES"

"Behold, I send you forth as sheep in the midst of wolves: be ye therefore wise as serpents, and harmless as doves. But beware of men: for they will deliver you up to the councils, and they will scourge you in their synagogues; and ye shall be brought before governors and kings for my sake, for a testimony against them and the Gentiles. But when they deliver you up, take no thought how or what ye shall speak: for it shall be given you in that same hour what ye shall speak. For it is not ye that speak, but the Spirit of your Father which speaketh in you. And the brother shall deliver up the brother to death, and the father the child: and the children shall rise up against their parents, and cause them to be put to death. And ye shall be hated of all men for my name's sake: but he that endureth to the end shall be saved. But when they persecute you in this city, flee ye into another: for verily I say unto you, ye shall not have gone over the cities of Israel, till the Son of man be come.

## THE DISCIPLE IS NOT ABOVE HIS MASTER

"The disciple is not above his master, nor the servant above his lord. It is enough for the disciple that he be as his master, and the servant as his lord. If they have called the master of the house Beelzebub, how much more shall they call them of his household? Fear them not therefore: for there is nothing covered, that shall not be revealed; and hid, that shall not be known. What I tell you in darkness, that speak ye in light: and what ye hear in the ear, that preach ye upon the house-tops. And fear not them which kill the body, but are not able to kill the soul: but rather fear him which is able to destroy both soul and body in hell."

### NOT A SPARROW FALLS WITHOUT GOD'S NOTICE

"Are not two sparrows sold for a farthing? And one of them shall not fall on the ground without your Father. But the very hairs of your head are all numbered. Fear ye not therefore, ye are of more value than many sparrows. Whosoever therefore shall confess me before men, him will I confess also before my Father which is in heaven. But whosoever shall deny me before men, him will I also deny before my Father which is in heaven.

"Think not that I am come to send peace on earth: I came not to send peace, but a sword. For I am come to set a man at variance against his father, and the daughter against her mother, and the daughter-in-law against her mother-in-law. And a man's foes shall be they of his own household. He that loveth father or mother more than me is not worthy of me: and he that loveth son or daughter more than me is not worthy of me. And he that taketh not his cross, and followeth after me, is not worthy of me. He that findeth his life shall lose it: and he that loseth his life for my sake shall find it.

"He that receiveth you receiveth me, and he that receiveth me receiveth him that sent me. He that receiveth a prophet in the name of a prophet shall receive a prophet's reward; and he that receiveth a righteous man in the name of a righteous man shall receive a righteous man's reward.

"And whosoever shall give to drink unto one of these little ones a cup of cold water only in the name of a disciple, verily I say unto you, he shall in no wise lose his reward."

And it came to pass, when Jesus had made an end of commanding his twelve disciples, he departed thence to teach and to preach in their cities. — Matthew 9:36; 11:1.

## The Death of John the Baptist

At a height of 3800 feet above the Dead Sea are the ruins of the old fortress town of Machaerus. Two dungeons may still be seen: one of them deep down in the solid rock with small holes still visible where staples of wood or iron had once been fixed, perhaps the very dungeon in which John was confined. In the hot stifling depths of this dark prison, for ten months, the free spirit of the desert dweller chafed in confinement.

In the palace of Machaerus there was wild revelry. Herod, on his birthday, made a supper for his lords and the high captains and the chief men of Galilee. The daughter of Herodias danced before the king and he offered to give her anything to the half of his kingdom. The head of John the Baptist was what she asked, for her mother hated the prophet, since he had boldly rebuked the king for his illegal marriage. Herod was exceedingly sorry, but his royal word had been passed. That same night a soldier carried out the order of the king. A weak king, an evil woman, a dancing girl, and the life of one of the greatest souls of all the ages! How dramatic and how tragic!

And King Herod heard of him; (for his name was spread abroad:) and he said, "John the Baptist was risen from the dead, and therefore mighty works do show forth themselves in him."

Others said, "It is Elias."

And others said, "It is a prophet, or as one of the prophets."

But when Herod heard thereof, he said, "It is John, whom I beheaded: he is risen from the dead."

For Herod himself had sent forth and laid hold upon John, and bound him in prison for Herodias' sake, his brother Philip's wife: for he had married her.

For John had said unto Herod, "It is not lawful for thee to have thy brother's wife." Therefore Herodias had a quarrel against him, and would have killed him; but she could not: for Herod feared John, knowing that he was a just man and an holy, and observed him;

and when he heard him, he did many things, and heard him gladly. And when a convenient day was come, that Herod on his birthday made a supper to his lords, high captains, and chief estates of Galilee; and when the daughter of the said Herodias came in, and danced, and pleased Herod and them that sat with him, the king said unto the damsel, "Ask of me whatsoever thou wilt, and I will give it thee."

And he sware unto her, "Whatsoever thou shalt ask of me, I will give it thee, unto the half of my kingdom."

And she went forth, and said unto her mother, "What shall I ask?"

And she said, "The head of John the Baptist."

And she came in straightway with haste unto the king, and asked, saying, "I will that thou give me by and by in a charger the head of John the Baptist."

And the king was exceeding sorry; yet for his oath's sake, and for their sakes which sat with him, he would not reject her. And immediately the king sent an executioner, and commanded his head to be brought: and he went and beheaded him in the prison, and brought his head in a charger, and gave it to the damsel: and the damsel gave it to her mother.

And when his disciples heard of it, they came and took up his corpse, and laid it in a tomb.  — Mark 6:14–29.

## FEEDING THE MULTITUDE

And the apostles gathered themselves together unto Jesus, and told him all things, both what they had done, and what they had taught. And he said unto them, "Come ye yourselves apart into a desert place, and rest a while": for there were many coming and going, and they had no leisure so much as to eat. And they departed into a desert place by ship privately.

And the people saw them departing, and many knew him, and ran afoot thither out of all cities, and outwent them, and came together unto him. And Jesus, when he came out, saw much people, and was moved with compassion toward them, because they were as sheep not having a shepherd: and he began to teach them many things. And when the day was now far spent, his disciples came unto him, and said, "This is a desert place, and now the time is far passed: send them away, that they may go into the country round about, and into the villages, and buy themselves bread: for they have nothing to eat."

He answered and said unto them, "Give ye them to eat."

And they say unto him, "Shall we go and buy two hundred pennyworth of bread, and give them to eat?"

He saith unto them, "How many loaves have ye? Go and see."

And when they knew, they say, "Five, and two fishes."

And he commanded them to make all sit down by companies upon the green grass. And they sat down in ranks, by hundreds, and by fifties. And when he had taken the five loaves and the two fishes, he looked up to heaven, and blessed, and brake the loaves, and gave them to his disciples to set before them; and the two fishes divided he among them all. And they did all eat, and were filled. And they took up twelve baskets full of the fragments, and of the fishes. And they that did eat of the loaves were about five thousand men. And straightway he constrained his disciples to get into the ship, and to go to the other side before unto Bethsaida, while he sent away the people. And when he had sent them away, he departed into a mountain to pray.

— Mark 6:30–46.

### Stilling the Storm

And when even was come, the ship was in the midst of the sea, and he alone on the land. And he saw them toiling in rowing; for the wind was contrary unto them: and about the fourth watch of the night he cometh unto them, walking upon the sea, and would have passed by them. But when they saw him walking upon the sea, they supposed it had been a spirit, and cried out: for they all saw him, and were troubled. And immediately he talked with them, and saith unto them, "Be of good cheer: it is I; be not afraid."          —Mark 6:47–50

### "Of a Truth Thou Art the Son of God"

And Peter answered him and said, "Lord, if it be thou, bid me come unto thee on the water." And he said, "Come." And when Peter was come down out of the ship, he walked on the water, to go to Jesus. But when he saw the wind boisterous, he was afraid; and beginning to sink, he cried, saying, "Lord save me." And immediately Jesus stretched forth his hand, and caught him, and said unto him, "O thou of little faith, wherefore didst thou doubt?" And when they were come into the ship, the wind ceased. Then they that were in the ship came and worshipped him, saying, "Of a truth thou art the Son of God."

And when they were gone over, they came into the land of Gennesaret. And when the men of that place had knowledge of him, they sent out into all that country round about, and brought unto him all that were diseased; and besought him that they might only touch the hem of his garment: and as many as touched were made perfectly whole.          — Matthew 14:28–36

## Evil Is from Within

Then came together unto him the Pharisees, and certain of the scribes, which came from Jerusalem. And when they saw some of his disciples eat bread with defiled, that is to say, with unwashen, hands, they found fault. For the Pharisees, and all the Jews, except they wash their hands oft, eat not, holding the tradition of the elders. And when they come from the market, except they wash, they eat not. And many other things there be, which they have received to hold, as the washing of cups, and pots, brazen vessels, and of tables.

Then the Pharisees and scribes asked him, "Why walk not thy disciples according to the tradition of the elders, but eat bread with unwashen hands?"

He answered and said unto them, "Well hath Esaias prophesied of you hypocrites, as it is written,

'This people honoureth me with their lips,
But their heart is far from me.
Howbeit in vain do they worship me,
Teaching for doctrines the commandments of men.'

"For laying aside the commandment of God, ye hold the tradition of men, as the washing of pots and cups: and many other such like things ye do."

And he said unto them, "Full well ye reject the commandment of God, that ye may keep your own tradition. For Moses said, 'Honour thy father and thy mother'; and, 'Whoso curseth father or mother, let him die the death': but ye say, 'If a man shall say to his father or mother, "It is Corban, that is to say, a gift, by whatsoever thou mightest be profited by me;' he shall be free." And ye suffer him no more to do ought for his father or his mother; making the word of God of none effect through your tradition, which ye have delivered: and many such like things do ye."

And when he had called all the people unto him, he said unto them, "Hearken unto me every one of you, and understand: there is nothing from without a man, that entering into him can defile him: but the things which come out of him, those are they that defile the man. If any man have ears to hear, let him hear."

And when he was entered into the house from the people, his disciples asked him concerning the parable. And he saith unto them, "Are ye so without understanding also? Do ye not perceive, that whatsoever thing from without entereth into the man, it cannot defile him; because it entereth not into his heart, but into the belly, and goeth out into the draught, purging all meats?"

. And he said, "That which cometh out of the man, that defileth the man. For from within, out of the heart of men, proceed evil thoughts, adulteries, fornications, murders, thefts, covetousness, wickedness, deceit, lasciviousness, an evil eye, blasphemy, pride, foolishness: all these evil things come from within, and defile the man."

— Mark 7:1-23.

A MOSES' SEAT

*Photograph by Frances Jenkins Olcott*

This is a real Moses' Seat among the ruins of an ancient synagogue in deserted Chorazin of the Bible.

Our Lord said of the proud and arrogant Pharisees, "The Scribes and the Pharisees sit in Moses' Seat." For the Moses' Seat in a synagogue was where the leading elders sat.

Today we climb a steep hill back of the Sea of Galilee, and cross a plain, and a gorge filled with black stones, and we are among the ruins of the synagogue of Chorazin. What did the Saviour say would happen to Chorazin? Matthew 11:20-24, page 95.

# The Story of the Master
## From the Gospels of Matthew, Mark and Luke

## Days of Service and Friendship

### THE JOURNEY TO THE REGION OF TYRE AND SIDON

While on this journey to Galilee the humility and the faith of the "Canaanitish woman" touched Jesus and won his commendation.

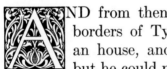ND from thence he arose, and went into the borders of Tyre and Sidon, and entered into an house, and would have no man know it: but he could not be hid. For a certain woman, whose young daughter had an unclean spirit, heard of him, and came and fell at his feet. The woman was a Greek, a Syrophenician by nation; and she besought him that he would cast forth the devil out of her daughter. But Jesus said unto her, "Let the children first be filled: for it is not meet to take the children's bread, and to cast it unto the dogs."

And she answered and said unto him, "Yes, Lord: yet the dogs under the table eat of the children's crumbs."

And he said unto her, "For this saying go thy way; the devil is gone out of thy daughter."

And when she was come to her house, she found the devil gone out, and her daughter laid upon the bed.

— Mark 7:24–30.

### HEALING THE DEAF MAN

And again, departing from the coasts of Tyre and Sidon, he came unto the sea of Galilee, through the midst of the coasts of Decapolis. And they bring unto him one

126

that was deaf, and had an impediment in his speech; and they beseech him to put his hand upon him. And he took him aside from the multitude, and put his fingers into his ears, and he spit, and touched his tongue; and looking up to heaven, he sighed, and saith unto him, "Ephphatha," that is, "Be opened."

And straightway his ears were opened, and the string of his tongue was loosed, and he spake plain. And he charged them that they should tell no man: but the more he charged them, so much the more a great deal they published it; and were beyond measure astonished, saying, "He hath done all things well: he maketh both the deaf to hear, and the dumb to speak."    — Mark 7:31-37.

## The Second Feeding of the Multitude

Then Jesus called his disciples unto him, and said, "I have compassion on the multitude, because they continue with me now three days, and have nothing to eat: and I will not send them away fasting lest they faint in the way."

And his disciples say unto him, "Whence should we have so much bread in the wilderness, as to fill so great a multitude?"

And Jesus saith unto them, "How many loaves have ye?"

And they said, "Seven, and a few little fishes."

And he commanded the multitude to sit down on the ground. And he took the seven loaves and the fishes, and gave thanks, and brake them, and gave to his disciples, and the disciples to the multitude. And they did all eat, and were filled: and they took up of the broken meat that was left seven baskets full. And they that did eat were four thousand men, beside women and children.    — Matthew 15:32-38.

## The Pharisees Seek a Sign
## But No Sign Is Given Them

And he sent away the multitude, and took ship, and came into the coasts of Magdala. The Pharisees also with the Sadducees came, and tempting desired him that he would show them a sign from heaven. He answered and said unto them, "When it is evening, ye say, 'It will be fair weather: for the sky is red.' And in the morning, 'It will be foul weather to-day: for the sky is red and lowering.' O ye hypocrites, ye can discern the face of the sky; but can ye not discern the signs of the times? A wicked and adulterous generation seeketh after a sign; and there shall no sign be given unto it, but the sign of the prophet Jonas." And he left them, and departed. And when his disciples were come to the other side, they had forgotten to take bread.

Then Jesus said unto them, "Take heed and beware of the leaven of the Pharisees and of the Sadducees."

And they reasoned among themselves, saying, "It is because we have taken no bread."

Which when Jesus perceived, he said unto them, "O ye of little faith, why reason ye among yourselves, because ye have brought no bread? Do ye not yet understand, neither remember the five loaves of the five thousand, and how many baskets ye took up? Neither the seven loaves of the four thousand, and how many baskets ye took up? How is it that ye do not understand that I spake it not to you concerning bread, that ye should beware of the leaven of the Pharisees and of the Sadducees?"

Then understood they how that he bade them not beware of the leaven of bread, but of the doctrine of the Pharisees and of the Sadducees. — Matthew 15:39; 16:1-12.

## The Blind Man of Bethsaida

And he cometh to Bethsaida; and they bring a blind man unto him, and besought him to touch him. And he took the blind man by the hand, and led him out of the town; and when he had spit on his eyes, and put his hands upon him, he asked him if he saw aught. And he looked up, and said, "I see men as trees, walking."

After that he put his hands again upon his eyes, and made him look up: and he was restored, and saw every man clearly. And he sent him away to his house, saying, "Neither go into the town, nor tell it to any in the town."                               —Mark 8:22–26.

## The Confession of Peter "The Rock"

When Jesus came into the coasts of Cæsarea Philippi, he asked his disciples, saying, "Who do men say that I the Son of man am?"

And they said, "Some say that thou art John the Baptist: some, Elias; and others, Jeremias, or one of the prophets."

He saith unto them, "But who say ye that I am?"

And Simon Peter answered and said, "Thou art the Christ, the Son of the living God."

And Jesus answered and said unto him, "Blessed art thou, Simon Bar-jona: for flesh and blood hath not revealed it unto thee, but my Father which is in heaven. And I say also unto thee, 'Thou art Peter, and upon this rock I will build my church; and the gates of hell shall not prevail against it. And I will give unto thee the keys of the kingdom of heaven: and whatsoever thou shalt bind on earth shall be bound in heaven: and whatsoever thou shalt loose on earth shall be loosed in heaven.'"

Then charged he his disciples that they should tell no man that he was Jesus the Christ.

—Matthew 16:13–20.

## JESUS REBUKES PETER

From that time forth began Jesus to show unto his disciples, how that he must go unto Jerusalem, and suffer many things of the elders and chief priests and scribes, and be killed, and be raised again the third day.

Then Peter took him, and began to rebuke him, saying, "Be it far from thee, Lord: this shall not be unto thee."

But he turned, and said unto Peter, "Get thee behind me, Satan: thou art an offence unto me: for thou savourest not the things that be of God, but those that be of men."

Then said Jesus unto his disciples, "If any man will come after me, let him deny himself, and take up his cross, and follow me. For whosoever will save his life shall lose it: and whosoever will lose his life for my sake shall find it. For what is a man profited, if he shall gain the whole world, and lose his own soul? Or what shall a man give in exchange for his soul? For the Son of man shall come in the glory of his Father with his angels; and then he shall reward every man according to his works. Verily I say unto you, there be some standing here, which shall not taste of death, till they see the Son of man coming in his kingdom."

— Matthew 16:21–28.

## THE TRANSFIGURATION

It was supposed by early writers that Mount Tabor was the Mount of Transfiguration. It is generally held to-day, however, that the splendid height, Mount Hermon, which lifts its snow-clad summit 9000 feet above the sea, is the mountain to which Jesus took his disciples "and was transfigured before them."

# The Transfiguration

By Fra Angelico da Fiesole (1387-1455)
Fresco in the Monastery of San Marco, Florence, Italy
Color Photograph by Alinari Brothers, Florence

THE Bible account of the Transfiguration of Christ is given on page 131.

This beautiful presentation of the Transfiguration shows Christ clothed in a long white robe standing on the holy mount with arms extended in the form of a cross. On either side the heads of Moses and Elias appear through the clouds. Below them are the Virgin and St. Dominic, figures additional to those that generally compose this scene. At the foot of the rocky platform Peter, James, and John kneel in wonder and astonishment. The central figure of Christ is the crown of them all, radiant, majestic, with a strong head full of austere beauty and sweet dignity.

This painting adorns a wall in one of the cells in the monastery of San Marco at Florence and was intended for the private devotions of the brother occupying the cell. Fra Angelico, the Dominican artist monk, lived within this monastery for about eleven years. During this time Cosimo de' Medici, who had presented the convent to the Dominican friars and caused it to be rebuilt for them, commissioned Fra Angelico to adorn the walls with frescoes. The master and his helpers painted fifty or more such pictures, the work occupying Fra Angelico for the greater part of the time he was in residence here. Fra Angelico was here painting for deeply religious men, for scholars who had the Scriptures at their finger tips, and for this reason perhaps he rejected all smaller realisms, reducing his compositions to the mere figures. Thus, the San Marco frescoes are more concise even than those of Giotto (see pages 308 and 332) and they reach at their best a simple sublimity. The fresco we have is considered one of Fra Angelico's masterpieces.

And it came to pass about eight days after these sayings, he took Peter and John and James, and went up into a mountain to pray. And as he prayed, the fashion of his countenance was altered, and his raiment was white and glistering. And, behold, there talked with him two men, which were Moses and Elias: who appeared in glory, and spake of his decease which he should accomplish at Jerusalem. But Peter and they that were with him were heavy with sleep: and when they were awake, they saw his glory, and the two men that stood with him. And it came to pass, as they departed from him, Peter said unto Jesus, "Master, it is good for us to be here: and let us make three tabernacles; one for thee, and one for Moses, and one for Elias": not knowing what he said. While he thus spake, there came a cloud, and overshadowed them: and they feared as they entered into the cloud.

And there came a voice out of the cloud, saying, "This is my beloved Son: hear him."

And when the voice was past, Jesus was found alone. And they kept it close, and told no man in those days any of those things which they had seen.

And when he came to his disciples, he saw a great multitude about them, and the scribes questioning with them. And straightway all the people, when they beheld him, were greatly amazed, and running to him saluted him. And he asked the scribes, "What question ye with them?"

And one of the multitude answered and said, "Master, I have brought unto thee my son, which hath a dumb spirit; and wheresoever he taketh him, he teareth him: and he foameth, and gnasheth with his teeth, and pineth away: and I spake to thy disciples that they should cast him out; and they could not."

He answereth him, and saith, "O faithless generation, how long shall I be with you? How long shall I suffer you? Bring him unto me."

And they brought him unto him: and when he saw him, straightway the spirit tare him; and he fell on the ground, and wallowed foaming. And he asked his father, "How long is it ago since this came unto him?"

And he said, "Of a child. And ofttimes it hath cast him into the fire, and into the waters, to destroy him: but if thou canst do anything, have compassion on us, and help us."

Jesus said unto him, "If thou canst believe, all things are possible to him that believeth."

And straightway the father of the child cried out, and said with tears, "Lord, I believe; help thou mine unbelief."

When Jesus saw that the people came running together, he rebuked the foul spirit, saying unto him, "Thou dumb and deaf spirit, I charge thee, come out of him, and enter no more into him."

And the spirit cried, and rent him sore, and came out of him: and he was as one dead; insomuch that many said, "He is dead." But Jesus took him by the hand, and lifted him up; and he arose. And when he was come into the house, his disciples asked him privately, "Why could not we cast him out?"

And he said unto them, "This kind can come forth by nothing but by prayer and fasting."

— Luke 9:28–36; Mark 9:14–29.

## The Shadow of the Cross

And they departed thence, and passed through Galilee; and he would not that any man should know it. For he taught his disciples, and said unto them,

"The Son of man is delivered into the hands of men, and they shall kill him; and after that he is killed, he shall rise the third day." But they understood not that saying, and were afraid to ask him.    —Mark 9:30-32.

### THE SHEKEL IN THE FISH'S MOUTH

And when they were come to Capernaum, they that received tribute money came to Peter, and said. "Doth not your master pay tribute?"

He saith, "Yes."

And when he was come into the house, Jesus prevented him, saying, "What thinkest thou, Simon? Of whom do the kings of the earth take custom or tribute? Of their own children, or of strangers?"

Peter saith unto him, "Of strangers."

Jesus saith unto him, "Then are the children free. Notwithstanding, lest we should offend them, go thou to the sea, and cast an hook, and take up the fish that first cometh up; and when thou hast opened his mouth, thou shalt find a piece of money: that take, and give unto them for me and thee."    —Matthew 17:24-27.

### "WHO IS THE GREATEST"

And he came to Capernaum: and being in the house he asked them, "What was it that ye disputed among yourselves by the way?"

But they held their peace: for by the way they had disputed among themselves, who should be the greatest. And he sat down, and called the twelve, and saith unto them, "If any man desire to be first, the same shall be last of all, and servant of all."

And he took a child, and set him in the midst of them: and when he had taken him in his arms, he said unto them, "Whosoever shall receive one of such children in my name, receiveth me: and whosoever shall receive me, receiveth not me, but him that sent me."

—Mark 9:33-37.

## "He that Is Not Against Us Is on Our Part"

And John answered him, saying, "Master, we saw one casting out devils in thy name, and he followeth not us: and we forbade him, because he followeth not us."

But Jesus said, "Forbid him not: for there is no man which shall do a miracle in my name, that can lightly speak evil of me. For he that is not against us is on our part. For whosoever shall give you a cup of water to drink in my name, because ye belong to Christ, verily I say unto you, he shall not lose his reward. And whosoever shall offend one of these little ones that believe in me, it is better for him that a millstone were hanged about his neck, and he were cast into the sea. And if thy hand offend thee, cut it off: it is better for thee to enter into life maimed, than having two hands to go into hell, into the fire that never shall be quenched: where their worm dieth not, and the fire is not quenched. And if thy foot offend thee, cut it off: it is better for thee to enter halt into life, than having two feet to be cast into hell, into the fire that never shall be quenched: where their worm dieth not, and the fire is not quenched. And if thine eye offend thee, pluck it out: it is better for thee to enter into the kingdom of God with one eye, than having two eyes to be cast into hell fire: where their worm dieth not, and the fire is not quenched. For every one shall be salted with fire, and every sacrifice shall be salted with salt. Salt is good: but if the salt have lost his saltness, wherewith will ye season it? Have salt in yourselves, and have peace one with another."

— Mark 9:38-50.

### "Despise Not These Little Ones"

"Take heed that ye despise not one of these little ones; for I say unto you, that in heaven their angels do always behold the face of my Father which is in heaven. For the Son of man is come to save that which was lost. How think ye? If a man have an hundred sheep, and one of them be gone astray, doth he not leave the ninety and nine, and goeth into the mountains, and seeketh that which is gone astray? And if so be that he find it, verily I say unto you, he rejoiceth more of that sheep, than of the ninety and nine which went not astray. Even so it is not the will of your Father which is in heaven, that one of these little ones should perish.

"Moreover if thy brother shall trespass against thee, go and tell him his fault between thee and him alone: if he shall hear thee, thou hast gained thy brother. But if he will not hear thee, then take with thee one or two more, that in the mouth of two or three witnesses every word may be established."     — Matthew 18:10–16.

### The Great Law of Forgiveness

"And if he shall neglect to hear them, tell it unto the church: but if he neglect to hear the church, let him be unto thee as an heathen man and a publican. Verily I say unto you, whatsoever ye shall bind on earth shall be bound in heaven: and whatsoever ye shall loose on earth shall be loosed in heaven. Again I say unto you, that if two of you shall agree on earth as touching anything that they shall ask, it shall be done for them of my Father which is in heaven. For where two or three are gathered together in my name, there am I in the midst of them." Then came Peter to him, and said, "Lord, how oft shall my brother sin against me, and I forgive him? Till seven times?"

Jesus saith unto him, "I say not unto thee, until seven times: but until seventy times seven."

— Matthew 18:17–22.

## The Story of the Unjust Steward

"Therefore is the kingdom of heaven likened unto a certain king, which would take account of his servants. And when he had begun to reckon, one was brought unto him which owed him ten thousand talents. But forasmuch as he had not to pay, his lord commanded him to be sold, and his wife, and children, and all that he had, and payment to be made. The servant therefore fell down, and worshiped him, saying, 'Lord, have patience with me, and I will pay thee all.' Then the lord of that servant was moved with compassion, and loosed him, and forgave him the debt. But the same servant went out, and found one of his fellowservants, which owed him an hundred pence: and he laid hands on him, and took him by the throat, saying, 'Pay me that thou owest.' And his fellowservant fell down at his feet, and besought him, saying, 'Have patience with me, and I will pay thee all.' And he would not: but went and cast him into prison, till he should pay the debt. So when his fellowservants saw what was done, they were very sorry, and came and told unto their lord all that was done. Then his lord, after that he had called him, said unto him, 'O thou wicked servant, I forgave thee all that debt, because thou desiredst me: shouldest not thou also have had compassion on thy fellowservant, even as I had pity on thee?' And his lord was wroth, and delivered him to the tormentors, till he should pay all that was due unto him. So likewise shall my heavenly Father do also unto you, if ye from your hearts forgive not every one his brother their trespasses."

— Matthew 18:23–35.

# The Story of the Master

## From the Gospels of Matthew, Mark and Luke

## The Last Days of Service

### JESUS SETS HIS FACE TOWARD JERUSALEM

AND it came to pass, when the time was come that he should be received up, he steadfastly set his face to go to Jerusalem, and sent messengers before his face: and they went, and entered into a village of the Samaritans, to make ready for him. And they did not receive him, because his face was as though he would go to Jerusalem. And when his disciples James and John saw this, they said, "Lord, wilt thou that we command fire to come down from heaven, and consume them, even as Elias did?"

But he turned, and rebuked them, and said, "Ye know not what manner of spirit ye are of. For the Son of man is not come to destroy men's lives, but to save them." And they went to another village.

### "LET THE DEAD BURY THEIR DEAD"

And it came to pass, that, as they went in the way, a certain man said unto him, "Lord, I will follow thee whithersoever thou goest."

And Jesus said unto him, "Foxes have holes, and birds of the air have nests; but the Son of man hath not where to lay his head."

And he said unto another, "Follow me."

But he said, "Lord, suffer me first to go and bury my father."

Jesus said unto him, "Let the dead bury their dead: but go thou and preach the kingdom of God."

And another also said, "Lord, I will follow thee; but let me first go bid them farewell, which are at home at my house."

COURTYARD OF AN INN

*Photograph by Professor Lewis Bayles Paton*

The khans or inns of Palestine are often not over-attractive to the weary traveler.

In this one it seems to be washing day. Probably the inn of Bethlehem and the inn of the Good Samaritan were not much better than this.

"But a certain Samaritan, as he journeyed, came where he was: and when he saw him, he had compassion on him, and went to him, and bound up his wounds, pouring in oil and wine, and set him on his own beast, and brought him to an inn, and took care of him."— *Luke 10:33.*

And Jesus said unto him, "No man, having put his hand to the plough, and looking back, is fit for the kingdom of God."                              —Luke 9:51-62.

## THE MISSION OF THE SEVENTY DISCIPLES

After these things the Lord appointed other seventy also, and sent them two and two before his face into every city and place, whither he himself would come. Therefore said he unto them, "The harvest truly is great, but the labourers are few: pray ye therefore the Lord of the harvest, that he would send forth labourers into his harvest. Go your ways: behold, I send you forth as lambs among wolves. Carry neither purse, nor scrip, nor shoes: and salute no man by the way. And into whatsoever house ye enter, first say, 'Peace be to this house.' And if the son of peace be there, your peace shall rest upon it: if not, it shall turn to you again. And in the same house remain, eating and drinking such things as they give: for the labourer is worthy of his hire. Go not from house to house. And into whatsoever city ye enter, and they receive you, eat such things as are set before you: and heal the sick that are therein, and say unto them, 'The kingdom of God is come nigh unto you.' But into whatsoever city ye enter, and they receive you not, go your ways out into the streets of the same, and say, 'Even the very dust of your city, which cleaveth on us, we do wipe off against you: notwithstanding be ye sure of this, that the kingdom of God is come nigh unto you.' But I say unto you, that it shall be more tolerable in that day for Sodom, than for that city. Woe unto thee, Chorazin! Woe unto thee, Bethsaida! For if the mighty works had been done in Tyre and Sidon, which have been done in you, they had a great while ago repented, sitting in sackcloth and ashes. But it shall be more tolerable for Tyre and Sidon at the judgment, than for you. And thou, Capernaum, which art exalted to heaven, shalt be thrust down to hell. He that heareth you heareth me; and he that despiseth you despiseth me; and he that despiseth me despiseth him that sent me."

And the seventy returned again with joy, saying, "Lord, even the devils are subject unto us through thy name."

And he said unto them, "I beheld Satan as lightning fall from heaven.  Behold, I give unto you power to tread on serpents and scorpions, and over all the power of the enemy: and nothing shall by any means hurt you. Notwithstanding in this rejoice not, that the spirits are subject unto you; but rather rejoice, because your names are written in heaven."

In that hour Jesus rejoiced in spirit, and said, "I thank thee, O Father, Lord of heaven and earth, that thou hast hid these things from the wise and prudent, and hast revealed them unto babes: even so, Father; for so it seemed good in thy sight. All things are de- livered to me of my Father: and no man knoweth who the Son is, but the Father; and who the Father is, but the Son, and he to whom the Son will reveal him."

And he turned him unto his disciples, and said pri- vately, "Blessed are the eyes which see the things that ye see: for I tell you, that many prophets and kings have desired to see those things which ye see, and have not seen them; and to hear those things which ye hear, and have not heard them."                    — Luke 10:1-24.

## THE STORY OF THE GOOD SAMARITAN

This is one of the most beautiful and effective of the stories told by Jesus. It is as clear-cut as a cameo. There is not a superfluous word, and yet the story unfolds until it is a complete drama of human life, and it lives on in a marvelous way.

And, behold, a certain lawyer stood up, and tempted him, saying, "Master, what shall I do to inherit eternal life?"

He said unto him, "What is written in the law? How readest thou?"

And he answering said, "Thou shalt love the LORD thy God with all thy heart, and with all thy soul, and

INN OF THE GOOD SAMARITAN

*Photograph by W. A. Pottenger expressly for The Book of Life*

This ancient building has been known for centuries as the Inn of the Good Samaritan. Its walls were shattered by shell fire during World War I.

with all thy strength, and with all thy mind; and thy neighbour as thyself."

And he said unto him, "Thou hast answered right: this do, and thou shalt live."

But he, willing to justify himself, said unto Jesus, "And who is my neighbour?"

And Jesus answering said, "A certain man went down from Jerusalem to Jericho, and fell among thieves, which stripped him of his raiment, and wounded him, and departed, leaving him half dead. And by chance there came down a certain priest that way: and when he saw him, he passed by on the other side. And likewise a Levite, when he was at the place, came and looked on him, and passed by on the other side. But a certain Samaritan, as he journeyed, came where he was: and when he saw him, he had compassion on him, and went to him, and bound up his wounds, pouring in oil and wine, and set him on his own beast, and brought him to an inn, and took care of him. And on the morrow when he departed, he took out two pence, and gave them to

RUINS OF THE HOUSE OF SIMON THE LEPER IN BETHANY
*Photograph by W. A. Pottenger expressly for The Book of Life*

"Now when Jesus was in Bethany, in the house of Simon the leper, there came unto him a woman having an alabaster box of very precious ointment, and poured it on his head, as he sat at meat."—*Matthew 26:6.*

the host, and said unto him, 'Take care of him; and whatsoever thou spendest more, when I come again, I will repay thee.' Which now of these three, thinkest thou, was neighbour unto him that fell among the thieves?"

And he said, "He that showed mercy on him."

Then said Jesus unto him, "Go, and do thou likewise."

— Luke 10:25-37.

## MARY AND MARTHA

In the little village of Bethany in the uplands of Judea, not far from Jerusalem, but hidden from it by the Mount of Olives, lived a family of means, Lazarus and his two sisters, Mary and Martha. Tradition holds that Lazarus was a gentle and holy rabbi, whose name is mentioned in the Talmud, and that Martha was a widow whose husband had been Simon the Leper. Nothing is surely known about them except that, as John tells us, Jesus loved these hospitable and friendly people and that he often found rest and refreshment at their home.

Now it came to pass, as they went, that he entered into a certain village: and a certain woman named Martha received him into her house. And she had a sister called Mary, which also sat at Jesus' feet, and heard his word. But Martha was cumbered about much serving, and came to him, and said, "Lord, dost thou not care that my sister hath left me to serve alone? Bid her therefore that she help me."

And Jesus answered and said unto her, "Martha, Martha, thou art careful and troubled about many things: but one thing is needful: and Mary hath chosen that good part, which shall not be taken away from her."

— Luke 10:38–42.

### "LORD, TEACH US TO PRAY"

And it came to pass, that, as he was praying in a certain place, when he ceased, one of his disciples said unto him, "Lord, teach us to pray, as John also taught his disciples."

And he said unto them, "When ye pray, say, 'Our Father which art in heaven, hallowed be thy name. Thy kingdom come. Thy will be done, as in heaven, so in earth. Give us day by day our daily bread. And forgive us our sins; for we also forgive every one that is indebted to us. And lead us not into temptation; but deliver us from evil.'"

And he said unto them, "Which of you shall have a friend, and shall go unto him at midnight, and say unto him, 'Friend, lend me three loaves; for a friend of mine in his journey is come to me, and I have nothing to set before him?' And he from within shall answer and say, 'Trouble me not: the door is now shut, and my children are with me in bed; I cannot rise and give thee.'

"I say unto you, though he will not rise and give him, because he is his friend, yet because of his importunity

he will rise and give him as many as he needeth.
And I say unto you, ask, and it shall be given you; seek,
and ye shall find; knock, and it shall be opened unto you.
For every one that asketh receiveth; and he that seeketh findeth; and to him that knocketh it shall be opened.
If a son shall ask bread of any of you that is a father,
will he give him a stone? Or if he ask a fish, will he for
a fish give him a serpent? Or if he shall ask an egg, will
he offer him a scorpion? If ye then, being evil, know
how to give good gifts unto your children: how much
more shall your heavenly Father give the Holy Spirit
to them that ask him?"          — Luke 11:1–13.

### "The Outside of the Cup"

And as he spake, a certain Pharisee besought him
to dine with him: and he went in, and sat down to
meat. And when the Pharisee saw it, he marveled that
he had not first washed before dinner. And the Lord
said unto him, "Now do ye Pharisees make clean the
outside of the cup and the platter; but your inward
part is full of ravening and wickedness. Ye fools, did
not he that made that which is without make that which
is within also? But rather give alms of such things as
ye have; and, behold, all things are clean unto you.

"But woe unto you, Pharisees! for ye tithe mint and
rue and all manner of herbs, and pass over judgment and
the love of God: these ought ye to have done, and not
to leave the other undone.

"Woe unto you, Pharisees! for ye love the uppermost
seats in the synagogues, and greetings in the markets.

"Woe unto you, scribes and Pharisees, hypocrites!
for ye are as graves which appear not, and the men that
walk over them are not aware of them."

Then answered one of the lawyers, and said unto
him, "Master, thus saying thou reproachest us also."

And he said, "Woe unto you also, ye lawyers! for ye lade men with burdens grievous to be borne, and ye yourselves touch not the burdens with one of your fingers. Woe unto you! for ye build the sepulchers of the prophets, and your fathers killed them. Truly ye bear witness that ye allow the deeds of your fathers: for they indeed killed them, and ye build their sepulchers. Therefore also said the wisdom of God, 'I will send them prophets and apostles, and some of them they shall slay and persecute: that the blood of all the prophets, which was shed from the foundation of the world, may be required of this generation; from the blood of Abel unto the blood of Zacharias, which perished between the altar and the temple.' Verily I say unto you, it shall be required of this generation.

"Woe unto you, lawyers! for ye have taken away the key of knowledge: ye entered not in yourselves, and them that were entering in ye hindered."

And as he said these things unto them, the scribes and the Pharisees began to urge him vehemently, and to provoke him to speak of many things: laying wait for him, and seeking to catch something out of his mouth, that they might accuse him. — Luke 11:37-54.

## The Teaching of the Kingdom

### WARNINGS AGAINST PHARISEEISM

In the mean time, when there were gathered together an innumerable multitude of people, insomuch that they trod one upon another, he began to say unto his disciples first of all, "Beware ye of the leaven of the Pharisees, which is hypocrisy. For there is nothing covered, that shall not be revealed; neither hid, that shall not be known. Therefore whatsoever ye have spoken in darkness shall be heard in the light; and that which ye have spoken in the ear in closets shall be proclaimed upon the housetops. And I say unto you my friends, be not afraid of them that kill the body, and after that have no more that they can do. But I will forewarn you whom ye shall fear: fear him, which after he hath killed hath power to cast into hell; yea, I say unto you, fear him. Are not five sparrows sold for two farthings, and not one of them is forgotten before God? But even the very hairs of your head are all numbered. Fear not therefore: ye are of more value than many sparrows. Also I say unto you, whosoever shall confess me before men, him shall the Son of man also confess before the angels of God: but he that denieth me before men shall be denied before the angels of God. And whosoever shall speak a word against the Son of man, it shall be forgiven him: but unto him that blasphemeth against the Holy Ghost it shall not be forgiven. And when they bring you unto the synagogues, and unto magistrates, and powers, take ye no thought how or what thing ye shall answer, or what ye shall say: for the Holy Ghost shall teach you in the same hour what ye ought to say."

And one of the company said unto him, "Master, speak to my brother, that he divide the inheritance with me."

And he said unto him, "Man, who made me a judge or a divider over you?"

And he said unto them, "Take heed, and beware of covetousness: for a man's life consisteth not in the abundance of the things which he possesseth."

### THE STORY OF THE RICH MAN WHOSE SOUL WAS REQUIRED OF HIM IN THE NIGHT

And he spake a parable unto them, saying, "The ground of a certain rich man brought forth plentifully:

and he thought within himself, saying, 'What shall I do, because I have no room where to bestow my fruits?'

"And he said, 'This will I do: I will pull down my barns, and build greater; and there will I bestow all my fruits and my goods. And I will say to my soul, "Soul, thou hast much goods laid up for many years; take thine ease, eat, drink, and be merry."'

"But God said unto him, 'Thou fool, this night thy soul shall be required of thee: then whose shall those things be, which thou hast provided?' So is he that layeth up treasure for himself, and is not rich toward God."

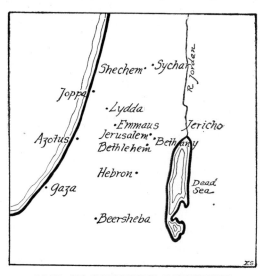

MAP OF SOUTHERN PALESTINE

## "FEAR NOT, LITTLE FLOCK"

And he said unto his disciples, "Therefore I say unto you, take no thought for your life, what ye shall eat; neither for the body, what ye shall put on. The life is more than meat, and the body is more than raiment. Consider the ravens: for they neither sow nor reap; which neither have storehouse nor barn; and God feedeth them: how much more are ye better than the fowls? And which of you with taking thought can add to his stature one cubit? If ye then be not able to do that thing which is least, why take ye thought for the rest?

Consider the lilies how they grow: they toil not, they spin not; and yet I say unto you, that Solomon in all his glory was not arrayed like one of these. If then God so clothe the grass, which is to-day in the field, and to-morrow is cast into the oven; how much more will he clothe you, O ye of little faith? And seek not ye what ye shall eat, or what ye shall drink, neither be ye of doubtful mind. For all these things do the nations of the world seek after: and your Father knoweth that ye have need of these things. But rather seek ye the kingdom of God; and all these things shall be added unto you. Fear not, little flock; for it is your Father's good pleasure to give you the kingdom.

"Sell that ye have, and give alms; provide yourselves bags which wax not old, a treasure in the heavens that faileth not, where no thief approacheth, neither moth corrupteth. For where your treasure is, there will your heart be also. Let your loins be girded about, and your lights burning; and ye yourselves like unto men that wait for their lord, when he will return from the wedding; that when he cometh and knocketh, they may open unto him immediately. Blessed are those servants, whom the lord when he cometh shall find watching: verily I say unto you, that he shall gird himself, and make them to sit down to meat, and will come forth and serve them. And if he shall come in the second watch, or come in the third watch, and find them so, blessed are those servants. And this know, that if the goodman of the house had known what hour the thief would come, he would have watched, and not have suffered his house to be broken through. Be ye therefore ready also: for the Son of man cometh at an hour when ye think not."

Then Peter said unto him, "Lord, speakest thou this parable unto us, or even to all?"

### THE FAITHFUL STEWARD

And the Lord said, "Who then is that faithful and wise steward, whom his lord shall make ruler over his household, to give them their portion of meat in due season? Blessed is that servant, whom his lord when he cometh shall find so doing. Of a truth I say unto you, that he will make him ruler over all that he hath. But and if that servant say in his heart, 'My lord delayeth his coming': and shall begin to beat the menservants and maidens, and to eat and drink, and to be drunken; the lord of that servant will come in a day when he looketh not for him, and at an hour when he is not aware, and will cut him in sunder, and will appoint him his portion with the unbelievers. And that servant, which knew his lord's will, and prepared not himself, neither did according to his will, shall be beaten with many stripes. But he that knew not, and did commit things worthy of stripes, shall be beaten with few stripes. For unto whomsoever much is given, of him shall be much required: and to whom men have committed much, of him they will ask the more."

### NOT PEACE BUT DIVISION

"I am come to send fire on the earth; and what will I, if it be already kindled? But I have a baptism to be baptized with; and how am I straitened till it be accomplished! Suppose ye that I am come to give peace on earth? I tell you, Nay; but rather division: for from henceforth there shall be five in one house divided, three against two, and two against three. The father shall be divided against the son, and the son against the father; the mother against the daughter, and the daughter against the mother; the mother-in-law against her daughter-in-law, and the daughter-in-law against her mother-in-law."

And he said also to the people, "When ye see a cloud rise out of the west, straightway ye say, 'There cometh a shower'; and so it is. And when ye see the south wind blow, ye say, 'There will be heat; and it cometh to pass.' Ye hypocrites, ye can discern the face of the sky and of the earth; but how is it that ye do not discern this time? Yea, and why even of yourselves judge ye not what is right?

"When thou goest with thine adversary to the magistrate, as thou art in the way, give diligence that thou mayest be delivered from him; lest he hale thee to the judge, and the judge deliver thee to the officer, and the officer cast thee into prison. I tell thee, thou shalt not depart thence, till thou hast paid the very last mite."

And he was teaching in one of the synagogues on the sabbath. And, behold, there was a woman which had a spirit of infirmity eighteen years, and was bowed together, and could in no wise lift up herself. And when Jesus saw her, he called her to him, and said unto her, "Woman, thou art loosed from thine infirmity." And he laid his hands on her: and immediately she was made straight, and glorified God. And the ruler of the synagogue answered with indignation, because that Jesus had healed on the sabbath day, and said unto the people, "There are six days in which men ought to work: in them therefore come and be healed, and not on the sabbath day."

The Lord then answered him, and said, "Thou hypocrite, doth not each one of you on the sabbath loose his ox or his ass from the stall, and lead him away to watering? And ought not this woman, being a daughter of Abraham, whom Satan hath bound, lo, these eighteen years, be loosed from this bond on the sabbath day?"

### The Glorious Things Done by Jesus

And when he had said these things, all his adversaries were ashamed: and all the people rejoiced for all the glorious things that were done by him.

Then said he, "Unto what is the kingdom of God like and whereunto shall I resemble it?  It is like a grain of mustard seed, which a man took, and cast into his garden; and it grew, and waxed a great tree; and the fowls of the air lodged in the branches of it."

And again he said, "Whereunto shall I liken the kingdom of God?  It is like leaven, which a woman took and hid in three measures of meal, till the whole was leavened."                      — Luke 12; Luke 13:10–21.

### "Enter in at the Strait Gate"

And he went through the cities and villages, teaching, and journeying toward Jerusalem.  Then said one unto him, "Lord, are there few that be saved?"

And he said unto them, "Strive to enter in at the strait gate: for many, I say unto you, will seek to enter in, and shall not be able.  When once the master of the house is risen up, and hath shut to the door, and ye begin to stand without, and to knock at the door, saying, 'Lord, Lord, open unto us'; and he shall answer and say unto you, 'I know you not whence ye are': then shall ye begin to say, 'We have eaten and drunk in thy presence, and thou hast taught in our streets.'

"But he shall say, 'I tell you, I know you not whence ye are;  depart from me, all ye workers of iniquity.'

"There shall be weeping and gnashing of teeth, when ye shall see Abraham, and Isaac, and Jacob, and all the prophets, in the kingdom of God, and you yourselves thrust out.  And they shall come from the east, and from the west, and from the north, and from the south, and shall sit down in the kingdom of God. And, behold, there are last which shall be first, and there are first which shall be last." — Luke 13:22-30.

## THE PITY OF JESUS FOR JERUSALEM

The same day there came certain of the Pharisees, saying unto him, "Get thee out, and depart hence: for Herod will kill thee."

And he said unto them, "Go ye, and tell that fox, 'Behold, I cast out devils, and I do cures to-day and to-morrow, and the third day I shall be perfected.' Nevertheless I must walk to-day, and to-morrow, and the day following: for it cannot be that a prophet perish out of Jerusalem.

"O Jerusalem, Jerusalem, which killest the prophets, and stonest them that are sent unto thee; how often would I have gathered thy children together, as a hen doth gather her brood under her wings, and ye would not! Behold, your house is left unto you desolate: and verily I say unto you, ye shall not see me, until the time come when ye shall say, 'Blessed is he that cometh in the name of the LORD.'" — Luke 13:31-35.

## AT A PHARISEE'S TABLE

And it came to pass, as he went into the house of one of the chief Pharisees to eat bread on the sabbath day, that they watched him. And, behold, there was a certain man before him which had the dropsy.

And Jesus answering spake unto the lawyers and Pharisees, saying, "Is it lawful to heal on the sabbath day?"

And they held their peace. And he took him, and healed him, and let him go; and answered them, saying, "Which of you shall have an ass or an ox fallen into a pit, and will not straightway pull him out on the sabbath day?" And they could not answer him again to these things.

### THE STORY OF THE GUESTS AT THE FEAST

And he put forth a parable to those which were bidden, when he marked how they chose out the chief rooms; saying unto them, "When thou art bidden of any man to a wedding, sit not down in the highest room; lest a more honourable man than thou be bidden of him; and he that bade thee and him come and say to thee, 'Give this man place'; and thou begin with shame to take the lowest room. But when thou art bidden, go and sit down in the lowest room; that when he that bade thee cometh, he may say unto thee, 'Friend, go up higher': then shalt thou have worship in the presence of them that sit at meat with thee. For whosoever exalteth himself shall be abased; and he that humbleth himself shall be exalted."

Then said he also to him that bade him, "When thou makest a dinner or a supper, call not thy friends, nor thy brethren, neither thy kinsmen, nor thy rich neighbours; lest they also bid thee again, and a recompense be made thee. But when thou makest a feast, call the poor, the maimed, the lame, the blind: and thou shall be blessed; for they cannot recompense thee: for thou shalt be recompensed at the resurrection of the just."

### THE STORY OF THE GUESTS WHO MADE EXCUSE

And when one of them that sat at meat with him heard these things, he said unto him, "Blessed is he that shall eat bread in the kingdom of God."

Then said he unto him, "A certain man made a great supper, and bade many: and sent his servant at supper time to say to them that were bidden, 'Come; for all things are now ready.' And they all with one consent began to make excuse. The first said unto him, 'I have bought a piece of ground, and I must needs go and see it: I pray thee have me excused.'

"And another said, 'I have bought five yoke of oxen, and I go to prove them: I pray thee have me excused.'

"And another said, 'I have married a wife, and therefore I cannot come.'

"So that servant came, and showed his lord these things. Then the master of the house being angry said to his servant, 'Go out quickly into the streets and lanes of the city, and bring in hither the poor, and the maimed, and the halt, and the blind.'

"And the servant said, 'Lord, it is done as thou hast commanded, and yet there is room.'

"And the lord said unto the servant, 'Go out into the highways and hedges, and compel them to come in, that my house may be filled. For I say unto you, that none of those men which were bidden shall taste of my supper.'" — Luke 14:1–24.

## COUNTING THE COST

And there went great multitudes with him: and he turned, and said unto them, "If any man come to me, and hate not his father, and mother, and wife, and children, and brethren, and sisters, yea, and his own life also, he cannot be my disciple. And whosoever doth not bear his cross, and come after me, cannot be my disciple. For which of you intending to build a tower, sitteth not down first, and counteth the cost, whether he have sufficient to finish it? Lest haply, after he hath laid the foundation, and is not able to finish it, all that behold it begin to mock him, saying, 'This man began to build, and was not able to finish.' Or what king, going to make war against another king, sitteth not down first, and consulteth whether he be able with ten thousand to meet him that cometh against him with twenty thousand? Or else, while the other is yet a great way off, he sendeth an ambassage, and desireth conditions of peace. So likewise, whosoever he be of you that forsaketh not all that he hath, he cannot be my disciple.

"Salt is good: but if the salt have lost his savour, wherewith shall it be seasoned? It is neither fit for the land, nor yet for the dunghill; but men cast it out. He that hath ears to hear, let him hear." — Luke 14:25-35.

### STORIES OF THE LOVE OF GOD FOR MEN

#### THE STORY OF THE NINETY AND NINE

Then drew near unto him all the publicans and sinners for to hear him. And the Pharisees and scribes murmured, saying, "This man receiveth sinners, and eateth with them."

And he spake this parable unto them, saying, "What man of you, having an hundred sheep, if he lose one of them, doth not leave the ninety and nine in the wilderness, and go after that which is lost, until he find it? And when he hath found it, he layeth it on his shoulders, rejoicing. And when he cometh home, he calleth together his friends and neighbours, saying unto them, 'Rejoice with me; for I have found my sheep which was lost.' I say unto you, that likewise joy shall be in heaven over one sinner that repenteth, more than over ninety and nine just persons, which need no repentance."
— Luke 15:1-7.

#### THE STORY OF THE WOMAN WHO LOST A PIECE OF SILVER

"Either what woman having ten pieces of silver, if she lose one piece, doth not light a candle, and sweep the house, and seek diligently till she find it? And when she hath found it, she calleth her friends and her neighbours together, saying, 'Rejoice with me; for I have found the piece which I had lost.' Likewise, I say unto you, there is joy in the presence of the angels of God over one sinner that repenteth." — Luke 15:8–10.

### THE STORY OF THE PRODIGAL SON

The story of the Prodigal Son is, by common consent, the most tender and beautiful and perfect story ever written. It is matchless in form, in grace of expression. It is the story of the gospel, the supreme expression of the love of Jesus who came to seek and to save that which is lost. It has been the theme of more appeals to repentance and it has touched the hearts of more wanderers in the far country than any words ever written; and still its power is unimpaired. It belongs, not simply to the group of people to whom it was uttered, but to all the ages.

And he said, "A certain man had two sons: and the younger of them said to his father, 'Father, give me the portion of goods that falleth to me.' And he divided unto them his living.

"And not many days after, the younger son gathered all together, and took his journey into a far country, and there wasted his substance with riotous living. And when he had spent all, there arose a mighty famine in that land; and he began to be in want. And he went and joined himself to a citizen of that country; and he sent him into his fields to feed swine. And he would fain have filled his belly with the husks that the swine did eat: and no man gave unto him. And when he came to himself, he said, 'How many hired servants of my father's have bread enough and to spare, and I perish with hunger! I will arise and go to my father, and will say unto him, "Father, I have sinned against heaven,

# The Prodigal Son

By Albrecht Dürer (1471-1528)
Preliminary Sketch in the British Museum,
London, England

THE Bible story of the Prodigal Son, that matchless story of a father's love, begins on page 156.

In this copper engraving the artist has depicted the moment when the Prodigal "comes to himself" and, in a rush of deep feeling, falls to his knees in repentant supplication. In spirit he is no longer held by his degrading surroundings, symbolized by the littered farmyard, the gluttonous, half-wild swine snarling about the feed trough, and the sinister monster looming over the housetops. He is suddenly free in his heart to say, "I will arise and go to my father and ask forgiveness."

Albrecht Dürer, "prince of German artists," was one of eighteen children of an humble goldsmith in the busy medieval city of Nuremberg. First learning the goldsmith's trade, he was apprenticed at fifteen for three years to the painter Wohlgemuth. Like his great contemporary Leonardo da Vinci, Dürer had a scientific mind, interested in all the world and all the forces in it. Everything about him he sketched repeatedly to see how best it might be portrayed, revealing in his subjects a devout nature and in his meticulous craftmanship one of the world's great draughtsmen. Besides being a remarkable painter, Dürer perfected the art of engraving on wood and copper, becoming the greatest master of this art who has ever lived. His industry was astonishing—his own list of works numbers 1,254 pieces —and his enthusiasm for Venetian art had a profound influence on the Netherlands' artists.

Living in the critical age of the Renaissance and Church Reformation, Dürer wrote treatises on art in which he gives the young artist this advice: "Attentively regard Nature . . . do not depart from her . . . for your power is pure nothingness compared with the creative activity of God."

and before thee, and am no more worthy to be called thy son: make me as one of thy hired servants.''' "And he arose, and came to his father. But when he was yet a great way off, his father saw him, and had compassion, and ran and fell on his neck, and kissed him. And the son said unto him, 'Father, I have sinned against heaven, and in thy sight, and am no more worthy to be called thy son.'

"But the father said to his servants, 'Bring forth the best robe, and put it on him; and put a ring on his hand, and shoes on his feet: and bring hither the fatted calf, and kill it; and let us eat, and be merry: for this my son was dead, and is alive again; he was lost, and is found.' And they began to be merry.

"Now his elder son was in the field: and as he came and drew nigh to the house, he heard music and dancing. And he called one of the servants, and asked what these things meant. And he said unto him, 'Thy brother is come; and thy father hath killed the fatted calf, because he hath received him safe and sound.' And he was angry, and would not go in: therefore came his father out, and intreated him.

"And he answering said to his father, 'Lo, these many years do I serve thee, neither transgressed I at any time thy commandment: and yet thou never gavest me a kid, that I might make merry with my friends: but as soon as this thy son was come, which hath devoured thy living with harlots, thou hast killed for him the fatted calf.'

"And he said unto him, 'Son, thou art ever with me, and all that I have is thine. It was meet that we should make merry, and be glad: for this thy brother was dead, and is alive again; and was lost, and is found.'"

— Luke 15:11–32.

## THE STORY OF THE UNJUST STEWARD

And he said also unto his disciples, "There was a certain rich man, which had a steward; and the same was accused unto him that he had wasted his goods. And he called him, and said unto him, 'How is it that I hear this of thee? Give an account of thy stewardship; for thou mayest be no longer steward.'

"Then the steward said within himself, 'What shall I do? For my lord taketh away from me the stewardship: I cannot dig; to beg I am ashamed. I am resolved what to do, that, when I am put out of the stewardship, they may receive me into their houses.'

"So he called every one of his lord's debtors unto him, and said unto the first, 'How much owest thou unto my lord?'

"And he said, 'An hundred measures of oil.'

"And he said unto him, 'Take thy bill, and sit down quickly, and write fifty.'

"Then said he to another, 'And how much owest thou?'

"And he said, 'An hundred measures of wheat.'

"And he said unto him, 'Take thy bill, and write fourscore.'

"And the lord commended the unjust steward, because he had done wisely: for the children of this world are in their generation wiser than the children of light. And I say unto you, 'Make to yourselves friends of the mammon of unrighteousness; that, when ye fail, they may receive you into everlasting habitations. He that is faithful in that which is least is faithful also in much: and he that is unjust in the least is unjust also in much. If therefore ye have not been faithful in the unrighteous mammon, who will commit to your trust the true riches? And if ye have not been faithful in that which is another man's, who shall give you that which is your own?"

"No servant can serve two masters: for either he will hate the one, and love the other; or else he will hold to the one, and despise the other. Ye cannot serve God and mammon. And the Pharisees also, who were covetous, heard all these things: and they derided him. And he said unto them, Ye are they which justify yourselves before men; but God knoweth your hearts: for that which is highly esteemed among men is abomination in the sight of God. The law and the prophets were until John: since that time the kingdom of God is preached, and every man presseth into it. And it is easier for heaven and earth to pass, than one tittle of the law to fail. Whosoever putteth away his wife, and marrieth another, committeth adultery: and whosoever marrieth her that is put away from her husband committeth adultery.                      — Luke 16:1–18.

### THE STORY OF THE BEGGAR LAZARUS

"There was a certain rich man, which was clothed in purple and fine linen, and fared sumptuously every day: and there was a certain beggar named Lazarus, which was laid at his gate, full of sores, and desiring to be fed with the crumbs which fell from the rich man's table: moreover the dogs came and licked his sores. And it came to pass, that the beggar died, and was carried by the angels into Abraham's bosom: the rich man also died, and was buried; and in hell he lift up his eyes, being in torments, and seeth Abraham afar off, and Lazarus in his bosom.

"And he cried and said, 'Father Abraham, have mercy on me, and send Lazarus, that he may dip the tip of his finger in water, and cool my tongue; for I am tormented in this flame.'

"But Abraham said, 'Son, remember that thou in thy lifetime receivedst thy good things, and likewise Lazarus evil things: but now he is comforted, and thou art tormented. And beside all this, between us and you there is a great gulf fixed: so that they which would pass from hence to you cannot; neither can they pass to us, that would come from thence.'

"Then he said, 'I pray thee therefore, father, that thou wouldest send him to my father's house: for I have five brethren; that he may testify unto them, lest they also come in to this place of torment.'

"Abraham saith unto him, 'They have Moses and the prophets; let them hear them.'

"And he said, 'Nay, Father Abraham: but if one went unto them from the dead, they will repent.'

"And he said unto him, 'If they hear not Moses and the prophets, neither will they be persuaded, though one rose from the dead.'"     — Luke 16:19–31.

## "LORD, INCREASE OUR FAITH"

Then said he unto the disciples, "It is impossible but that offences will come: but woe unto him, through whom they come! It were better for him that a millstone were hanged about his neck, and he cast into the sea, than that he should offend one of these little ones.

"Take heed to yourselves: if thy brother trespass against thee, rebuke him; and if he repent, forgive him. And if he trespass against thee seven times in a day, and seven times in a day turn again to thee, saying, 'I repent'; thou shalt forgive him."

And the apostles said unto the Lord, "Increase our faith."

And the Lord said, "If ye had faith as a grain of mustard seed, ye might say unto this sycamine tree, 'Be thou plucked up by the root, and be thou planted in the sea'; and it should obey you. But which of you, having a servant plowing or feeding cattle, will say unto him by and by, when he is come from the field, 'Go and sit down to meat'? And will not rather say unto him, 'Make ready wherewith I may sup, and gird thyself, and serve me, till I have eaten and drunken; and afterward thou shalt eat and drink'? Doth he thank that servant because he did the things that were commanded him? I trow not. So likewise ye, when ye shall have done all those things which are commanded you, say, 'We are unprofitable servants: we have done that which was our duty to do.'"

— Luke 17:1-10.

### THE TEN LEPERS

And it came to pass, as he went to Jerusalem, that he passed through the midst of Samaria and Galilee. And as he entered into a certain village, there met him ten men that were lepers, which stood afar off: and they lifted up their voices, and said, "Jesus, Master, have mercy on us."

And when he saw them, he said unto them, "Go show yourselves unto the priests." And it came to pass, that, as they went, they were cleansed.

And one of them, when he saw that he was healed, turned back, and with a loud voice glorified God, and fell down on his face at his feet, giving him thanks: and he was a Samaritan. And Jesus answering said, "Were there not ten cleansed? But where are the nine? There are not found that returned to give glory to God, save this stranger."

And he said unto him, "Arise, go thy way: thy faith hath made thee whole."

— Luke 17:11-19.

## A Warning to Be Prepared

And when he was demanded of the Pharisees, when the kingdom of God should come, he answered them and said, "The kingdom of God cometh not with observation: neither shall they say, 'Lo here!' or, 'Lo there!' for, behold, the kingdom of God is within you."

And he said unto the disciples, "The days will come, when ye shall desire to see one of the days of the Son of man, and ye shall not see it. And they shall say to you, 'See here'; or, 'See there': go not after them, nor follow them. For as the lightning, that lighteneth out of the one part under heaven, shineth unto the other part under heaven; so shall also the Son of man be in his day. But first must he suffer many things, and be rejected of this generation. And as it was in the days of Noe, so shall it be also in the days of the Son of man. They did eat, they drank, they married wives, they were given in marriage, until the day that Noe entered into the ark, and the flood came, and destroyed them all. Likewise also as it was in the days of Lot; they did eat, they drank, they bought, they sold, they planted, they builded; but the same day that Lot went out of Sodom it rained fire and brimstone from heaven, and destroyed them all. Even thus shall it be in the day when the Son of man is revealed. In that day, he which shall be upon the housetop, and his stuff in the house, let him not come down to take it away: and he that is in the field, let him likewise not return back. Remember Lot's wife. Whosoever shall seek to save his life shall lose it; and whosoever shall lose his life shall preserve it. I tell you, in that night there shall be two men in one bed; the one shall be taken, and the other shall be left. Two women shall be grinding together; the one shall be taken

# Christ and the Rich Young Man

By Heinrich Hofmann (1824-1911)
In the Riverside Church, New York City

THE story of the rich young man who asked Jesus what "good thing" he should do that he might "inherit eternal life" is told in Matthew, Mark, and Luke. You will find the selection from Matthew on pages 169-170.

This beautifully expressive picture gives us a spiritual tragedy in briefest compass. Jesus is offering the youth a chance to leave his present life of ease and serve the Lord, thus winning for himself "treasure in heaven," and he is going to refuse.

See how skillfully Hofmann has embodied the essentials of the narrative. The young man, elegantly attired, is very attractive. His refined face shows that he has been delicately reared, that he is a youth of good impulses, of ideals, but habituated to the easy, superficial goodness of his own privileged social set. He needs will power and a wider sympathy. Jesus, divining this, sternly pronounces the conditions that alone will save the youth from eternal remorse, the fate hinted at in the parable of the Rich Man and the Beggar Lazarus (see page 161).

The kindly eyes of Jesus are searching the young man's soul. These are the eyes of one who knows life, who sees the issues involved here: not so much the monetary difference it will make to the poor if the riches are divided, but the spiritual difference in the lives of this youth and of those he can help if he will break the golden chains which bind him and go meet the world's need which Jesus points out to him.

Compare this picture, painted in 1889, with that on page 168 painted about 1894 by the distinguished English artist Watts.

Other Hofmann paintings are on pages 264, 336, and in Volume I, pages 50 and 56.

and the other left. Two men shall be in the field; the one shall be taken, and the other left.

And they answered and said unto him, "Where, LORD?" And he said unto them, "Wheresoever the body is, thither will the eagles be gathered together."

— Luke 17:20–37.

## THE STORY OF THE UNJUST JUDGE

And he spake a parable unto them to this end, that men ought always to pray, and not to faint; saying, "There was in a city a judge, which feared not God, neither regarded man: and there was a widow in that city; and she came unto him, saying, 'Avenge me of mine adversary.'

"And he would not for a while: but afterward he said within himself, 'Though I fear not God, nor regard man; yet because this widow troubleth me, I will avenge her, lest by her continual coming she weary me.'"

And the Lord said, "Hear what the unjust judge saith. And shall not God avenge his own elect, which cry day and night unto him, though he bear long with them? I tell you that he will avenge them speedily. Nevertheless when the Son of man cometh, shall he find faith on the earth?"

— Luke 18:1–8.

## THE STORY OF THE PHARISEE AND THE PUBLICAN

And he spake this parable unto certain which trusted in themselves that they were righteous, and despised others: "Two men went up into the temple to pray; the one a Pharisee, and the other a publican. The Pharisee stood and prayed thus with himself, 'God, I thank thee, that I am not as other men are, extortioners, unjust, adulterers, or even as this publican. I fast twice in the week, I give tithes of all that I possess.'

"And the publican, standing afar off, would not lift up so much as his eyes unto heaven, but smote upon his breast, saying, 'God oe merciful to me a sinner.' I tell you, this man went down to his house justified rather than the other: for every one that exalteth himself shall be abased; and he that humbleth himself shall be exalted." —Luke 18:9-14.

"FOR HE HAD GREAT
POSSESSIONS"

*By George F. Watts (1818-1904)*
*In the National (Tate) Gallery, London*

The young man "who had many possessions" has turned away from Jesus with hanging head. Compare with the picture by Hofmann. Does it make a stronger picture to have only the one downcast figure?

And the Pharisees came to him, and asked him, "Is it lawful for a man to put away his wife?" tempting him. And he answered and said unto them, "What did Moses command you?"

And they said, "Moses suffered to write a bill of divorcement, and to put her away."

And Jesus answered and said unto them, "For the hardness of your heart he wrote you this precept. But from the beginning of the creation God made them male and female. For this cause shall a man leave his father and mother, and cleave to his wife; and they twain shall be one flesh: so then they are no more twain, but one flesh. What therefore God hath joined together, let not man put asunder."

And in the house his disciples asked him again of the same matter. And he saith unto them, "Whosoever shall put away his wife, and marry another, committeth adultery against her. And if a woman shall put away her husband, and be married to another, she committeth adultery."

—Luke 18:9–14; Mark 10:2–12.

### JESUS AND THE LITTLE CHILDREN

And they brought young children to him, that he should touch them: and his disciples rebuked those that brought them. But when Jesus saw it, he was much displeased, and said unto them, "Suffer the little children to come unto me, and forbid them not: for of such is the kingdom of God. Verily I say unto you, whosoever shall not receive the kingdom of God as a little child, he shall not enter therein." And he took them up in his arms, put his hands upon them, and blessed them.

— Mark 10:13–16.

### THE RICH YOUNG MAN

And behold, one came and said unto him, "Good Master, what good thing shall I do, that I may have eternal life?"

And he said unto him, "Why callest thou me good? There is none good but one, that is, God: but if thou wilt enter into life, keep the commandments."

He saith unto him, "Which?"

Jesus said, "Thou shalt do no murder, Thou shalt not commit adultery, Thou shalt not steal, Thou shalt not bear false witness, Honour thy father and thy mother: and, Thou shalt love thy neighbour as thyself."

The young man saith unto him, "All these things have I kept from my youth up: what lack I yet?"

Jesus said unto him, "If thou wilt be perfect, go and

sell that thou hast, and give to the poor, and thou shalt have treasure in heaven: and come and follow me."

But when the young man heard that saying, he went away sorrowful: for he had great possessions.

Then said Jesus unto his disciples, "Verily I say unto you, that a rich man shall hardly enter into the kingdom of heaven. And again I say unto you, it is easier for a camel to go through the eye of a needle, than for a rich man to enter into the kingdom of God."

When his disciples heard it they were exceedingly amazed, saying, "Who then can be saved?"

But Jesus beheld them, and said unto them, "With men this is impossible; but with God all things are possible."

Then answered Peter and said unto him, "Behold, we have forsaken all, and followed thee; what shall we have therefore?"

And Jesus said unto them, "Verily I say unto you, that ye which have followed me, in the regeneration when the Son of man shall sit in the throne of his glory, ye also shall sit upon twelve thrones, judging the twelve tribes of Israel. And every one that hath forsaken houses, or brethren, or sisters, or father, or mother, or wife, or children, or lands, for my name's sake, shall receive an hundredfold, and shall inherit everlasting life. But many that are first shall be last; and the last shall be first."                    — Matthew 19:16–30.

### The Story of the Man Who Hired Laborers for His Vineyard

"For the kingdom of heaven is like unto a man that is an householder, which went out early in the morning to hire labourers into his vineyard. And when he had agreed with the labourers for a penny a day, he sent them into his vineyard. And he went out about the third hour, and saw others standing idle in the marketplace, and said unto them: 'Go ye also into the vineyard, and whatsoever is right I will give you.' And they went their way. Again he went out about the sixth and ninth hour, and did likewise.

"And about the eleventh hour he went out, and found others standing idle, and saith unto them, 'Why stand ye here all the day idle?'

"They say unto him, 'Because no man hath hired us.'

"He saith unto them, 'Go ye also into the vineyard; and whatsoever is right, that shall ye receive.'

"THE LAST SHALL BE FIRST AND THE FIRST LAST"

"So when even was come, the lord of the vineyard saith unto his steward, 'Call the labourers, and give them their hire, beginning from the last unto the first.'

"And when they came that were hired about the eleventh hour, they received every man a penny. But when the first came, they supposed that they should have received more; and they likewise received every man a penny. And when they had received it, they murmured against the goodman of the house, saying, 'These last have wrought but one hour, and thou hast made them equal unto us, which have borne the burden and heat of the day.'

"But he answered one of them, and said, 'Friend, I do thee no wrong: didst not thou agree with me for a penny? Take that thine is, and go thy way: I will give unto this last, even as unto thee. Is it not lawful for me to do what I will with mine own? Is thine eye evil, because I am good?'

"So the last shall be first, and the first last: for many be called, but few chosen."                    — Matthew 20:1–16.

## Again the Shadow of the Cross

And they were in the way going up to Jerusalem; and Jesus went before them: and they were amazed; and as they followed, they were afraid. And he took again the twelve, and began to tell them what things should happen unto him, saying, "Behold, we go up to Jerusalem; and the Son of man shall be delivered unto the chief priests, and unto the scribes; and they shall condemn him to death, and shall deliver him to the Gentiles: and they shall mock him, and shall scourge him, and shall spit upon him, and shall kill him: and the third day he shall rise again." — Mark 10:32–34.

## "Whosoever Will Be Chief Among You, Let Him Be Your Servant"

Then came to him the mother of Zebedee's children with her sons, worshiping him, and desiring a certain thing of him. And he said unto her, "What wilt thou?"

She saith unto him, "Grant that these my two sons may sit, the one on thy right hand, and the other on the left, in thy kingdom."

But Jesus answered and said, "Ye know not what ye ask. Are ye able to drink of the cup that I shall drink of, and to be baptized with the baptism that I am baptized with?"

They say unto him, "We are able."

And he saith unto them, "Ye shall drink indeed of my cup, and be baptized with the baptism that I am baptized with: but to sit on my right hand, and on my left, is not mine to give, but it shall be given to them for whom it is prepared of my Father."

And when the ten heard it, they were moved with indignation against the two brethren. But Jesus called them unto him, and said, "Ye know that the princes of the Gentiles exercise dominion over them, and they that are great exercise authority upon them. But it shall not be so among you: but whosoever will be great among you, let him be your minister; and whosoever will be chief among you, let him be your servant: even as the Son of man came not to be ministered unto, but to minister, and to give his life a ransom for many."

And they came to Jericho: and as he went out of Jericho with his disciples and a great number of people, blind Bartimæus, the son of Timæus, sat by the highway side begging. And when he heard that it was Jesus of Nazareth, he began to cry out, and say, "Jesus, thou son of David, have mercy on me." And many charged him that he should hold his peace: but he cried the more a great deal, "Thou son of David, have mercy on me."

And Jesus stood still, and commanded him to be called. And they call the blind man, saying unto him, "Be of good comfort, rise; he calleth thee."

And he, casting away his garment, rose, and came to Jesus.

And Jesus answered and said unto him, "What wilt thou that I should do unto thee?"

The blind man said unto him, "Lord, that I might receive my sight."

And Jesus said unto him, "Go thy way; thy faith hath made thee whole." And immediately he received his sight, and followed Jesus in the way. — Matthew 20:20–28; Mark 10:46–52.

## THE MAN IN THE TREE

The publican, Zacchæus, climbed a tree in his eagerness to see Jesus. His repentance and his honesty gained for him high favor with the Master.

And Jesus entered and passed through Jericho. And, behold, there was a man named Zacchæus, which was the chief among the publicans, and he was rich. And he sought to see Jesus who he was; and could not for the press, because he was little of stature. And he ran before, and climbed up into a sycamore tree to see him: for he was to pass that way.

And when Jesus came to the place, he looked up, and saw him and said unto him, "Zacchæus, make haste, and come down; for to-day I must abide at thy house."

## THE CHIEF PUBLICAN ENTERTAINS THE MASTER AND MAKES RESTITUTION FOR HIS PAST MISDEEDS

And he made haste, and came down, and received him joyfully. And when they saw it, they all murmured, saying that he was gone to be guest with a man that is a sinner. And Zacchæus stood, and said unto the Lord: "Behold, Lord, the half of my goods I give to the poor; and if I have taken anything from any man by false accusation, I restore him fourfold."

And Jesus said unto him, "This day is salvation come to this house, forsomuch as he also is a son of Abraham. For the Son of man is come to seek and to save that which was lost." — Luke 19:1–10.

## THE STORY OF THE TALENTS

And as they heard these things, he added and spake a parable, because he was nigh to Jerusalem, and because they thought that the kingdom of God should immediately appear.

He said therefore, "A certain nobleman went into a far country to receive for himself a kingdom, and to return. And he called his ten servants, and delivered them ten pounds, and said unto them, 'Occupy till I come.'

"But his citizens hated him, and sent a message after him, saying, 'We will not have this man to reign over us'

"And it came to pass, that when he was returned, having received the kingdom, then he commanded these servants to be called unto him, to whom he had given the money, that he might know how much every man had gained by trading. Then came the first, saying, 'Lord, thy pound hath gained ten pounds.'

"And he said unto him, 'Well, thou good servant: because thou hast been faithful in a very little, have thou authority over ten cities.'

"And the second came, saying, 'Lord, thy pound hath gained five pounds.'

"And he said likewise to him, 'Be thou also over five cities.'

"And another came, saying, 'Lord, behold, here is thy pound, which I have kept laid up in a napkin: for I feared thee, because thou art an austere man: thou takest up that thou layedst not down, and reapest that thou didst not sow.'

"And he saith unto him, 'Out of thine own mouth will I judge thee, thou wicked servant. Thou knewest that I was an austere man, taking up that I laid not down, and reaping that I did not sow. Wherefore then gavest not thou my money into the bank, that at my coming I might have required mine own with usury?'

"And he said unto them that stood by, 'Take from him the pound, and give it to him that hath ten pounds.'

"And they said unto him, 'Lord, he hath ten pounds.'

" 'For I say unto you, that unto every one which hath shall be given; and from him that hath not, even that he hath shall be taken away from him. But those mine enemies, which would not that I should reign over them, bring hither, and slay them before me.' "

And when he had thus spoken, he went before, ascending up to Jerusalem. — Luke 19:11–28.

### THE BOX OF OINTMENT

Now when Jesus was in Bethany, in the house of Simon the leper, there came unto him a woman having an alabaster box of very precious ointment, and poured it on his head, as he sat at meat. But when his disciples saw it, they had indignation, saying, "To what purpose is this waste? For this ointment might have been sold for much, and given to the poor."

When Jesus understood it, he said unto them, "Why trouble ye the woman? For she hath wrought a good work upon me. For ye have the poor always with you; but me ye have not always. For in that she hath poured this ointment on my body, she did it for my burial. Verily I say unto you, wheresoever this gospel shall be preached in the whole world, there shall also this, that this woman hath done. be told for a memorial of her."        — Matthew 26:6–13.

SYCAMORE TREE
IN JERICHO

*Photograph by*
*Frances Jenkins Olcott*

Here in Jericho still grow the stately sycamores, tall and shade-casting. Their top-shaped figs are sweet and aromatic.

Into such a tree in the Jericho of the Lord's day, did Zacchaeus the rich publican climb, for he was too short to see the Lord Jesus over the heads of the crowd.

There are three Jerichos in the deep gorge of the Jordan Valley—the massive ruins of the Jericho that fell before Joshua and the army of Israel; the bare mound that indicates the site of the Jericho of our Lord's day, and modern Jericho in its palm trees.

Read Luke 19:1-10, pages 173-4.

# The Triumphal Entry Into Jerusalem

By Fra Angelico da Fiesole (1387-1455)

In the Museum of the Monastery of San Marco, Florence

Photograph by Alinari Brothers, Florence, Italy

THE Triumphal Entry occurred on what we now
call Palm Sunday. The story of this event is given
in all four Gospels. The scene as presented in Fra
Angelico's picture follows the account in Matthew.
How do we know this? You will find the Bible story in
this Volume beginning on page 179.

In this picture we have another of those severely
simple yet tremendously moving portrayals by the
great artist saint of Florence. The Master rides upon
an ass, the little colt trotting by its side. The disciples
follow close behind while other believers lead the way,
one spreading his cloak upon the ground, others strew-
ing the path with palm branches.

The artist has made the scene an entirely serious one,
as has also Giotto, another early master, in his painting
on page 350 in Volume I. Here the Master's face is
thoughtful and sad. The faces of those who attend him
seem to reflect this mood as though they, too, realized
that after the day of triumph would come the Cross.

This painting is one of thirty-five little panel pictures
which originally ornamented the silver-press of one of
the chapels in the Church of the Annunciation in
Florence. It is believed that these panels were painted
by order of Cosimo de' Medici, a wealthy and powerful
merchant of Florence, who spent large sums of money
in beautifying this chapel. The series of pictures depict
important scenes from the life of Christ closing with
the Last Judgment. As you study the paintings by
Fra Angelico you will find that the cloistered painter
was gifted with a deep feeling for the spiritual and
mystical qualities of the medieval conception of Christianity and a consummate artistic skill for portraying
this feeling.

# The Story of the Master

### From the Gospels of Matthew, Mark and Luke

## The Last Week of the Master's Life

### SUNDAY

#### THE TRIUMPHAL ENTRY INTO JERUSALEM

AND it came to pass, when he was come nigh to Bethphage and Bethany, at the mount called the Mount of Olives, he sent two of his disciples, saying, "Go ye into the village over against you; in the which at your entering ye shall find a colt tied, whereon yet never man sat: loose him, and bring him hither. And if any man ask you, 'Why do ye loose him?' thus shall ye say unto him, 'Because the LORD hath need of him.'"

And they that were sent went their way, and found even as he had said unto them. And as they were loosing the colt, the owners thereof said unto them, "Why loose ye the colt?"

And they said, "The Lord hath need of him."

And they brought him to Jesus: and they cast their garments upon the colt, and they set Jesus thereon. And as he went, they spread their clothes in the way. And when he was come nigh, even now at the descent of the Mount of Olives, the whole multitude of the disciples began to rejoice and praise God with a loud voice for all the mighty works that they had seen; saying, "Blessed be the King that cometh in the name of the Lord: peace in heaven, and glory in the highest."

And some of the Pharisees from among the multitude said unto him, "Master, rebuke thy disciples."

And he answered and said unto them, "I tell you that, if these should hold their peace, the stones would immediately cry out."

And when he was come near, he beheld the city, and wept over it, saying, "If thou hadst known, even thou, at least in this thy day, the things which belong unto thy peace! But now they are hid from thine eyes. For the days shall come upon thee, that thine enemies shall cast a trench about thee, and compass thee round, and keep thee in on every side, and shall lay thee even with the ground, and thy children within thee; and they shall not leave in thee one stone upon another; because thou knewest not the time of thy visitation."

And when he was come into Jerusalem, all the city was moved, saying, "Who is this?"

And the multitude said, "This is Jesus the prophet of Nazareth of Galilee."

And Jesus entered into Jerusalem, and into the temple: and when he had looked round about upon all things, and now the eventide was come, he went out unto Bethany with the twelve. And in the day time he was teaching in the temple; and at night he went out, and abode in the mount that is called the Mount of Olives.

— Luke 19:29–44; Matthew 21:10–11; Mark 11:11; Luke 21:37.

## MONDAY

### THE BARREN FIG-TREE

Now in the morning as he returned into the city, he hungered. And when he saw a fig-tree in the way, he came to it, and found nothing thereon, but leaves only and said unto it, "Let no fruit grow on thee henceforward forever." And presently the fig-tree withered away. And when the disciples saw it, they marveled, saying, "How soon is the fig-tree withered away!" Jesus answered and said unto them, "Verily I say unto you, if ye have faith, and doubt not, ye shall not only do this which is done to the fig-tree, but also if ye shall say unto this mountain, 'Be thou removed, and be thou cast into the sea'; it shall be done. And all things, whatsoever ye shall ask in prayer, believing, ye shall receive." —Matthew 21:18-22.

### THE CLEANSING OF THE TEMPLE

And Jesus went into the temple of God, and cast out all them that sold and bought in the temple, and overthrew the tables of the money-changers, and the seats of them that sold doves, and said unto them, "It is written, 'My house shall be called the house of prayer'; but ye have made it a den of thieves."

And the blind and the lame came to him in the temple; and he healed them. And when the chief priests and scribes saw the wonderful things that he did, and the children crying in the temple, and saying, "Hosanna to the son of David;" they were sore displeased, and said unto him, "Hearest thou what these say?"

And Jesus saith unto them, "Yea; have ye never read, 'Out of the mouth of babes and sucklings thou hast perfected praise'?"

And he left them, and went out of the city into Bethany; and he lodged there. —Matthew 21:12-17.

### TUESDAY

#### THE WITHERED FIG-TREE

And in the morning, as they passed by, they saw the fig-tree dried up from the roots. And Peter calling to remembrance saith unto him, "Master, behold, the fig-tree which thou cursedst is withered away."

And Jesus answering saith unto them, "Have faith in God. For verily I say unto you, that whosoever shall say unto this mountain, 'Be thou removed, and be thou cast into the sea'; and shall not doubt in his heart, but shall believe that those things which he saith shall come to pass; he shall have whatsoever he saith. Therefore I say unto you, what things soever ye desire, when ye pray, believe that ye receive them, and ye shall have them. And when ye stand praying, forgive, if ye have ought against any: that your Father also which is in heaven may forgive you your trespasses." — Mark 11:20–25.

## "BY WHAT AUTHORITY DOEST THOU THESE THINGS?"

### THE CHALLENGE TO JESUS' AUTHORITY

And they come again to Jerusalem: and as he was walking in the temple, there come to him the chief priests, and the scribes, and the elders, and say unto him, "By what authority doest thou these things? And who gave thee this authority to do these things?"

And Jesus answered and said unto them, "I will also ask of you one question, and answer me, and I will tell you by what authority I do these things. The baptism of John, was it from heaven, or of men? Answer me."

And they reasoned with themselves, saying, "If we shall say, 'From heaven': he will say, 'Why then did ye not believe him?' But if we shall say, 'Of men—' " they feared the people: for all men counted John, that he was a prophet indeed.

And they answered and said unto Jesus, "We cannot tell."

And Jesus answering saith unto them, "Neither do I tell you by what authority I do these things."
— Mark 11:27–33.

## THE STORY OF THE TWO SONS WHO WERE SENT TO WORK IN THE VINEYARD

"But what think ye? A certain man had two sons; and he came to the first, and said, 'Son, go work to-day in my vineyard.'

"He answered and said, 'I will not'; but afterward he repented and went.

"And he came to the second, and said likewise. And he answered and said, 'I go, sir': and went not.

"Whether of them twain did the will of his father?" They say unto him, "The first."

Jesus saith unto them, "Verily I say unto you, that the publicans and the harlots go into the kingdom of God before you. For John came unto you in the way of righteousness, and ye believed him not: but the publicans and the harlots believed him: and ye, when ye had seen it, repented not afterward, that ye might believe him."

## THE STORY OF THE WICKED AND UNFAITHFUL SERVANTS

"Hear another parable: There was a certain householder, which planted a vineyard, and hedged it round about, and digged a wine-press in it, and built a tower, and let it out to husbandmen, and went into a far country: and when the time of the fruit drew near, he sent his servants to the husbandmen, that they might receive the fruits of it. And the husbandmen took his servants, and beat one, and killed another, and stoned another. Again, he sent other servants more than the first: and they did unto them likewise. But last of all he sent unto them his son, saying, 'They will reverence my son.'

"But when the husbandmen saw the son, they said among themselves, 'This is the heir; come, let us kill him, and let us seize on his inheritance.'

"And they caught him, and cast him out of the vineyard, and slew him. When the lord therefore of the vineyard cometh, what will he do unto those husbandmen?"

They say unto him, "He will miserably destroy those
wicked men, and will let out his vineyard unto other husbandmen, which shall render him the fruits in their seasons."

Jesus saith unto them, "Did ye never read in the
scriptures,

'The stone which the builders rejected,
The same is become the head of the corner:
This is the LORD's doing
And it is marvellous in our eyes'?

"Therefore say I unto you, the kingdom of God shall
be taken from you, and given to a nation bringing forth
the fruits thereof. And whosoever shall fall on this stone
shall be broken: but on whomsoever it shall fall, it will
grind him to powder."

### THE PHARISEES FEAR THE MULTITUDE

And when the chief priests and Pharisees had heard
his parables, they perceived that he spake of them. But
when they sought to lay hands on him, they feared the
multitude, because they took him for a prophet.

### THE STORY OF THE ROYAL MARRIAGE

And Jesus answered and spake unto them again by parables, and said, "The kingdom of heaven is like unto a
certain king, which made a marriage for his son, and sent
forth his servants to call them that were bidden to the
wedding: and they would not come. Again, he sent forth
other servants, saying, 'Tell them which are bidden,
"Behold, I have prepared my dinner: my oxen and my

# The Kiss of Judas

By Antoine Auguste Ernest Hébert (1817-1908)
In the Louvre Museum, Paris, France

ALL four Gospels tell the story of Jesus' betrayal in Gethsemane, and Matthew, Mark, and Luke each tell us that a kiss, the customary expression of salutation and special regard, was to be the sign by which Judas would identify Jesus.

John describes the scene thus, page 342: "Judas then, having received a band of men and officers from the chief priests and Pharisees, cometh thither with lanterns and torches and weapons." Matthew's account page 211, continues: "And forthwith Judas came to Jesus and said, 'Hail, master;' and kissed him. And Jesus said unto him, 'Friend, wherefore art thou come?'" When the soldiers then laid hands on him, Jesus spoke, Luke 23:52-3: "Be ye come out, as against a thief, with swords and staves? When I was daily with you in the temple, ye stretched forth no hands against me: but this is your hour, and the power of darkness."

This black deed seeks the cloak of black night. The sharp lantern light, barely piercing the nearest shadows, reveals the innermost group. Jesus, strengthened by prayer, see pages 208 and 336, endures with unreproachful dignity the salutation of the cringing Judas and by his very fearlessness checks the hasty brutality of the captors. Long spears are sharply silhouetted against the distant glow of the night sky.

Ernest Hébert, French historical and portrait artist born at Grenoble, painted this well-known picture in 1853.

In comparing Hébert with his contemporaries in other countries, pages 107, 324, 336, and in France, Volume I, pages 65, 282, 366, we find many similarities in the work of the school-trained or academic painters. Which artists differ?

fatlings are killed, and all things are ready: come unto the marriage.'"

"But they made light of it, and went their ways, one to his farm, another to his merchandise: and the remnant took his servants, and entreated them spitefully, and slew them. But when the king heard thereof, he was wroth: and he sent forth his armies, and destroyed those murderers, and burned up their city.

"Then saith he to his servants, 'The wedding is ready, but they which were bidden were not worthy. Go ye therefore into the highways, and as many as ye shall find, bid to the marriage.'

"So those servants went out into the highways, and gathered together all as many as they found, both bad and good: and the wedding was furnished with guests.

"And when the king came in to see the guests, he saw there a man which had not on a wedding garment: and he saith unto him, 'Friend, how camest thou in hither not having a wedding garment?' And he was speechless.

"Then said the king to the servants, 'Bind him hand and foot, and take him away, and cast him into outer darkness; there shall be weeping and gnashing of teeth.' For many are called, but few are chosen."

— Matthew 21:28–22:14.

### THE THREE QUESTIONS

And they send unto him certain of the Pharisees and of the Herodians, to catch him in his words. And when they were come, they say unto him, "Master, we know that thou art true, and carest for no man: for thou regardest not the person of men, but teachest the way of God in truth. Is it lawful to give tribute to Cæsar, or not? Shall we give, or shall we not give?"

But he, knowing their hypocrisy, said unto them, "Why tempt ye me? Bring me a penny that I may see it."

And they brought it.   And he saith unto them, "Whose is this image and superscription?"

And they said unto him, "Cæsar's."

And Jesus answering said unto them, "Render to Cæsar the things that are Cæsar's, and to God the things that are God's." And they marveled at him.

Then come unto him the Sadducees, which say there is no resurrection; and they asked him, saying, "Master, Moses wrote unto us, 'If a man's brother die, and leave his wife behind him, and leave no children, that his brother should take his wife, and raise up seed unto his brother.' Now there were seven brethren: and the first took a wife, and dying left no seed. And the second took her, and died, neither left he any seed: and the third likewise. And the seven had her, and left no seed: last of all the woman died also. In the resurrection therefore, when they shall rise, whose wife shall she be of them? For the seven had her to wife."

## "THE GOD OF THE LIVING"

And Jesus answering said unto them, "Do ye not therefore err, because ye know not the scriptures, neither the power of God? For when they shall rise from the dead, they neither marry, nor are given in marriage; but are as the angels which are in heaven. And as touching the dead, that they rise: have ye not read in the book of Moses, how in the bush God spake unto him, saying, 'I am the God of Abraham, and the God of Isaac, and the God of Jacob'? He is not the God of the dead, but the God of the living: ye therefore do greatly err."

And one of the scribes came, and having heard them reasoning together, and perceiving that he had answered them well, asked him, "Which is the first commandment of all?"

# The Tribute Money

By Titian, Tiziano Vecellio (c. 1477-1576)
In the Royal Picture Gallery, Dresden, Germany

HERE is pictured that tensely dramatic moment in which Jesus, the popular friend of the people, is being challenged by his enemies to declare openly whether he thinks it is lawful for the Romans to exact tribute from the people. The shrewdly phrased question of the Pharisee and Jesus' masterly reply are given on pages 187-8.

After such a reply, is it any wonder that the Pharisees "marveled at him"? And when we study this picture, which, in a few sweeping lines and finely modelled dark and light masses both fathoms and conveys the essence of the forces involved, we have double cause to marvel. Christ, parrying the Pharisee's cunning challenge, is gentle, a little sad, showing none of the exultation or condescension with which any mere man would accompany such a crushing retort. In His noble countenance and refined gesture we discern, intellectual power, sympathetic insight, calm purity, unwavering justness.

The Pharisee, also, is singularly dignified. Here is no petty trickster or obstructionist. He shows rather the sternness of a man sure of his case and seeking to expose a dangerous impostor. In his controlled fanaticism, he is akin to the great persecutors.

Titian took greatest pains with this painting, the finest religious picture of his early maturity, painted in 1514-15, because he wished to interest Albrecht Dürer, the great German artist, then in Venice. Dürer, see page 158, undoubtedly recognized this painting, as both a technical achievement and a triumph of psychological interpretation.

For other pictures by Titian, one of the greatest painters the world has known, see page 222 and Volume I, page 260.

And Jesus answered him, "The first of all the commandments is, 'Hear, O Israel; The LORD our God is one LORD: and thou shalt love the LORD thy God with all thy heart, and with all thy soul, and with all thy mind, and with all thy strength.' This is the first commandment. And the second is like, namely this, 'Thou shalt love thy neighbour as thyself.' There is none other commandment greater than these."

And the scribe said unto him, "Well, Master, thou hast said the truth: for there is one God; and there is none other but he: and to love him with all the heart, and with all the understanding, and with all the soul, and with all the strength, and to love his neighbour as himself, is more than all whole burnt offerings and sacrifices." And when Jesus saw that he answered discreetly, he said unto him, "Thou art not far from the kingdom of God." And no man after that durst ask him any question.

— Mark 12:13–34.

### THE QUESTION OF JESUS WHICH NO ONE COULD ANSWER

While the Pharisees were gathered together, Jesus asked them, saying, "What think ye of Christ? Whose son is he?"

They say unto him, "The son of David."

He saith unto them, "How then doth David in spirit call him LORD, saying,

'The LORD said unto my LORD,
Sit thou on my right hand,
Till I make thine enemies thy footstool'?

"If David then call him LORD, how is he his son?"

And no man was able to answer him a word, neither durst any man from that day forth ask him any more questions. And the common people heard him gladly.

— Matthew 22:41–46.

THE CONDEMNATIONS OF THE SCRIBES AND PHARISEES

Then spake Jesus to the multitude, and to his disciples, saying, "The scribes and the Pharisees sit in Moses' seat: all therefore whatsoever they bid you observe, that observe and do; but do not ye after their works for they say, and do not. For they bind heavy burdens and grievous to be borne, and lay them on men's shoulders; but they themselves will not move them with one of their fingers. But all their works they do for to be seen of men: they make broad their phylacteries, and enlarge the borders of their garments, and love the uppermost rooms at feasts, and the chief seats in the synagogues, and greetings in the markets, and to be called of men, 'Rabbi, Rabbi.' But be not ye called 'Rabbi': for one is your Master, even Christ; and all ye are brethren. And call no man your father upon the earth: for one is your Father, which is in heaven. Neither be ye called masters: for one is your Master, even Christ. But he that is greatest among you shall be your servant. And whosoever shall exalt himself shall be abased; and he that shall humble himself shall be exalted.

"But woe unto you, scribes and Pharisees, hypocrites! For ye shut up the kingdom of heaven against men: for ye neither go in yourselves, neither suffer ye them that are entering to go in.

"Woe unto you, scribes and Pharisees, hypocrites! For ye devour widows' houses, and for a pretence make long prayer: therefore ye shall receive the greater damnation.

"Woe unto you, scribes and Pharisees, hypocrites! For ye compass sea and land to make one proselyte, and when he is made, ye make him twofold more the child of hell than yourselves.

"Woe unto you, ye blind guides, which say, 'Whosoever shall swear by the temple, it is nothing; but whosoever shall swear by the gold of the temple, he is a debtor!' Ye fools and blind: for whether is greater, the gold or the temple that sanctifieth the gold? And, 'Whosoever shall swear by the altar, it is nothing; but whosoever sweareth by the gift that is upon it, he is guilty.' Ye fools and blind: for whether is greater, the gift or the altar that sanctifieth the gift? Whoso therefore shall swear by the altar, sweareth by it, and by all things thereon. And whoso shall swear by the temple, sweareth by it, and by him that dwelleth therein. And he that shall swear by heaven, sweareth by the throne of God, and by him that sitteth thereon.

"Woe unto you, scribes and Pharisees, hypocrites! For ye pay tithe of mint and anise and cummin, and have omitted the weightier matters of the law, judgment, mercy, and faith: those ought ye to have done, and not to leave the other undone. Ye blind guides, which strain at a gnat, and swallow a camel.

"Woe unto you, scribes and Pharisees, hypocrites! For ye make clean the outside of the cup and of the platter, but within they are full of extortion and excess. Thou blind Pharisee, cleanse first that which is within the cup and platter, that the outside of them may be clean also.

"Woe unto you, scribes and Pharisees, hypocrites! For ye are like unto whited sepulchers, which indeed appear beautiful outward, but are within full of dead men's bones, and of all uncleanness. Even so ye also outwardly appear righteous unto men, but within ye are full of hypocrisy and iniquity.

"Woe unto you, scribes and Pharisees, hypocrites! Because ye build the tombs of the prophets, and garnish the sepulchers of the righteous, and say, 'If we had been in the days of our fathers, we would not have been partakers with them in the blood of the prophets.' Wherefore ye be witnesses unto yourselves, that ye are the children of them which killed the prophets. Fill ye up then the measure of your fathers. Ye serpents, ye generation of vipers, how can ye escape the damnation of hell?

"Wherefore, behold, I send unto you prophets, and wise men, and scribes: and some of them ye shall kill and crucify; and some of them shall ye scourge in your synagogues, and persecute them from city to city: that upon you may come all the righteous blood shed upon the earth, from the blood of righteous Abel unto the blood of Zacharias, son of Barachias, whom ye slew between the temple and the altar. Verily I say unto you, all these things shall come upon this generation.

"O Jerusalem, Jerusalem, thou that killest the prophets, and stonest them which are sent unto thee, how often would I have gathered thy children together, even as a hen gathereth her chickens under her wings, and ye would not! Behold, your house is left unto you desolate. For I say unto you, ye shall not see me henceforth, till ye shall say, 'Blessed is he that cometh in the name of the Lord.' "

— Matthew 23.

### THE WIDOW AND HER TWO MITES

And Jesus sat over against the treasury, and beheld how the people cast money into the treasury: and many that were rich cast in much. And there came a certain poor widow, and she threw in two mites, which make a farthing. And he called unto him his disciples, and saith unto them, "Verily I say unto you, that this poor widow hath cast more in, than all they which have cast into the treasury: for all they did cast in of their abundance; but she of her want did cast in all that she had, even all her living."

— Mark 12:41–44.

### WARNING OF THE DESTRUCTION WHICH WAS IMPENDING

The Jews could not believe that the holy city of Jerusalem could be destroyed, but it was only a few years before the Roman armies swept over Palestine, laying waste all her towns and cities, making of Jerusalem and the Temple a heap of ruins, slaughtering thousands of the people. There would be many in those days who would remember the words of warning solemnly spoken by Jesus.

And Jesus went out, and departed from the temple: and his disciples came to him for to show him the buildings of the temple. And Jesus said unto them, "See ye not all these things? Verily I say unto you, there shall not be left here one stone upon another, that shall not be thrown down."

And as he sat upon the Mount of Olives, the disciples came unto him privately, saying, "Tell us, when shall these things be? And what shall be the sign of thy coming, and of the end of the world?"

And Jesus answered and said unto them, "Take heed that no man deceive you. For many shall come in my name, saying, 'I am Christ'; and shall deceive many. And ye shall hear of wars and rumours of wars: see that ye be not troubled: for all these things must come to pass, but the end is not yet. For nation shall rise against nation, and kingdom against kingdom: and there shall be famines, and pestilences, and earthquakes, in divers places. All these are the beginning of sorrows. Then shall they deliver you up to be afflicted, and shall kill you: and ye shall be hated of all nations for my name's sake. And then shall many be offended, and shall betray one another, and shall hate one another. And many false prophets shall rise, and shall deceive many. And because iniquity shall abound, the love of many shall wax cold. But he that shall endure unto the end, the same shall be saved. And this gospel of the kingdom shall be preached in all the world for a witness unto all nations; and then shall the end come. When ye therefore shall see the abomination of desolation, spoken of by Daniel the prophet, stand in the holy place (whoso readeth, let him understand), then let them which be in Judæa flee into the mountains: let him which is on

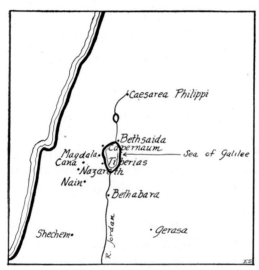

MAP OF NORTHERN PALESTINE IN THE TIME OF JESUS

the housetop not come down to take anything out of his house: neither let him which is in the field return back to take his clothes. And woe unto them that are with child, and to them that give suck in those days! But pray ye that your flight be not in the winter, neither on the sabbath day: for

then shall be great tribulation, such as was not since the beginning of the world to this time, no, nor ever shall be. And except those days should be shortened, there should no flesh be saved: but for the elect's sake those days shall be shortened. Then if any man shall say unto you, 'Lo, here is Christ,' or, 'There'; believe it not. For there shall arise false Christs, and false prophets, and shall show great signs and wonders; insomuch that, if it were possible, they shall deceive the very elect. Behold, I have told you before. Wherefore if they shall say unto you, 'Behold, he is in the desert'; go not forth; 'Behold, he is in the secret chambers'; believe it not. For as the lightning cometh out of the east, and shineth even unto the west; so shall also the coming of the Son of man be. For wheresoever the carcase is, there will the eagles be gathered together.

"Immediately after the tribulation of those days shall the sun be darkened, and the moon shall not give her light, and the stars shall fall from heaven, and the powers of the heavens shall be shaken: and then shall appear the sign of the Son of man in heaven: and then shall all the tribes of the earth mourn, and they shall see the Son of man coming in the clouds of heaven with power and great glory. And he shall send his angels with a great sound of a trumpet, and they shall gather together his elect from the four winds, from one end of heaven to the other.

"Now learn a parable of the fig-tree: when his branch is yet tender, and putteth forth leaves, ye know that summer is nigh: so likewise ye, when ye shall see all these things, know that it is near, even at the doors. Verily I say unto you, this generation shall not pass, till all these things be fulfilled. Heaven and earth shall pass away, but my words shall not pass away.

### "THE DAY AND THE HOUR NO MAN KNOWS"

"But of that day and hour knoweth no man, no, not the angels of heaven, but my Father only. But as the days of Noe were, so shall also the coming of the Son of man be. For as in the days that were before the flood they were eating and drinking, marrying and giving in marriage, until the day that Noe entered into the ark, and knew not until the flood came, and took them all away; so shall also the coming of the Son of man be. Then shall two be in the field; the one shall be taken, and the other left. Two women shall be grinding at the mill; the one shall be taken, and the other left. Watch therefore: for ye know not what hour your Lord doth come. But know this, that if the goodman of the house had known in what watch the thief would come, he would have watched, and would not have suffered his house to be broken up. Therefore be ye also ready: for in such an hour as ye think not the Son of man cometh. Who then is a faithful and wise servant, whom his lord hath made ruler over his household, to give them meat in due season? Blessed is that servant, whom his lord when he cometh shall find so doing. Verily I say unto you, that he shall make him ruler over all his goods. But if that evil servant shall say in his heart, 'My lord delayeth his coming'; and shall begin to smite his fellowservants, and to eat and drink with the drunken; the lord of that servant shall come in a day when he looketh not for him, and in an hour that he is not aware of, and shall cut him asunder, and appoint him his portion with the hypocrites: there shall be weeping and gnashing of teeth."          —Matthew 24.

### THE STORY OF THE WISE AND THE FOOLISH VIRGINS

"Then shall the kingdom of heaven be likened unto ten virgins, which took their lamps, and went forth to meet the bridegroom. And five of them were wise, and five were foolish. They that were foolish took their lamps, and took no oil with them: but the wise took oil in their vessels with their lamps. While the bridegroom tarried, they all slumbered and slept. And at midnight there was a cry made, 'Behold, the bridegroom cometh; go ye out to meet him.' Then all those virgins arose, and trimmed their lamps. And the foolish said unto the wise, 'Give us of your oil; for our lamps are gone out.'

"But the wise answered, saying, 'Not so; lest there be not enough for us and you: but go ye rather to them that sell, and buy for yourselves.'

"And while they went to buy, the bridegroom came; and they that were ready went in with him to the marriage: and the door was shut.

"Afterward came also the other virgins, saying, 'Lord, Lord, open to us.'

"But he answered and said, 'Verily I say unto you, I know you not.' Watch therefore, for ye know neither the day nor the hour wherein the Son of man cometh."

### THE STORY OF THE TALENTS

"For the kingdom of heaven is as a man traveling into a far country, who called his own servants, and delivered unto them his goods. And unto one he gave five talents, to another two, and to another one; to every man according to his several ability; and straightway took his journey. Then he that had received the five talents went and traded with the same, and made them other five talents. And likewise he that had received two, he also gained other two. But he that had received one went and digged in the earth, and hid his lord's money. After a long time the lord of those servants cometh, and reckoned with them. And so he that had received five talents came and brought other five talents, saying, 'Lord, thou deliveredst unto me five talents: behold, I have gained beside them five talents more.'

"His lord said unto him, 'Well done, thou good and faithful servant: thou hast been faithful over a few things, I will make thee ruler over many things: enter thou into the joy of thy lord.'

"He also that had received two talents came and said, 'Lord, thou deliveredst unto me two talents: behold, I have gained two other talents beside them.'

"His lord said unto him, 'Well done, good and faithful servant; thou hast been faithful over a few things, I will make thee ruler over many things: enter thou into the joy of thy lord.'

"Then he which had received the one talent came and said, 'Lord, I knew thee that thou art an hard man, reaping where thou hast not sown, and gathering where thou hast not strowed: and I was afraid, and went and hid thy talent in the earth: lo, there thou hast that is thine.'

"His lord answered and said unto him, 'Thou wicked and slothful servant, thou knewest that I reap where I sowed not, and gather where I have not strowed: thou oughtest therefore to have put my money to the exchangers, and then at my coming I should have received mine own with usury.' Take therefore the talent from him, and give it unto him which hath ten talents. For unto every one that hath shall be given, and he shall have abundance: but from him that hath not shall be taken away even that which he hath. And cast ye the unprofitable servant into outer darkness: there shall be weeping and gnashing of teeth."

### THE TEST OF DISCIPLESHIP

"When the Son of man shall come in his glory, and all the holy angels with him, then shall he sit upon the throne of his glory: and before him shall be gathered all nations: and he shall separate them one from another, as a shepherd divideth his sheep from the goats: and he shall set the sheep on his right hand, but the goats on the left.

"Then shall the King say unto them on his right hand, 'Come, ye blessed of my Father, inherit the kingdom prepared for you from the foundation of the world: for I was an hungred, and ye gave me meat: I was thirsty, and ye gave me drink: I was a stranger, and ye took me in: naked, and ye clothed me: I was sick, and ye visited me: I was in prison, and ye came unto me.'

THE GARDEN OF GETHSEMANE
*Photograph by W. A. Pottenger expressly for The Book of Life*

"Then shall the righteous answer him, saying, 'Lord, when saw we thee an hungered, and fed thee? or thirsty, and gave thee drink? When saw thee we a stranger, and took thee in? or naked, and clothed thee? Or when saw we thee sick, or in prison, and came unto thee?'

"And the King shall answer and say unto them, 'Verily I say unto you, inasmuch as ye have done it unto one of the least of these my brethren, ye have done it unto me.'

"Then shall he say also unto them on the left hand, 'Depart from me, ye cursed, into everlasting fire, prepared for the devil and his angels: for I was an hungered, and ye gave me no meat: I was thirsty, and ye gave me no drink: I was a stranger, and ye took me not in: naked, and ye clothed me not: sick, and in prison, and ye visited me not.'

"Then shall they also answer him, saying, 'Lord, when saw we thee an hungered, or athirst, or a stranger, or naked, or sick, or in prison, and did not minister unto thee?'

ENTRANCE TO THE GARDEN OF GETHSEMANE
*Photograph by W. A. Pottenger expressly for The Book of Life*

The Garden of Gethsemane is now enclosed and still there are very ancient olives in the sacred place where Jesus agonized in spirit alone.

"When Jesus had spoken these words, he went forth with his disciples over the brook Cedron, where was a garden, into the which he entered, and his disciples."—*John 18:1.*

"Then shall he answer them, saying, 'Verily I say unto you, inasmuch as ye did it not to one of the least of these, ye did it not to me.' And these shall go away into everlasting punishment: but the righteous into life eternal."

And it came to pass, when Jesus had finished all these sayings, he said unto his disciples, "Ye know that after two days is the feast of the passover, and the Son of man is betrayed to be crucified." — Matthew 24, 25, 26:1, 2.

### JUDAS BARGAINS WITH THE CHIEF PRIESTS

After two days was the feast of the passover, and of unleavened bread: and the chief priests and the scribes sought how they might take him by craft, and put him to death. But they said, "Not on the feast day, lest there be an uproar of the people."

Then one of the twelve, called Judas Iscariot, went unto the chief priests, and said unto them, "What will ye give me, and I will deliver him unto you?" And they covenanted with him for thirty pieces of silver. And from that time he sought opportunity to betray him.

—Mark 14:1-2; Matthew 26:14-16.

[There is no record of events on Wednesday.]

## THURSDAY

### THE LAST SUPPER

The communion in one form or another is observed by nearly all Christian churches, and even those who do not follow any outward form, recognize the spiritual beauty of this symbolic act of fellowship.

Break Thou the bread of life,
    Dear Lord, to me,
As Thou didst break the loaves
    Beside the sea;
Beyond the sacred page
    I seek Thee, Lord;
My spirit pants for Thee
    O living Word!
Bless Thou the truth, dear Lord,
    To me—to me—
As Thou didst bless the bread
    By Galilee;
Then shall all bondage cease,
    All fetters fall;
And I shall find my peace,
    My All in All.

—*Mary A. Lathbury.*

Then came the day of unleavened bread, when the passover must be killed. And he sent Peter and John, saying, "Go and prepare us the passover, that we may eat."

And they said unto him, "Where wilt thou that we prepare?"

And he said unto them, "Behold, when ye are entered into the city, there shall a man meet you, bearing a pitcher of water; follow him into the house where he entereth in. And ye shall say unto the goodman of the house, 'The Master saith unto thee, "Where is the guestchamber, where I shall eat the passover with my disciples?"'

ROOTS OF AN ANCIENT OLIVE-
TREE IN THE GARDEN OF
GETHSEMANE

*Photograph by W. A. Pottenger expressly
for The Book of Life*

"And he shall show you a large upper room furnished: there make ready." And they went, and found as he had said unto them: and they made ready the passover.

And when the hour was come, he sat down, and the twelve apostles with him. And he said unto them, "With desire I have desired to eat this passover with you before I suffer: for I say unto you, I will not any more eat thereof, until it be fulfilled in the kingdom of God."

And he took the cup, and gave thanks, and said, "Take this, and divide it among yourselves: for I say unto you, I will not drink of the fruit of the vine, until the kingdom of God shall come."

And he took bread, and gave thanks, and brake it, and gave unto them, saying, "This is my body which is given for you: this do in remembrance of me."

# The Thirty Pieces of Silver

By Fra Angelico da Fiesole (1387-1455)
In the Museum of the Monastery of San Marco, Florence
Photograph by Alinari Brothers, Florence, Italy

THE Biblical account of Judas' bargain with the high priests is given on page 202 of this Volume. What a study in human character we have here! Judas, the faithless disciple, having promised to make it possible for the chief priests to capture Christ, is being given his pay in advance, "thirty pieces of silver." A designing, unscrupulous character is written in his face and a selfish, secretive nature is shown in his clenched hand which draws the robe close to his body. The priests, with their crafty expressions and hypocritical gestures of piety, are unable to conceal their satisfaction at seeing their plans so near a successful completion. And yet notice how the old priest despises the traitor while giving him his price.

This is one of thirty-five pictures which were painted originally on the doors of a silver-press of a church in Florence. Critics tell us that Fra Angelico was assisted by other artists in the painting of this cycle of pictures, as was the custom. This being the case, it seems probable that the building here was left to a helper who is responsible for this queer structure with two retreating walls showing an incorrect perspective. But some painters of the period had mastered this problem of representing objects as they recede from the eye into distance. We can see in another picture of this same series on page 318 that Fra Angelico, or some other assistant of his, understood how to do this for the courtyard there is perfectly rendered. But, while the architectural background of this picture of Judas receiving the price of his betrayal is unsatisfying, the faces are the beautiful and finely executed revelations of thought and emotion for which Fra Angelico is so famous.

Likewise also the cup after supper, saying, "This cup is the new testament in my blood, which is shed for you. But, behold, the hand of him that betrayeth me is with me on the table. And truly the Son of man goeth, as it was determined: but woe unto that man by whom he is betrayed!" And they began to enquire among themselves, which of them it was that should do this thing.

And there was also a strife among them, which of them should be accounted the greatest. And he said unto them, "The kings of the Gentiles exercise lordship over them; and they that exercise authority upon them are called benefactors. But ye shall not be so: but he that is greatest among you, let him be as the younger; and he that is chief, as he that doth serve. For whether is greater, he that sitteth at meat, or he that serveth? Is not he that sitteth at meat? But I am among you as he that serveth. Ye are they which have continued with me in my temptations. And I appoint unto you a kingdom, as my Father hath appointed unto me; that ye may eat and drink at my table in my kingdom, and sit on thrones judging the twelve tribes of Israel."

And as they did eat, he said, "Verily I say unto you, that one of you shall betray me." And they were exceeding sorrowful, and began every one of them to say unto him, "Lord, is it I?"

And he answered and said, "He that dippeth his hand with me in the dish, the same shall betray me. The Son of man goeth as it is written of him: but woe unto that man by whom the Son of man is betrayed! It had been good for that man if he had not been born."

Then Judas, which betrayed him, answered and said, "Master, is it I?"

He said unto him, "Thou hast said."

And as they were eating, Jesus took bread, and blessed

it, and brake it, and gave it to the disciples, and said, "Take, eat; this is my body."

And he took the cup, and gave thanks, and gave it to them, saying, "Drink ye all of it; for this is my blood of the new testament, which is shed for many for the remission of sins. But I say unto you, I will not drink henceforth of this fruit of the vine, until that day when I drink it new with you in my Father's kingdom." And when they had sung an hymn, they went out into the Mount of Olives. And Jesus saith unto them, "All ye shall be offended because of me this night: for it is written, 'I will smite the shepherd, and the sheep shall be scattered.' But after that I am risen, I will go before you into Galilee."

But Peter said unto him, "Although all shall be offended, yet will not I."

And Jesus saith unto him, "Verily I say unto thee, that this day, even in this night, before the cock crow twice, thou shalt deny me thrice."

But he spake the more vehemently, "If I should die with thee, I will not deny thee in any wise." Likewise also said they all.	— Luke 22:7–30; Matthew 26:21–30; Mark 14:27–31.

### FRIDAY

'Tis midnight; and on Olive's brow
The star is dimmed that lately shone:
'Tis midnight; in the garden, now,
The suffering Saviour prays alone.'
—*William B. Tappan.*

### THE AGONY IN THE GARDEN

Then cometh Jesus with them unto a place called Gethsemane, and saith unto the disciples, "Sit ye here, while I go and pray yonder." And he took with him Peter and the two sons of Zebedee, and began to be sorrowful and very heavy.

# The Arrest of Jesus

By Fra Angelico da Fiesole (1387-1455)
In the Museum of the Monastery of San Marco, Florence
Photograph by Alinari Brothers, Florence, Italy

THIS picture depicts the arrest of Jesus in the Garden of Gethsemane the Biblical account of which begins on page 211.

The scene shows the moment when Christ is seized. The Roman soldiers in medieval armor are about to bind him. The apostle Peter is cutting off the servant's ear. A high priest in his long robe directs the movements of the soldiers behind whom Judas stands holding his money bag. Judas' face shows that he is just beginning to realize what they intend to do with his Master. Christ is resigned, already forgiving these men who "know not what they do."

Here is another of the thirty-five little pictures representing the Life of Christ which were painted on the doors of a silver cupboard in the Church of the Annunciation in Florence. In this series of pictures the artist monk, Fra Angelico, created one of his most beautiful representations of compassionate Christianity as taught a century earlier by the preaching monk, St. Francis of Assisi. In this painting the lovely, hilly background receding into the distance is one of Fra Angelico's many studies of nature which marked the beginning of landscape painting in Italian art.

Let us compare this picture with the one on page 186 by the modern French artist, Ernest Hebert. We notice immediately that Fra Angelico has made no mention of the fact that the scene took place at night. This is because in Fra Angelico's day painters had not yet discovered how to create such lighting effects. In comparing these two pictures we must be careful not to judge the older picture unfavorably just because it seems less skillfully drawn than the modern picture. Each is a vivid and sincere representation of the arrest of Jesus and each has its own special merit.

ECCE DATA SVNT SVPER TE VINCVLA ET LIGABVNT TE IN EIS. EÇECHIEL. III. C

AT ILLI TENĒTES YHM DVXERVT EV LIGATV AD CHAIPHAN PNCIPĒ IVDEOR̄ M XXVII C

Then saith he unto them, "My soul is exceeding sorrowful, even unto death: tarry ye here, and watch with me."

And he went a little farther, and fell on his face, and prayed, saying, "O my Father, if it be possible, let this cup pass from me: nevertheless not as I will, but as thou wilt."

And he cometh unto the disciples, and findeth them asleep, and saith unto Peter, "What, could ye not watch with me one hour? Watch and pray, that ye enter not into temptation: the spirit indeed is willing, but the flesh is weak."

He went away again the second time, and prayed, saying, "O my Father, if this cup may not pass away from me, except I drink it, thy will be done."

And he came and found them asleep again: for their eyes were heavy. And he left them, and went away again, and prayed the third time, saying the same words. Then cometh he to his disciples, and saith unto them, "Sleep on now, and take your rest: behold, the hour is at hand, and the Son of man is betrayed into the hands of sinners. Rise, let us be going: behold, he is at hand that doth betray me."

### THE BETRAYAL

And while he yet spake, lo, Judas, one of the twelve, came, and with him a great multitude with swords and staves, from the chief priests and elders of the people. Now he that betrayed him gave them a sign, saying, "Whomsoever I shall kiss, that same is he: hold him fast."

And forthwith he came to Jesus, and said, "Hail, master"; and kissed him. And Jesus said unto him, "Friend, wherefore art thou come?"

Then came they, and laid hands on Jesus, and took him. And, behold, one of them which were with Jesus stretched out his hand, and drew his sword, and struck a servant of the high priest's, and smote off his ear.

Then said Jesus unto him, "Put up again thy sword into his place: for all they that take the sword shall perish with the sword. Thinkest thou that I cannot now pray to my Father, and he shall presently give me more than twelve legions of angels? But how then shall the scriptures be fulfilled, that thus it must be?"

In that same hour said Jesus to the multitudes, "Are ye come out as against a thief with swords and staves for to take me? I sat daily with you teaching in the temple, and ye laid no hold on me." But all this was done, that the scriptures of the prophets might be fulfilled. Then all the disciples forsook him, and fled.        — Matthew 26:36-56.

### THE TRIAL BEFORE THE COUNCIL

And there followed him a certain young man, having a linen cloth cast about his naked body; and the young men laid hold on him: and he left the linen cloth, and fled from them naked.

And they led Jesus away to the high priest: and with him were assembled all the chief priests and the elders and the scribes. And Peter followed him afar off, even into the palace of the high priest: and he sat with the servants, and warmed himself at the fire. And the chief priests and all the council sought for witness against Jesus to put him to death; and found none. For many bare false witness against him, but their witness agreed not together. And there arose certain, and bare false witness against him, saying, "We heard him say, 'I will destroy this temple that is made with hands, and within three days I will build another made without hands.'" But neither so did their witness agree together. And the high priest stood up in the midst, and asked Jesus, saying, "Answerest thou nothing? What is it which these witness against thee?"

# The Soldiers Mocking Jesus

By Fra Angelico da Fiesole (1387-1455)
In the Museum of the Monastery of San Marco, Florence
Photograph by Alinari Brothers, Florence, Italy

THIS picture shows the mocking of Jesus after He
has been condemned to die because of his teaching.
You will find the Bible versions on pages 215 and 220.

"Then the soldiers of the governor took Jesus into
the common hall . . . And they stripped him, and put
on him a scarlet robe. And when they had platted a
crown of thorns, they put it on his head, and a reed in
his right hand: and they bowed the knee before him,
saying, 'Hail, King of the Jews!' And they spit upon
him, and took the reed, and smote him on the head."
Here the Roman soldiers and other attendants are
dressed in the garments of the painter's own time. The
Saviour sits upon a throne with blindfolded eyes holding the improvised scepter and orb of royal authority
given him by his tormentors. One of the attendants
lifts his cap in mock reverence and others are striking
and insulting him in various ways. Through the doorway we see Peter talking with the maid to whom he
denied knowing Jesus.

This is another of the expressive little panel pictures
which were painted originally on the doors of a silver
cabinet belonging to a church in Florence. The pictures
were long since removed from this cabinet and may
now be seen in the Museum connected with the Monastery of San Marco in Florence. Fra Angelico was commissioned to do this work by Cosimo de' Medici, a
wealthy and powerful merchant of Florence renowned
for his generous patronage of arts and letters as well as
for his energetic manner of ruling Florentine politics.
Thus, by building chapels and beautifying churches,
did the man of the Renaissance seek renown. Other
pictures from this series by Fra Angelico are on pages
300, 318, 340, 344 and 352.

But he held his peace, and answered nothing. Again the high priest asked him, and said unto him, "Art thou the Christ, the Son of the Blessed?"

And Jesus said, "I am: and ye shall see the Son of man sitting on the right hand of power, and coming in the clouds of heaven."

Then the high priest rent his clothes, and saith, "What need we any further witnesses? Ye have heard the blasphemy. What think ye?" And they all condemned him to be guilty of death.

And some began to spit on him, and to cover his face, and to buffet him, and to say unto him, "Prophesy": and the servants did strike him with the palms of their hands.

ENTRANCE TO THE CHURCH OF THE HOLY SEPULCHER
*Photograph by W. A. Pottenger expressly for The Book of Life*

PETER'S DENIAL

And as Peter was beneath in the palace, there cometh one of the maids of the high priest: and when she saw Peter warming himself, she looked upon him, and said, "And thou also wast with Jesus of Nazareth."

But he denied, saying, "I know not, neither understand I what thou sayest." And he went out into the porch; and the cock crew. And a maid saw him again, and began to say to them that stood by, "This is one of them." And he denied it again. And a little after, they that stood by said again to Peter, "Surely thou art one of them: for thou art a Galilæan, and thy speech agreeth thereto."

But he began to curse and to swear, saying, "I know not this man of whom ye speak."

And the second time the cock crew. And Peter called to mind the word that Jesus said unto him, "Before the cock crow twice, thou shalt deny me thrice." And when he thought thereon, he wept. — Mark 14:51-72.

### THE REMORSE OF JUDAS

Then Judas, which had betrayed him, when he saw that he was condemned, repented himself, and brought again the thirty pieces of silver to the chief priests and elders, saying, "I have sinned in that I have betrayed the innocent blood."

And they said, "What is that to us? See thou to that."

And he cast down the pieces of silver in the temple, and departed, and went and hanged himself. And the chief priests took the silver pieces, and said, "It is not lawful for to put them into the treasury, because it is the price of blood." And they took counsel, and bought with them the potter's field, to bury strangers in. Wherefore that field was called the field of blood, unto this day.

Then was fulfilled that which was spoken by Jeremy the prophet, saying, "And they took the thirty pieces of silver, the price of him that was valued, whom they of the children of Israel did value; and gave them for the potter's field, as the Lord appointed me." — Matthew 27:3-10.

### THE TRIAL BEFORE PILATE

And the whole multitude of them arose, and led him unto Pilate. And they began to accuse him, saying, "We found this fellow perverting the nation, and forbidding to give tribute to Cæsar, saying that he himself is Christ a King."

# Christ Before Pilate

By Mihály Munkácsy (1844-1900)
In the Rodman Wanamaker Collection, Philadelphia

THE scene is the judgment hall in Jerusalem with Pilate on the judgment seat. On Pilate's right are the chief priests, there to bring charges and listen to the trial. Before Pilate stands the Saviour with hands tied. Beyond are the rabble who have pressed into the hall to add noise and clamor to the evidence.

Caiaphas, the high priest, is presenting his charges against Jesus who stands composed in the midst of this tumult. The very vehemence of Caiaphas' manner indicates the necessity of deceit to achieve his purpose of destroying Jesus. Pilate appears to be pondering his course of action. How can he satisfy his own conscience if he delivers this innocent man to his enemies? How can he meet the vindictive anger of the chief priests and the mob if he saves Jesus' life? The question of justice has been lost sight of in a maze of intrigue and mob passion. The decision which Pilate finally made you will find on page 220.

The artist, Mihály Munkácsy, whose real name was Michael Lieb, was born in 1846 in the Hungarian village of Munkács. His parents died when he was very young, and a poor uncle took care of him. Mihály was first apprenticed to a carpenter but at thirteen decided he wanted to be a painter. The rest of his youth was spent studying and painting in various European art centers, earning his living, as he went, by his art. In 1872 he settled in Paris where his works found great favor.

This picture, CHRIST BEFORE PILATE, was finished in 1881 and shown in many places in Europe before it was brought to America and exhibited in New York in 1886. There it was purchased by Mr. John Wanamaker and brought to Philadelphia where it now is.

And Pilate asked him, saying, "Art thou the King of the Jews?"

And he answered him and said, "Thou sayest it."

Then said Pilate to the chief priests and to the people, "I find no fault in this man."

And they were the more fierce, saying, "He stirreth up the people, teaching throughout all Jewry, beginning from Galilee to this place."

When Pilate heard of Galilee, he asked whether the man were a Galilæan. And as soon as he knew that he belonged unto Herod's jurisdiction, he sent him to Herod, who himself also was at Jerusalem at that time.

And when Herod saw Jesus, he was exceeding glad: for he was desirous to see him of a long season, because he had heard many things of him; and he hoped to have seen some miracle done by him. Then he questioned with him in many words; but he answered him nothing. And the chief priests and scribes stood and vehemently accused him. And Herod with his men of war set him at naught, and mocked him, and arrayed him in a gorgeous robe, and sent him again to Pilate. And the same day Pilate and Herod were made friends together: for before they were at enmity between themselves.

And Pilate, when he had called together the chief priests and the rulers and the people, said unto them, "Ye have brought this man unto me, as one that perverteth the people: and, behold, I, having examined him before you, have found no fault in this man touching those things whereof ye accuse him: no, nor yet Herod: for I sent you to him; and lo, nothing worthy of death is done unto him. I will therefore chastise him, and release him." For of necessity he must release one unto them at the feast. And they cried out all at once, saying, "Away with this man, and release unto us Barabbas." Who for a certain sedition made in the city, and for murder, was cast into prison.

Pilate therefore, willing to release Jesus, spake again to them. But they cried, saying, "Crucify him, crucify him."

And he said unto them the third time, "Why, what evil hath he done? I have found no cause of death in him: I will therefore chastise him, and let him go."

And they were instant with loud voices, requiring that he might be crucified. And the voices of them and of the chief priests prevailed. And Pilate gave sentence that it should be as they required. And he released unto them him that for sedition and murder was cast into prison, whom they had desired; but he delivered Jesus to their will.

Then the soldiers of the governor took Jesus into the common hall, and gathered unto him the whole band of soldiers. And they stripped him, and put on him a scarlet robe. And when they had platted a crown of thorns, they put it upon his head, and a reed in his right hand: and they bowed the knee before him, and mocked him, saying, "Hail, King of the Jews!" And they spit upon him, and took the reed, and smote him on the head.

—Luke 23:1-25; Matthew 27:27-30.

### THE CRUCIFIXION

And they compel one Simon, a Cyrenian, who passed by, coming out of the country, the father of Alexander and Rufus, to bear his cross. And they bring him unto the place Golgotha, which is, being interpreted, The place of a skull. And they gave him to drink wine mingled with myrrh: but he received *it* not. And when they had crucified him, they parted his garments, casting lots upon them, what every man should take. And it was the third hour, and they crucified him.         —Mark 15:21-25.

# The Entombment of Jesus

By Titian, Tiziano Vecellio (1477-1576)
In the Louvre, Paris, France

THIS moving representation of the burial of Jesus helps us to visualize the biblical accounts by Mark and John found on pages 227 and 353, respectively.

We have here a vision of profound human sympathy in action. On the right, tenderly supporting the weight of the Saviour's body, is Joseph of Arimathaea who had gone "boldly unto Pilate" to ask for Jesus' body and had provided the linen and sepulchre. At the left, Nicodemus, who had brought spices for the burial, pauses in his action of wrapping the body to gaze reverently upon the Master's face. Between them, John compassionately holds up a wounded hand for Mary, mute and stark with grief, to see, while Mary Magdalene protectingly comforts her. All share the desolating anguish of this hour, epitomized by the crown of thorns resting against the base of the tomb.

How powerfully the artist has conveyed the reserve, nobility and pathos of this moment and these actions! The central group looms against the sky with the grandeur of a great dome. All lines converge upon the central figure of Christ and are held there by the curved, oblique and vertical lines of draperies and forms, by the horizontal lines of sepulchre and sky, and by the over-all arrangement of light and dark masses. Magnificent are the contrasts between the sublime nude form and the rich stuffs in which the attendants are clothed, between the immobility of the dead Christ and the compassionate, vigorous actions of those ministering unto him.

Titian, the celebrated Venetian painter, finished this noble painting about 1525 when he was midway in his remarkably long, creative life. Another of Titian's masterpieces is on page 190.

Then said Jesus, "Father, forgive them; for they know not what they do."

And the people stood beholding. And the rulers also with them derided *him*, saying, "He saved others; let him save himself, if he be Christ, the chosen of God."

And the soldiers also mocked him, coming to him, and offering him vinegar, and saying, "If thou be the king of the Jews, save thyself." And a superscription also was written over him in letters of Greek, and Latin and Hebrew. THIS IS THE KING OF THE JEWS.

And with him they crucify two thieves; the one on his right hand, and the other on his left. And the Scripture was fulfilled, which saith, "And he was numbered with the transgressors."

And one of the malefactors which were hanged railed on him, saying, "If thou be Christ, save thyself and us."

But the other answering rebuked him, saying, "Dost not thou fear God, seeing thou art in the same condemnation? And we indeed justly; for we receive the due reward of our deeds: but this man hath done nothing amiss."

And he said unto Jesus, "Lord, remember me when thou comest into thy kingdom."

And Jesus said unto him, "Verily I say unto thee, To-day shalt thou be with me in paradise."

And it was about the sixth hour, and there was a darkness over all the earth until the ninth hour. And the sun was darkened, and the veil of the temple was rent in the midst.

And at the ninth hour Jesus cried with a loud voice, saying, "Eloi, Eloi, lama sabachthani?" which is, being interpreted, "My God, my God, why hast thou forsaken me?"

And when Jesus had cried with a loud voice, he said, "Father, into thy hands I commend my spirit": and having said thus, he gave up the ghost.

And when the centurion, which stood over against him, saw that he so cried out, and gave up the ghost, he said, "Truly this man was the Son of God."

And all the people that came together to that sight, beholding the things which were done, smote their breasts, and returned. And all his acquaintance, and the women that followed him from Galilee, stood afar off, beholding these things.

—Luke 23:34–38; Mark 15:27, 28; Luke 23:39–45; Mark 15:34; Luke 23:46; Mark 15:39; Luke 23:48, 49.

## IN THE CROSS OF CHRIST I GLORY

In the cross of Christ I glory;
  Towering o'er the wrecks of time,
All the light of sacred story
  Gathers round its head sublime.

When the woes of life o'ertake me,
  Hopes deceive, and fears annoy,
Never shall the cross forsake me;
  Lo! it glows with peace and joy.

When the sun of bliss is beaming
  Light and love upon my way,
From the cross the radiance streaming
  Adds new lustre to the day.

Bane and blessing, pain and pleasure,
  By the cross are sanctified;
Peace is there, that knows no measure,
  Joys that through all time abide.

In the cross of Christ I glory;
  Towering o'er the wrecks of time,
All the light of sacred story
  Gathers round its head sublime.—*John Bowring.*

# Pietà

**By Andrea** del Sarto (1486-1531)
**In the** Pitti Gallery, Florence, Italy
**Photograph** by Alinari Brothers, Florence

THIS picture shows John "the beloved disciple" supporting Jesus' body while Mary sits contemplating sorrowfully the pierced hand of her Son. At the Saviour's feet kneels grief-worn Mary Magdalene, clasping her hands in despair. Behind her is St. Catherine, her face eloquently compassionate. On the left Peter stands mourning, with the look of a man who has grown old overnight. To the right stands Paul, his arm outstretched as if to ward off the grievous sight which he beholds. The scene is laid out-of-doors in a rocky place, suggesting the sepulchre.

In Italian, the word "pietà" means "pity," and in Italian art, a work so named represents the dead Christ with Mary the mother often alone, sorrowing over his body. Here, for artistic and devotional purposes, del Sarto has introduced several personages, one of whom was not living in Jesus' lifetime.

This fine, dramatic picture was painted in 1523-4 for the Convent of St. Peter in Luco, whither del Sarto had fled with his family to escape that dreaded illness, the plague, to which a few years later he fell a victim.

Andrea's fellow-townspeople called him "The Faultless Painter." Certainly his skill in drawing the human figure and draperies, his understanding of balanced composition, and his mastery of subdued, rich coloring complete a perfection of work rarely attained. But the great gifts of this admirable painter were in some subtle manner limited. While the secret of visible beauty was truly his, Andrea lacked, or lost, the vision of spiritual beauty which mark the supreme masters.

Nevertheless, we know that del Sarto's placid harmonies are among the treasures of our heritage.

### THE BURIAL OF JESUS

And now when the even was come, because it was the preparation, that is, the day before the Sabbath, Joseph of Arimathæa, an honourable counsellor, which also waited for the kingdom of God, came, and went in boldly unto Pilate, and craved the body of Jesus. And Pilate marveled if he were already dead: and calling unto him the centurion, he asked him whether he had been any while dead. And when he knew it of the centurion, he gave the body to Joseph. And he bought fine linen, and took him down, and wrapped him in the linen, and laid him in a sepulcher which was hewn out of a rock, and rolled a stone unto the door of the sepulcher. And Mary Magdalene and Mary the mother of Joses beheld where he was laid.

— Mark 15:42–47.

## Saturday

### THE ROMAN SOLDIERS WATCH AT THE SEPULCHER

Now the next day, that followed the day of the preparation, the chief priests and Pharisees came together unto Pilate, saying, "Sir, we remember that that deceiver said, while he was yet alive, 'After three days I will rise again.' Command therefore that the sepulcher be made sure until the third day, lest his disciples come by night, and steal him away, and say unto the people, 'He is risen from the dead': so the last error shall be worse than the first."

Pilate said unto them, "Ye have a watch: go your way, make it as sure as ye can." So they went, and made the sepulcher sure, sealing the stone, and setting a watch.

— Matthew 27:62–66.

## A GUARD OF THE SEPULCHER

I was a Roman soldier in my prime;
Now age is on me and the yoke of time.
I saw your Risen Christ, for I am he
Who reached the hyssop to Him on the tree;
And I am one of two who watched beside
The Sepulcher of Him we crucified.

All that last night I watched with sleepless eyes;
Great stars arose and crept across the skies.
The world was all too still for mortal rest,
For pitiless thoughts were busy in the breast.
That night was long, so long, it seemed at last
I had grown old and a long life had passed.
Far off, the hills of Moab, touched with light,
Were swimming in the hollow of the night.
I saw Jerusalem all wrapped in a cloud,
Stretched like a dead thing folded in a shroud.

Once in the pauses of our whispered talk
I heard a something on the garden walk.
Perhaps it was a crisp leaf lightly stirred,
Perhaps the dream-note of a waking bird.
Then suddenly an angel burning white
Came down with earthquake in the breaking light,
And rolled the great stone from the Sepulcher,
Mixing in the morning with a scent of myrrh.
And lo, the Dead had risen with the day:
The man of Mystery had gone his way!

Years have I wandered, carrying my shame;
Now let the tooth of time eat out my name.
For we, who all the wonder might have told,
Kept silence, for our mouths were stopt with gold.

*—Edwin Markham.*

# Appearance of the Risen Christ to Mary Magdalene

By Giotto di Bondone (1266-1336)
In the Chapel of the Arena at Padua, Italy
Photograph by Alinari Brothers, Florence

FOR the Bible story of this Resurrection scene turn to page 358 in this Volume.
The tomb in the picture is a great stone sarcophagus with angels seated upon it. The Roman guards lie asleep. Christ carries a pennant, a symbol of the resurrection, which bears the Latin words: "Victor Mortis," meaning: "Victor over Death." The face of Mary Magdalene is very fine. What is the Master saying to her?

This picture is one of a series of frescoes depicting the life of the Virgin and the life of Christ which adorns the interior walls of a chapel at Padua. The chapel was built in honor of the Virgin of the Annunciation by a rich citizen of the town, Enrico Scrovegni, perhaps in order to atone for the sins of his father, a notorious usurer. The building is near the ruins of a Roman amphitheatre and is therefore generally called the Chapel of the Arena.

These Paduan paintings have been called "the noblest cycle of pictures known to Christian art." Their creator, Giotto, was the first Florentine painter of genius. His talent led him away from the traditional Byzantine art of his age to the discovery of a realistic way of expressing human figures and emotions with brush and color. Thus Italian painting and hence modern painting are said truly to begin with Giotto.

This Giotto, a shepherd's son, was born at Colle near Florence in 1266. During his lifetime, he traveled thruout Italy painting on commission for lay and ecclesiastical patrons of art. He was from the first a kind of popular hero celebrated and quoted by poets and chroniclers not only for his amazing achievement in art but also for his wit in practical jest and repartee. One of his famous jokes is told in Volume VIII on page 125.

# The Story of the Master

From the Gospels of Matthew, Mark and Luke

## The Glorious Resurrection

### THE JOYOUS RESURRECTION MORNING

AND when the sabbath was past, Mary Magdalene, and Mary the mother of James, and Salome, had bought sweet spices, that they might come and anoint him. And very early in the morning the first day of the week, they came unto the sepulcher at the rising of the sun. And they said among themselves, "Who shall roll us away the stone from the door of the sepulcher?"

And they entered in, and found not the body of the Lord Jesus. And it came to pass, as they were much perplexed thereabout, behold, two men stood by them in shining garments: and as they were afraid, and bowed down their faces to the earth, they said unto them, "Why seek ye the living among the dead? He is not here, but is risen: remember how he spake unto you when he was yet in Galilee, saying, 'The Son of man must be delivered into the hands of sinful men, and be crucified, and the third day rise again.'"

And they remembered his words, and returned from the sepulcher, and told all these things unto the eleven, and to all the rest. It was Mary Magdalene, and Joanna, and Mary the mother of James, and other women that were with them, which told these things unto the apostles. And their words seemed to them as idle tales, and they believed them not. Then arose Peter, and ran unto the

231

sepulcher; and stooping down, he beheld the linen clothes laid by themselves, and departed, wondering in himself at that which was come to pass.   — Mark 16:1-3; Luke 24:3-12.

## The Report of the Guard at the Sepulcher

Now when they were going, behold, some of the watch came into the city, and showed unto the chief priests all the things that were done. And when they were assembled with the elders, and had taken counsel, they gave large money unto the soldiers, saying, "Say ye, 'His disciples came by night, and stole him away while we slept.' And if this come to the governor's ears, we will persuade him, and secure you." So they took the money, and did as they were taught: and this saying is commonly reported among the Jews until this day.   — Matthew 28:11-15.

## The Walk to Emmaus

And, behold, two of them went that same day to a village called Emmaus, which was from Jerusalem about threescore furlongs. And they talked together of all these things which had happened. And it came to pass, that, while they communed together and reasoned, Jesus himself drew near, and went with them. But their eyes were holden that they should not know him. And he said unto them, "What manner of communications are these that ye have one to another, as ye walk, and are sad?"

And the one of them, whose name was Cleopas, answering said unto him, "Art thou only a stranger in Jerusalem, and hast not known the things which are come to pass there in these days?"

And he said unto them, "What things?"

And they said unto him, "Concerning Jesus of Nazareth, which was a prophet mighty in deed and word before God and all the people: and how the chief priests and our

# On the Way to Emmaus

By Bernhard Plockhorst (1825-1907)
In the Louvre Museum, Paris, France

ACCOUNTS of various appearances of Jesus after his burial are recorded in the Gospels and bear witness to the intense desire of the early Christians to make clear to all, the certainty that Jesus had risen from the dead and still lived. The beautiful incident of Christ's joining two of his followers on the way to Emmaus (see map, page 147) and later revealing himself to them at supper is recorded in detail only by Luke. The Bible text begins on page 232.

This painting shows Jesus walking with Cleopas and his friend. The two have been telling the unknown Companion about their Messiah's death, which they fear means the end of his kingdom, and about their doubts concerning the women's testimony of having seen the risen Christ. From the Saviour's gesture, we gather that this is the moment when he asks: "Ought not Christ to have suffered these things, and to enter into his glory?"

The question penetrates to the very heart of their human uncertainties. And having asked it, the unknown Friend helps them find the answer by expounding the Scriptures to them. The younger man, with bent head, ponders the truths which this wise Stranger is uttering. The other, with arm extended as if he were about to ask a question, is silenced by some vague inner perception. Their hearts are burning within them, but they will not know why until Jesus breaks bread with them that evening, as depicted in Rembrandt's famous painting on page 238.

Plockhorst places this scene in Palestine. Contrast his conception with those of Rembrandt and of Lhermitte, Volume I, page 370, both of whom used settings and people of their own day, thus emphasizing the universality of the lesson in faith which Jesus taught on that long-ago evening in Emmaus.

rulers delivered him to be condemned to death, and have crucified him. But we trusted that it had been he which should have redeemed Israel: and beside all this, to-day is the third day since these things were done. Yea, and certain women also of our company made us astonished, which were early at the sepulcher; and when they found not his body, they came, saying, that they had also seen a vision of angels, which said that he was alive. And certain of them which were with us went to the sepulcher, and found it even so as the women had said: but him they saw not."

Then he said unto them, "O fools, and slow of heart to believe all that the prophets have spoken: ought not Christ to have suffered these things, and to enter into his glory?" And beginning at Moses and all the prophets, he expounded unto them in all the scriptures the things concerning himself.

And they drew nigh unto the village, whither they went: and he made as though he would have gone further. But they constrained him, saying, "Abide with us: for it is toward evening, and the day is far spent." And he went in to tarry with them.

And it came to pass, as he sat at meat with them, he took bread, and blessed it, and brake, and gave to them. And their eyes were opened, and they knew him; and he vanished out of their sight. And they said one to another, "Did not our heart burn within us, while he talked with us by the way, and while he opened to us the scriptures?"

And they rose up the same hour, and returned to Jerusalem, and found the eleven gathered together, and them that were with them, saying, "The Lord is risen indeed, and hath appeared to Simon." And they told what things were done in the way, and how he was known of them in breaking of bread.                                   — Luke 24:13-35.

## The Appearance of Jesus to the Disciples

And as they thus spake, Jesus himself stood in the midst of them, and saith unto them, "Peace be unto you." But they were terrified and affrighted, and supposed that they had seen a spirit.

And he said unto them, "Why are ye troubled? And why do thoughts arise in your hearts? Behold my hands and my feet, that it is I myself: handle me, and see; for a spirit hath not flesh and bones, as ye see me have." And when he had thus spoken, he showed them his hands and his feet.

And while they yet believed not for joy, and wondered, he said unto them, "Have ye here any meat?" And they gave him a piece of a broiled fish, and of an honeycomb. And he took it, and did eat before them.  — Luke 24:36–43.

## The Great Commission

Then the eleven disciples went away into Galilee, into a mountain where Jesus had appointed them. And when they saw him, they worshipped him: but some doubted. And Jesus came and spake unto them, saying, "All power is given unto me in heaven and in earth. Go ye therefore, and teach all nations, baptizing them in the name of the Father, and of the Son, and of the Holy Ghost: teaching them to observe all things whatsoever I have commanded you: and, lo, I am with you alway, even unto the end of the world. Amen."

And he said unto them, "These are the words which I spake unto you, while I was yet with you, that all things must be fulfilled, which were written in the law of Moses, and in the prophets, and in the psalms, concerning me." Then opened he their understanding, that they might understand the scriptures, and said unto them, "Thus it is written, and thus it behoved Christ to suffer, and to rise

# The Supper at Emmaus

By Rembrandt van Rijn (1607-1669)
In the Louvre Museum, Paris, France

THE Bible story which inspired this famous painting begins on page 232.

In a shadowed room Christ is seated at a table, with clasped hands, uplifted eyes and worn face, perfectly quiet and serene. The disciple at the left sits with hands folded in adoration as he recognizes the Guest. The one at the right has made a quick movement as recognition dawns, but remains transfixed as if still doubting. The stolid serving boy hesitates, puzzled at the scene.

The room is dim except for the brilliant light that falls on the tablecloth and the faces and hands of the figures. About the head of Christ is a deep glow subtly blending into the shadows of the large unadorned arch behind him. The light carries the eye directly and irresistibly to the center of interest—the figure of Christ —and plays into the other figures, tying them into a spiritual unity with the central one; the contour lines are blurred and finally fade into the shadows.

This magnificent contrasting of light and shade, or chiaroscuro, through which the forms and their meaning are as forcibly revealed as if they were sharply defined in clear light, is characteristic of Rembrandt's work, see Volume I, page 332.

While Rembrandt contributed tremendously to the art of portraiture and even more to the development of landscape, it is in religious composition that the complete Rembrandt is most fully revealed. The artist must have learned the Bible very thoroughly from his pious mother, for all through his life biblical subjects remained his favorites. Through his supreme intellectual and spiritual endowments, Rembrandt gave to his works a tenderness and a poignancy and a religious power which make them live as great art and great truth.

from the dead the third day: and that repentance and remission of sins should be preached in his name among all nations, beginning at Jerusalem. And ye are witnesses of these things. And, behold, I send the promise of my Father upon you: but tarry ye in the city of Jerusalem, until ye be endued with power from on high."

—Matthew 28:16–20; Luke 24:44-49.

## THE ASCENSION

And he led them out as far as to Bethany, and he lifted up his hands, and blessed them. And it came to pass, while he blessed them, he was parted from them, and carried up into heaven. And they worshiped him, and returned to Jerusalem with great joy: and were continually in the temple, praising and blessing God. Amen.

— Luke 24:50-53.

SCENE OF CHRIST'S ASCENSION

*Photograph by the Rev. Frederick J. Moore*

View on eastern slope of Mount of Olives, looking back on Bethany. Scene of Christ's ascension.

Read Luke 24:50-53 on this page.

## JESUS SHALL REIGN

Jesus shall reign where'er the sun
Does his successive journeys run;
His kingdom stretch from shore to shore,
Till moons shall wax and wane no more.

To Him shall endless prayer be made,
And endless praises crown His head;
His name, like sweet perfume, shall rise
With every morning sacrifice

People and realms of every tongue
Dwell on His love, with sweetest song;
And infant voices shall proclaim
Their early blessings on His name.

Blessings abound where'er He reigns;
The prisoner leaps to loose his chains;
The weary find eternal rest,
And all the sons of want are blest.

Let every creature rise and bring
Peculiar honors to our King;
Angels descend with songs again,
And earth repeat the loud Amen!

　　　　　　　　　— *Isaac Watts.*

# The Infant John the Baptist

By Murillo, Bartolomé Estéban (1617-1682)
In the Prado Gallery, Madrid, Spain

JOHN is shown here as much younger than in Murillo's other picture of him, at the beginning of his ministry. The same child is model for both paintings but here his child-like beauty is as yet untouched by the seriousness of the first.

The artist's boyhood, to the time when he was a painter of the "Feria," of Seville, is told with the earlier picture of John the Baptist, in Volume I, page 286. The story continues from there:

The turning-point in his life came in 1642. Pedro de Moya, a fellow artist in Castillo's school, returned from England, where he had studied with Van Dyck. So impressed was Murillo by the improvement in de Moya's style, and his tales of foreign art that Murillo himself felt spurred on to visit the wonders of Rome and Flanders.

To get money for the journey was the problem. Buying a huge piece of canvas, and cutting it up into various shapes, he quickly painted bright-colored pictures, to catch the popular fancy. On selling these, Murillo then set out on foot across the mountains, in search of new worlds of art.

After 250 miles he arrived at Madrid, Spain's capital, completely unknown and with his funds low. Courageously, he sought out his fellow-townsman, Velasquez, then at the height of fortune as court painter, for Philip IV. Murillo told his story and asked for letters to artists in Rome.

Then, at last, good fortune smiled on the youth, for Velasquez received him kindly. So pleased was he with Murillo, and his motives for undertaking such a journey, that he lodged him in his own house, and secured admission for him to the royal art galleries of Madrid.

More of Murillo's life is on page 254.

# John the Baptist Preaching in the Wilderness

By Raphael Sanzio (1483-1520)
In the Uffizi Gallery, Florence, Italy
Color Photograph by Alinari Brothers, Florence

HERE we see John the Baptist preaching in the wilderness. He is represented as a youth of about sixteen, seated in a rocky, mountainous place, a leopard skin thrown about him. One hand is pointing heavenward and the other holding a scroll on which we can see the word "Dei". This is the end of the phrase "Ecce Agnus Dei", "Behold the Lamb of God", which is usually introduced in pictures of John and refers to his mission as forerunner to Jesus. In the upper left corner is the reed cross, another of the symbols of the Baptist. The dark, ominous surroundings form a striking contrast to the light beauty of person and countenance of the inspired youth.

The conception of this picture is Raphael's but critics usually ascribe the actual painting to Raphael's pupil, Giulio Romano (c. 1492-1546), because of the murky shadows. The picture was executed in Rome some time between 1518 and 1520. Since 1515 Raphael had been superintending several great tasks at once. He had been appointed Bramante's successor as architect of the new St. Peter's and superintendent of all archeological excavations at Rome. Besides these heavy administrative charges, Raphael designed decorations for private palaces and chapels, altar-pieces, fifty-two Bible stories for the Vatican Loggia, and painted with his own hand several great altar-pieces, portraits, and part of the TRANSFIGURATION, (Volume VIII, frontispiece). After 1517 he had to rely upon assistants, as was the habit of the day, for the final painting of many of his designs. Even so, the amount of manual labor carried out by Raphael himself was phenomenal. The work he did with the help of assistants remains one of the largest undertakings known to painting.

Other works by Raphael are on pages 246, 360 and 428, and in Volumes I, VII and VIII.

# The
# Story of the Master
### from
# The Gospel of John

HE Gospel of John is an interpretation of the life of Jesus by the "beloved disciple." It is the gospel of love. It is full of poetic feeling. The life of Jesus was many sided. No one account could do justice to it. The other gospels are practical. Their writers tell the straightforward story of the life of Jesus. John sees the beauty and the glory of it, the divine nature shining through the human form. Luke reports the matchless stories of the Good Samaritan and the Prodigal Son. John alone tells us of the visit of Nicodemus, the talk with the woman of Samaria, and those wonderful words of the Master at the Last Supper: "Let not your heart be troubled. Ye believe in God; believe also in me. In my Father's house are many mansions." Matthew tells us of the birth of Jesus in the manger of Bethlehem. John tells of the "Word made flesh, the light of the world." For devotional reading, for comfort and spiritual help, for teaching the way of salvation, the Gospel of John is unsurpassed.

CANA OF GALILEE

*Photograph by Frances Jenkins Olcott*

Sweetly set among the hills, is the traditional Cana where we are shown a Christian Church in which marriages are performed in memory of that marriage at Cana of Galilee.

From Nazareth to Capernaum we drive along the highway, over Cana's hills, till standing on the brink of the Jordan gorge our heart thrills as we look down, down, down on the shores of the Sea of Galilee where the Saviour lived and taught. Read Matthew 4:13, page 63.

WATER POTS OF STONE

*Photograph by Frances Jenkins Olcott*

This is the very spring, so claimed, where the six water pots of stone were filled, whose water the Saviour made into wine at the marriage of Cana of Galilee.

And what wonderful thing did the Saviour do to the boy of Capernaum, at Cana of Galilee? Answer: John 4:46-54, page 269; John 2:1-11, page 255.

# The Sistine Madonna

By Raphael Sanzio (1483-1520)
In the Royal Picture Gallery, Dresden, Germany
Photograph by Hanfstaengl, Munich

THE SISTINE MADONNA is perhaps the most memorable of Raphael's Madonnas. From a quiet silvery cloudland emerges the mother of our Lord carrying the Infant in her arms. Her majestic beauty and noble mien proclaim her a vision from heaven. Yet she is surpassed by the Holy Child who looks out into the world with solemn, searching eyes and hair dishevelled, like that of a prophet. Below, Pope Sixtus, from whom the picture takes its name, gazes upward in rapt devotion, and St. Barbara, looking down at the exquisite child angels, adds her reverent presence. The effect of the whole is ineffably grand and gentle. With all the resources of the Renaissance, Raphael has expressed an emotion as intense and reverent as that of Fra Angelico.

This picture, the only one painted on canvas by Raphael, was executed in Rome about 1516. It was the last Madonna painted by him and the last work entirely by his own hand.

Raphael's father, Giovanni Santi, was court painter and poet to the cultivated Dukes of Urbino, Federigo Montefeltro and his son and successor, Guidobaldo. Raphael, the only one of three children to survive infancy, was born in 1483. Orphaned at eleven, he was brought up by an uncle, Simone Ciarla, whom Raphael called, "Dearest, in place of a father." Young Raphael studied four years with the eminent Pietro Perugino at Perugia and mastered the Umbrian sweetness of style and color. He went next to the great art center of Florence where he assimilated Florentine realism and composition. At twenty-five he settled in Rome and there was deeply influenced by classical art. He soon won wide renown as an artist and was universally loved. He died in 1520 mourned by all Rome.

Other of Raphael's pictures are on pages 243, 360 and 428.

# The Story of the Master

## From the Gospel of John

## In the Beginning

IN the beginning was the Word, and the Word was with God, and the Word was God. The same was in the beginning with God. All things were made by him; and without him was not any thing made that was made. In him was life; and the life was the light of men. And the light shineth in darkness; and the darkness comprehended it not.

There was a man sent from God, whose name was John. The same came for a witness, to bear witness of the Light, that all men through him might believe. He was not that Light, but was sent to bear witness of that Light.

That was the true Light, which lighteth every man that cometh into the world. He was in the world, and the world was made by him, and the world knew him not. He came unto his own, and his own received him not. But as many as received him, to them gave he power to become the sons of God, even to them that believe on his name: which were born, not of blood, nor of the will of the flesh, nor of the will of man, but of God. And the Word was made flesh, and dwelt among us, and we beheld his glory, the glory as of the only begotten of the Father, full of grace and truth.

John bare witness of him, and cried, saying, "This was he of whom I spake, 'He that cometh after me is preferred before me': for he was before me." And of his fulness have all we received, and grace for grace. For the law was given by Moses, but grace and truth came by Jesus Christ. No man hath seen God at any time; the only begotten Son, which is in the bosom of the Father, he hath declared him.

And this is the record of John, when the Jews sent priests and Levites from Jerusalem to ask him, "Who art thou?"

And he confessed, and denied not; but confessed, "I am not the Christ."

And they asked him, "What then? Art thou Elias?" And he saith, "I am not."

"Art thou that prophet?"

And he answered, "No."

Then said they unto him, "Who art thou? that we may give an answer to them that sent us. What sayest thou of thyself?"

He said, "I am the voice of one crying in the wilderness, 'Make straight the way of the LORD,' as said the prophet Esaias."

And they which were sent were of the Pharisees. And they asked him, and said unto him, "Why baptizest thou then, if thou be not that Christ, nor Elias, neither that prophet?"

John answered them, saying, "I baptize with water: but there standeth one among you, whom ye know not; he it is, who coming after me is preferred before me, whose shoe's latchet I am not worthy to unloose."

These things were done in Bethabara beyond Jordan, where John was baptizing. —John 1:1-28.

## THE BAPTISM OF JESUS

The next day John seeth Jesus coming unto him, and saith, "Behold the Lamb of God, which taketh away the sin of the world. This is he of whom I said, 'After me

# The First Miracle at Cana of Galilee

By Alessio Baldovinetti (1425-1499)
In the Museum of the Monastery of San Marco, Florence
Photograph by Alinari Brothers, Florence, Italy

THE first miracle that Jesus performed was at the wedding at Cana of Galilee. The Bible account is given on page 255.

In this painting we see Jesus, his Mother and four other persons seated at table. One servant is passing a plate while another, at Jesus' command, pours water into the empty vessels. The scene takes place in a simple room; the lower part of the wall is covered by material with a pattern of flowers.

We have here a picture by a young artist who collaborated with the famous Fra Angelico in the painting of a series of panels originally decorating a chapel cupboard in the Church of the Annunciation in Florence. Other pictures from this series are given on pages 178, 206, 210, 214, 300, 318, 340, 344 and 352. From these we can see the vast difference between the master and the young assistant in depth of spiritual feeling and in artistic skill. But Alessio must have been very promising for critics tell us that he painted three of the series of thirty-five pictures, which is more than any other collaborator was permitted to do. In those days it was the custom for a master, when commissioned to execute one or more paintings, to make the designs, paint certain principal figures and superintend the rest of the work which would be done by assistants.

Alessio's father was called Baldovinetto and came from an old patrician family of Florence. Records show that Alessio was inscribed in the company of painters in Florence in 1448, which was about the time that Fra Angelico started the cycle of pictures of which this is one. Besides being a painter, Baldovinetti also worked in mosaic and wrote a treatise on the subject. He died in August 1499 and is buried at Florence.

cometh a man which is preferred before me: for he was before me.' And I knew him not: but that he should be made manifest to Israel, therefore am I come baptizing with water."

And John bare record, saying, "I saw the Spirit descending from heaven like a dove, and it abode upon him. And I knew him not: but he that sent me to baptize with water, the same said unto me, 'Upon whom thou shalt see the Spirit descending, and remaining on him, the same is he which baptizeth with the Holy Ghost.'

"And I saw, and bare record that this is the Son of God."

—John 1:29-34.

Dear Lord and Father of mankind,
    Forgive our feverish ways!
Reclothe us in our rightful mind;
In purer lives Thy service find,
    In deeper reverence, praise.

In simple trust like theirs who heard,
    Beside the Syrian Sea,
The gracious calling of the Lord,
Let us, like them, without a word
    Rise up and follow Thee.

—*John G. Whittier.*

## The First Disciples

Again the next day after, John stood, and two of his disciples; and looking upon Jesus as he walked, he saith, "Behold the Lamb of God!" And the two disciples heard him speak, and they followed Jesus. Then Jesus turned, and saw them following, and saith unto them, "What seek ye?"

They said unto him, "Rabbi," (which is to say, being interpreted, "Master,") where dwellest thou?"

He saith unto them, "Come and see." They came and

saw where he dwelt, and abode with him that day: for it was about the tenth hour.

One of the two which heard John speak, and followed him, was Andrew, Simon Peter's brother. He first findeth his own brother Simon, and saith unto him, "We have found the Messias," which is, being interpreted, "the Christ." And he brought him to Jesus.

And when Jesus beheld him, he said, "Thou art Simon the son of Jona: thou shalt be called 'Cephas,' which is by interpretation, a stone."

The day following, Jesus would go forth into Galilee, and findeth Philip, and saith unto him, "Follow me."

Now Philip was of Bethsaida, the city of Andrew and Peter. Philip findeth Nathanael, and saith unto him, "We have found him, of whom Moses in the law, and the prophets, did write, Jesus of Nazareth, the son of Joseph."

And Nathanael said unto him, "Can there any good thing come out of Nazareth?"

Philip saith unto him, "Come and see."

Jesus saw Nathanael coming to him, and saith of him, "Behold an Israelite indeed, in whom is no guile!"

Nathanael saith unto him, "Whence knowest thou me?"

Jesus answered and said unto him, "Before that Philip called thee, when thou wast under the fig-tree, I saw thee."

Nathanael answered and saith unto him, "Rabbi, thou art the Son of God; thou art the King of Israel."

Jesus answered and said unto him, "Because I said unto thee, I saw thee under the fig-tree, believest thou? Thou shalt see greater things than these."

And he saith unto him, "Verily, verily, I say unto you, hereafter ye shall see heaven open, and the angels of God ascending and descending upon the Son of man."

# Holy Family

By Murillo, Bartolomé Estéban (1617-1682)
In the National Gallery, London

IN this picture the angel scene, with the bright opening in the heavens, gives lightness to the sombre background and to serious faces of the group of the Holy Family.

Joseph, the father, has an unusually strong face; his expression is rather sad, as if he had a presentiment of the trials in store for the Child. Mary, too, stretches her hands out toward Jesus, as if she felt He would soon be taken away from her.

The artist, Murillo, as we read on page 242, had been befriended by Velasquez, at Madrid, who got him admission to the splendid royal art galleries there.

Philip IV had been a weak and indifferent monarch, for Spain, except in his interest in collecting art treasures from other lands. Murillo, stimulated by this fine new world of art, worked intensely for nearly three years, studying and imitating the styles of various masters.

So marked was his progress that in 1644 Velasquez pronounced him ready for Rome, but Murillo returned to his native city, Seville, instead. His first commission there was for a series of pictures for a Franciscan monastery, and when they were completed, Murillo's fame was assured. From then on he enjoyed great popularity. In 1648 he married a wealthy woman of high social position and his house was the gathering-place for the leading artists of Spain.

Yet he didn't forget his early days of hardships, as artist of the Feria. The most beloved undertaking of his later years was the establishment of an art academy, where poor students could be taught free of charge.

## The First Miracle

And the third day there was a marriage in Cana of Galilee; and the mother of Jesus was there: and both Jesus was called, and his disciples, to the marriage. And when they wanted wine, the mother of Jesus saith unto him, "They have no wine."

Jesus saith unto her, "Woman, what have I to do with thee? Mine hour is not yet come."

His mother saith unto the servants, "Whatsoever he saith unto you, do it."

And there were set there six waterpots of stone, after the manner of the purifying of the Jews, containing two or three firkins apiece. Jesus saith unto them, "Fill the waterpots with water." And they filled them up to the brim. And he saith unto them, "Draw out now, and bear unto the governor of the feast." And they bare it.

When the ruler of the feast had tasted the water that was made wine, and knew not whence it was: (but the servants which drew the water knew;) the governor of the feast called the bridegroom, and saith unto him, "Every man at the beginning doth set forth good wine; and when men have well drunk, then that which is worse: but thou hast kept the good wine until now."

This beginning of miracles did Jesus in Cana of Galilee, and manifested forth his glory; and his disciples believed on him. — John 1:35–51; 2:1–11.

## A Brief Visit to Capernaum

After this he went down to Capernaum, he, and his mother, and his brethren, and his disciples: and they continued there not many days. — John 2:12.

# The Story of the Master

From the Gospel of John

## Early Ministry in Judæa

### THE CLEANSING OF THE TEMPLE

ND the Jews' passover was at hand, and Jesus went up to Jerusalem, and found in the temple those that sold oxen and sheep and doves, and the changers of money sitting. And when he had made a scourge of small cords, he drove them all out of the temple, and the sheep, and the oxen; and poured out the changers' money, and overthrew the tables; and said unto them that sold doves, "Take these things hence; make not my Father's house an house of merchandise."

And his disciples remembered that it was written, "The zeal of thine house hath eaten me up."

Then answered the Jews and said unto him, "What sign shewest thou unto us, seeing that thou doest these things?"

Jesus answered and said unto them, "Destroy this temple, and in three days I will raise it up."

Then said the Jews, "Forty and six years was this temple in building, and wilt thou rear it up in three days?"

But he spake of the temple of his body. When therefore he was risen from the dead, his disciples remembered that he had said this unto them; and they believed the scripture, and the word which Jesus had said.

Now when he was in Jerusalem at the passover, in the feast day, many believed in his name, when they saw the miracles which he did. But Jesus did not commit himself

### Jesus and Nicodemus

From an oil painting by Edwin John Prittie, painted
expressly for The Book of Life

One of the most striking scenes of the New
Testament is that of the interview between
the Master and the old ruler of the Jews,
Nicodemus, who comes to inquire the way
of life.

"There was a man of the Pharisees, named
Nicodemus, a ruler of the Jews:

"The same came to Jesus by night, and said
unto him, 'Rabbi, we know that thou art a
teacher come from God; for no man can do
these miracles that thou doest, except God
be with him.'" John 3:1, 2.

unto them, because he knew all men, and needed not that
any should testify of man: for he knew what was in man.

— John 2:13–25.

## The Visit of Nicodemus

This is one of the most dramatic incidents of Jesus' life. We may
imagine more than John tells us,—Nicodemus walking through the
quiet streets at night, his coming into Jesus' presence, the mys-
terious wind blowing outside the house.

There was a man of the Pharisees, named Nicodemus,
a ruler of the Jews. The same came to Jesus by night, and
said unto him, "Rabbi, we know that thou art a teacher
come from God: for no man can do these miracles that
thou doest, except God be with him."

Jesus answered and said unto him, "Verily, verily, I
say unto thee, except a man be born again, he cannot see
the kingdom of God."

Nicodemus saith unto him, "How can a man be born
when he is old?"

Jesus answered, "Verily, verily, I say unto thee, except a man be born of water and of the Spirit, he cannot
enter into the kingdom of God. That which is born of the
flesh is flesh; and that which is born of the Spirit is spirit.
Marvel not that I said unto thee, ye must be born again.
The wind bloweth where it listeth, and thou hearest the
sound thereof, but canst not tell whence it cometh, and
whither it goeth: so is every one that is born of the Spirit."

Nicodemus answered and said unto him, "How can
these things be?"

Jesus answered and said unto him, "Art thou a master
of Israel, and knowest not these things? Verily, verily, I
say unto thee, we speak that we do know, and testify that
we have seen; and ye receive not our witness. If I have
told you earthly things, and ye believe not, how shall ye

believe, if I tell you of heavenly things? And no man hath ascended up to heaven, but he that came down from heaven, even the Son of man which is in heaven. And as Moses lifted up the serpent in the wilderness, even so must the Son of man be lifted up: that whosoever believeth in him should not perish, but have eternal life. For God so loved the world, that he gave his only begotten Son, that whosoever believeth in him should not perish, but have everlasting life. For God sent not his Son into the world to condemn the world; but that the world through him might be saved. He that believeth on him is not condemned: but he that believeth not is condemned already, because he hath not believed in the name of the only begotten Son of God. And this is the condemnation, that light is come into the world, and men loved darkness rather than light, because their deeds were evil. For every one that doeth evil hateth the light, neither cometh to the light, lest his deeds should be reproved. But he that doeth truth cometh to the light, that his deeds may be made manifest, that they are wrought in God."          — John 3:1-21.

## JESUS BAPTIZES IN JUDÆA

After these things came Jesus and his disciples into the land of Judæa; and there he tarried with them, and baptized.          — John 3:22.

## THE QUESTION OF JOHN'S DISCIPLES

And John also was baptizing in Ænon near to Salim, because there was much water there: and they came, and were baptized. For John was not yet cast into prison.

Then there arose a question between some of John's disciples and the Jews about purifying. And they came unto John, and said unto him, "Rabbi, he that was with thee beyond Jordan, to whom thou barest witness, behold, the same baptizeth, and all men come to him."

# Jesus and Nicodemus

By John LaFarge (1835-1910)
Mural in Trinity Church, Boston, Massachusetts
From a Copley Print, Copyright by
Curtis and Cameron, Inc., Boston

THE power of John LaFarge to depict the human
soul is well shown in this painting of Jesus and
Nicodemus. Nicodemus is a Pharisee, a ruler and a
distinguished teacher of the Jews, and most of these
leaders were hostile to Jesus. But Nicodemus has heard
and pondered the Master's teachings. He has seen
miracles wrought by him and is deeply impressed.
Nicodemus senses that here is the Great Teacher sent
of God and, seeking to know more, "came to Jesus by
night."

In this picture we can imagine that Nicodemus has
just arrived at the place in Jerusalem where Jesus is
staying and is pouring out his questions while the
Master listens quietly. Note the earnest gestures of
Nicodemus and his anxious face, as contrasted with
the calm and wholly relaxed figure of the Lord. The
one is uneasy, doubting; the other, assured in mind
and at rest. After reading John III: 1-21 on page 257
of this Volume and studying the picture, what do you
think they are saying?

John LaFarge was born in New York City in 1835.
His maternal grandfather, Binnse de St. Victor, was a
well-known artist and became the boy's first teacher.
Most of LaFarge's training, however, came from within
himself for many hours of his youth and young man-
hood were spent in reading and in studying the paintings of the great masters. From them he learned the
beauty of color that was to manifest itself later in his
own paintings and in his beautiful works in stained
glass. LaFarge was a great artist; he loved all the finer
things in art; he loved beautiful colors and nature; he
reverenced spiritual things; and he was ever inspired
by the desire to portray a great soul. He died in Provi-
dence, Rhode Island, in 1910.

John answered and said, "A man can receive nothing, except it be given him from heaven. Ye yourselves bear me witness, that I said, 'I am not the Christ, but that I am sent before him.' He that hath the bride is the bridegroom: but the friend of the bridegroom, which standeth and heareth him, rejoiceth greatly because of the bridegroom's voice: this my joy therefore is fulfilled. He must increase, but I must decrease. He that cometh from above is above all: he that is of the earth is earthly, and speaketh of the earth: he that cometh from heaven is above all. And what he hath seen and heard, that he testifieth; and no man receiveth his testimony. He that hath received his testimony hath set to his seal that God is true. For he whom God hath sent speaketh the words of God: for God giveth not the Spirit by measure unto him. The Father loveth the Son, and hath given all things into his hand. He that believeth on the Son hath everlasting life: and he that believeth not the Son shall not see life, but the wrath of God abideth on him."

— John 3:23-35.

### Jesus Leaves Judæa for Galilee

When therefore the Lord knew how the Pharisees had heard that Jesus made and baptized more disciples than John, (though Jesus himself baptized not, but his disciples,) he left Judæa, and departed again into Galilee.

— John 4:1-3.

## Two Days in Samaria

### The Woman at Jacob's Well

This is another intensely dramatic incident. The Jews had no dealings with the Samaritans. Yet Jesus here by Jacob's well reveals some of the deepest truths of the kingdom to this woman of a despised sect.

I heard the voice of Jesus say,
"Behold, I freely give
The living water; thirsty one,
    Stoop down, and drink, and live."

I came to Jesus, and I drank
    Of that life-giving stream;
My thirst was quenched, my soul revived,
    And now I live in Him.

                              — *Horatius Bonar.*

And he must needs go through Samaria. Then cometh
he to a city of Samaria, which is called Sychar, near to the
parcel of ground that Jacob gave to his son Joseph. Now
Jacob's well was there. Jesus therefore, being wearied
with his journey, sat thus on the well: and it was about
the sixth hour. There cometh a woman of Samaria to draw
water: Jesus saith unto her, "Give me to drink:" For
his disciples were gone away unto the city to buy meat.

Then saith the woman of Samaria unto him, "How is it
that thou, being a Jew, askest drink of me, which am a
woman of Samaria? For the Jews have no dealings with
the Samaritans."

Jesus answered and said unto her, "If thou knewest
the gift of God, and who it is that saith to thee, 'Give me
to drink'; thou wouldest have asked of him, and he would
have given thee living water."

The woman saith unto him, "Sir, thou hast nothing to
draw with, and the well is deep: from whence then hast
thou that living water? Art thou greater than our father
Jacob, which gave us the well, and drank thereof himself,
and his children, and his cattle?"

Jesus answered and said unto her, "Whosoever drinketh of this water shall thirst again: but whosoever drinketh of the water that I shall give him shall never thirst;

# Jesus and the Woman of Samaria

## By Heinrich Hofmann (1824-1911)

THE Bible story from which the artist took his inspiration for this picture begins on page 261. How simply, yet effectively, Hofmann has portrayed the essence of Jesus' teaching: "The water that I shall give him shall be in him a well of water springing up into everlasting life." Surprise, deference, engrossed interest are all expressed in the Samaritan woman's bearing.

The setting is an ancient, vine-covered well in hilly Samaria. Springs and wells were precious natural resources in Jesus' day, essential to the lives of the people and their flocks. Stone shelters were often built at the wells so that those who came to draw water might rest, protected from the hot sun.

Heinrich Hofmann was born in Darmstadt, Germany, in 1824. He studied in the Dusseldorf and the Antwerp Academies of Art and later spent four years in Rome, where he was much influenced by a group of German artists devoted to the study of Renaissance Italian painters and the portrayal of religious subjects. In 1870 Hofmann was appointed professor at the Academy in Dresden, where he died in 1911.

Hofmann was gifted with a fine sense of color as shown in the lovely, colored reproduction of Jesus in the Midst of the Doctors, and diligently applied his skill to a wide range of subjects: portraits, landscape, themes from history and literature, particularly the Bible. His fame rests on his religious pictures of which the chief are: Jesus in Gethsemane, page 336; Christ and the Rich Young Man, page 166; and Jesus in the Midst of the Doctors. Hofmann's clear, simple, beautiful representations of the life of Jesus are so appealing that they are more widely used in Sunday Schools today than those of any other artist.

but the water that I shall give him shall be in him a well of water springing up into everlasting life."

The woman saith unto him, "Sir, give me this water, that I thirst not, neither come hither to draw."

Jesus saith unto her, "Go, call thy husband, and come hither."

The woman answered and said, "I have no husband."

Jesus said unto her, "Thou hast well said, 'I have no husband': for thou hast had five husbands; and he whom thou now hast is not thy husband: in that saidst thou truly."

The woman saith unto him, "Sir, I perceive that thou art a prophet. Our fathers worshiped in this mountain; and ye say that in Jerusalem is the place where men ought to worship."

Jesus saith unto her, "Woman, believe me, the hour cometh, when ye shall neither in this mountain, nor yet at Jerusalem, worship the Father. Ye worship ye know not what: we know what we worship: for salvation is of the Jews. But the hour cometh, and now is, when the true worshipers shall worship the Father in spirit and in truth: for the Father seeketh such to worship him. God is a Spirit: and they that worship him must worship him in spirit and in truth."

The woman saith unto him, "I know that Messias cometh, which is called Christ: when he is come, he will tell us all things."

Jesus saith unto her, "I that speak unto thee am he."

And upon this came his disciples, and marveled that he talked with the woman: yet no man said, "What seekest thou?" or, "Why talkest thou with her?"

The woman then left her waterpot, and went her way into the city, and saith to the men, "Come, see a man, which told me all things that ever I did. Is not this the

Christ?" Then they went out of the city, and came unto him.

In the meanwhile his disciples prayed him, saying, "Master, eat."

But he said unto them, "I have meat to eat that ye know not of."

Therefore said the disciples one to another, "Hath any man brought him aught to eat?"

Jesus saith unto them, "My meat is to do the will of him that sent me, and to finish his work. Say not ye, 'There are yet four months, and then cometh harvest'? Behold, I say unto you, lift up your eyes, and look on the fields; for they are white already to harvest. And he that reapeth receiveth wages, and gathereth fruit unto life eternal: that both he that soweth and he that reapeth may rejoice together. And herein is that saying true, 'One soweth, and another reapeth.' I sent you to reap that whereon ye bestowed no labour: other men laboured, and ye are entered into their labours."

And many of the Samaritans of that city believed on him for the saying of the woman, which testified, "He told me all that ever I did."

So when the Samaritans were come unto him, they besought him that he would tarry with them: and he abode there two days. And many more believed because of his own word; and said unto the woman, "Now we believe, not because of thy saying: for we have heard him ourselves, and know that this is indeed the Christ, the Saviour of the world."

Now after two days he departed thence, and went into Galilee. For Jesus himself testified that a prophet hath no honour in his own country. Then when he was come into Galilee, the Galilæans received him, having seen all the things that he did at Jerusalem at the feast: for they also went unto the feast.          —John 4:4-45.

# Mary and the Infants Jesus and John

By Bernardino Luini (c.1475-c.1533)
In the Gallery Ambrosiana, Milan, Italy
Photograph by Anderson, Rome

IN this lovely picture we see Mary holding the infant Jesus on her knee and little John the Baptist presenting him with a flower. The scene is in a garden where irises and other flowers are in bloom. John carries his cross-hilted staff, an attribute which is almost always given him. The cross is intended, it is said, to symbolize the fact that the forerunner was the first to use the cross as a symbol of the sacrifice made by the Saviour of the world.

Is this not a beautiful conception of the characters portrayed? A quiet serenity, an indefinable charm of deep religious feeling are given us. All of the attraction and power of the painter's art are here expressed. As Browning says in FRA FILIPPO LIPPI,

"We're so made that we love
First when we see them painted, things we have passed
Perhaps a hundred times nor cared to see."

Little exact information about Bernardino Luini has come down to us. It is supposed that he was born in Luino because he signed his pictures Bernardino of Luino. ("Of Luino" becomes "Luini" in Italian.) His paintings show that he was artistically influenced by Leonardo da Vinci. That he must have been a busy and popular artist is evidenced by the many works from his hand. If we study his pictures we conclude that he was a man of delicate poetic and religious feelings who loved the vivacity and joy of life yet was sensitive to the pathos and suffering. Luini's beautiful representations of the Christ Child, a curly-headed infant with expressive far-seeing eyes, have won for him the name, the Raphael of Lombardy.

Other paintings by Luini are given on pages 8 and 12, and in Volumes I and VIII.

# The Story of the Master

## From the Gospel of John

## Early Ministry in Galilee

### THE HEALING OF THE NOBLEMAN'S SON

SO Jesus came again into Cana of Galilee, where he made the water wine. And there was a certain nobleman, whose son was sick at Capernaum. When he heard that Jesus was come out of Judæa into Galilee, he went unto him, and besought him that he would come down and heal his son: for he was at the point of death.

Then said Jesus unto him, "Except ye see signs and wonders, ye will not believe."

The nobleman saith unto him, "Sir, come down ere my child die."

Jesus saith unto him, "Go thy way; thy son liveth." And the man believed the word that Jesus had spoken unto him, and he went his way.

And as he was now going down, his servants met him, and told him, saying, "Thy son liveth."

Then enquired he of them the hour when he began to amend. And they said unto him, "Yesterday at the seventh hour the fever left him."

So the father knew that it was at the same hour, in the which Jesus said unto him, "Thy son liveth": and himself believed, and his whole house.

This is again the second miracle that Jesus did, when he was come out of Judæa into Galilee. —John 4:46-54.

## The Pool of Bethesda

After this there was a feast of the Jews; and Jesus went up to Jerusalem. Now there is at Jerusalem by the sheep market a pool, which is called in the Hebrew tongue Bethesda, having five porches. In these lay a great multitude of impotent folk, of blind, halt, withered, waiting for the moving of the water. For an angel went down at a certain season into the pool, and troubled the water: whosoever then first after the troubling of the water stepped in was made whole of whatsoever disease he had. And a certain man was there, which had an infirmity thirty and eight years. When Jesus saw him lie, and knew that he had been now a long time in that case, he saith unto him, "Wilt thou be made whole?"

The impotent man answered him, "Sir, I have no man, when the water is troubled, to put me into the pool: but while I am coming, another steppeth down before me."

Jesus saith unto him, "Rise, take up thy bed, and walk." And immediately the man was made whole, and took up his bed, and walked: and on the same day was the sabbath.

The Jews therefore said unto him that was cured, "It is the sabbath day: it is not lawful for thee to carry thy bed."

He answered them, "He that made me whole, the same said unto me, 'Take up thy bed, and walk.'"

Then asked they him, "What man is that which said unto thee, 'Take up thy bed, and walk'?"

And he that was healed wist not who it was: for Jesus had conveyed himself away, a multitude being in that place.

Afterward Jesus findeth him in the temple, and said unto him, "Behold, thou art made whole: sin no more,

# Madonna and Child

By Correggio (Antonio Allegri, c.1494-1534)
In the Uffizi Gallery, Florence, Italy
Color Photograph by Alinari Brothers, Florence

THIS lovely picture shows Mary kneeling in de-
lighted adoration before her new-born Son, playfully trying to attract his attention. The scene is placed
midst quiet, overgrown ruins and bathed in light and
atmosphere.

The artist, Correggio, was noted for his portrayals of
joyous human emotion and beauty, and for his skillful
handling of light and shadow. In the art of chiaroscuro
(light and dark) the objects and figures of a picture
are made to seem enveloped in light and air, as in the
actual world. Leonardo da Vinci was among the first
to study how to produce these effects in painting, (see
Volume VIII, page 140). Here the contrast between
the lighted figures and the dark shadows gives a vivid
reality to the figures. Furthermore, by omitting the
source of the light, such as a candle, which would be
necessary to illumine a similar scene in real life, the
artist has procured a supernatural effect. We feel that
the light here comes from the Holy Child, and our
thoughts turn to him, the "light of the world." Thus,
we enter into the picture by instinctively supplying an
explanation for the light, and in the process are moved
to devotional thoughts. Such is part of the spell that
painting holds for men. Of chiaroscuro, Rembrandt (see
page 238) is the supreme master. Correggio's skill in
it is remarkable to this day.

Antonio Allegri, called Correggio from his birthplace,
is thought to have studied with Francia (see page 94)
in Bologna. He was evidently influenced by the works
of Andrea Mantegna (1431-1506) at Mantua, Italy,
and those of famous contemporary artists. His greatest
work, ceiling decorations of two churches in Parma,
foreshadowed later Baroque art, and proved Correggio an original as well as masterful artist. Another
of his pictures is in Volume I, page 72.

lest a worse thing come unto thee." The man departed, and told the Jews that it was Jesus, which had made him whole. And therefore did the Jews persecute Jesus, and sought to slay him, because he had done these things on the sabbath day.

### "MY FATHER WORKETH AND I WORK"

But Jesus answered them, "My Father worketh hitherto, and I work."

Therefore the Jews sought the more to kill him, because he not only had broken the sabbath, but said also that God was his Father, making himself equal with God.

Then answered Jesus and said unto them, "Verily, verily, I say unto you, the Son can do nothing of himself, but what he seeth the Father do: for what things soever he doeth, these also doeth the Son likewise. For the Father loveth the Son, and sheweth him all things that himself doeth: and he will shew him greater works than these, that ye may marvel. For as the Father raiseth up the dead, and quickeneth them; even so the Son quickeneth whom he will. For the Father judgeth no man, but hath committed all judgment unto the Son: that all men should honour the Son, even as they honour the Father. He that honoureth not the Son honoureth not the Father which hath sent him. Verily, verily, I say unto you, he that heareth my word, and believeth on him that sent me, hath everlasting life, and shall not come into condemnation; but is passed from death unto life. Verily, verily, I say unto you, the hour is coming, and now is, when the dead shall hear the voice of the Son of God: and they that hear shall live. For as the Father hath life in himself; so hath he given to the Son to have life in himself; and hath given him authority to execute judgment also, because he is the Son of man. Marvel not at this: for the hour is coming, in the which all that are in the graves shall hear his voice, and shall come forth; they that have done good, unto the resurrection of life; and they that have done evil, unto the resurrection of damnation.

"I can of mine own self do nothing: as I hear, I judge: and my judgment is just; because I seek not mine own will, but the will of the Father which hath sent me. If I bear witness of myself, my witness is not true."

### THE WITNESS OF JOHN

"There is another that beareth witness of me; and I know that the witness that he witnesseth of me is true. Ye sent unto John, and he bare witness unto the truth. But I receive not testimony from man: but these things I say that ye might be saved. He was a burning and a shining light: and ye were willing for a season to rejoice in his light.

"But I have greater witness than that of John: for the works which the Father hath given me to finish, the same works that I do, bear witness of me that the Father hath sent me. And the Father himself, which hath sent me, hath borne witness of me. Ye have neither heard his voice at any time, nor seen his shape. And ye have not his word abiding in you: for whom he hath sent, him ye believe not."

### "SEARCH THE SCRIPTURES"

"Search the scriptures; for in them ye think ye have eternal life: and they are they which testify of me. And ye will not come to me, that ye might have life. I receive not honour from men. But I know you, that ye have not the love of God in you. I am come in my Father's name, and ye receive me not: if another shall come in his own name, him ye will receive. How can ye believe, which receive honour one of another, and seek not the honour that cometh from God only? Do not think that I will accuse you to the Father: there is one that accuseth you, even Moses, in whom ye trust. For had ye believed Moses, ye would have believed me: for he wrote of me. But if ye believe not his writings, how shall ye believe my words?" — John 5.

### THE FEEDING OF THE MULTITUDE

After these things Jesus went over the sea of Galilee, which is the sea of Tiberias. And a great multitude followed him, because they saw his miracles which he did on them that were diseased. And Jesus went up into a mountain, and there he sat with his disciples. And the passover, a feast of the Jews, was nigh.

When Jesus then lifted up his eyes, and saw a great company come unto him, he saith unto Philip, "Whence shall we buy bread, that these may eat?"

And this he said to prove him: for he himself knew what he would do.

Philip answered him, "Two hundred pennyworth of bread is not sufficient for them, that every one of them may take a little."

### THE LAD WITH FIVE BARLEY LOAVES AND TWO SMALL FISHES

One of his disciples, Andrew, Simon Peter's brother, saith unto him, "There is a lad here, which hath five barley loaves, and two small fishes: but what are they among so many?"

And Jesus said, "Make the men sit down."

Now there was much grass in the place. So the men sat down, in number about five thousand. And Jesus took the loaves; and when he had given thanks, he distributed to the disciples, and the disciples to them that were set down; and likewise of the fishes as much as they would.

When they were filled, he said unto his disciples, "Gather up the fragments that remain, that nothing be lost."

Therefore they gathered them together, and filled twelve baskets with the fragments of the five barley loaves, which remained over and above unto them that had eaten.

Then those men, when they had seen the miracle that Jesus did, said, "This is of a truth that prophet that should come into the world."

When Jesus therefore perceived that they would come and take him by force, to make him a king, he departed again into a mountain himself alone.　　　　— John 6:1–15.

### "PEACE! IT IS I"

Fierce was the wild billow,
　Dark was the night,
Oars labored heavily,
　Foam glimmered white,
Trembled the mariners,
　Peril was nigh;
Then said the God of God,
　"Peace! It is I!"

Ridge of the mountain-wave
　Lower thy crest!
Wail of Euroclydon,
　Be thou at rest!
Sorrow can never be,
　Darkness must fly,
Where saith the Light of light,
　"Peace! It is I!"

Jesus, Deliverer,
　Come Thou to me:
Soothe Thou my voyaging
　Over life's sea;
Thou, when the storm of death
　Roars, sweeping by,
Whisper, Thou Truth of truth,
　"Peace! It is I!"
— *Anatolius 458. Translation by John Mason Neale.*

# Christ Walking on the Sea

By Charles Caryl Coleman (1840-1928)
In the Seamen's Church Institute, New York City
Copley Print, Copyright by Curtis and Cameron, Boston

A LONG wearying day for Jesus and His disciples had come to a close. The Master had gone up alone into a mountain. "When the even was come" the disciples entered their boat and began the journey over the Sea of Galilee toward Capernaum. Soon a dangerous storm arose. They were tossed with the tempest and were in great peril and fear. It seemed they must surely perish, when suddenly the Saviour appeared walking on the Sea toward them. Immediately all was well.

This painting is a powerful portrayal of the Christian's life. How often, when the trials and anxieties of everyday tasks seem about to overwhelm us, we turn to Jesus and find all is calm and safe! When trouble is nigh, our blessed Lord comes to our aid.

Charles Caryl Coleman's life helps us to understand something of the spirit behind this picture. At the age of nineteen Coleman left his native city of Buffalo, New York, to study art in Paris. When the Civil War broke out, he returned to America and served in the Union Army for three years. After the war, although still suffering from a serious wound, Coleman sailed for Europe and took up again an active life in his profession of painting. In later years, he made his home in Italy on the Island of Capri where he died in 1928. He became especially well known for his fine, deeply-felt religious pictures of which this is one of the best. It is an oil painting in various shades of brown.

How appropriate that this beautiful painting has come to rest in the Seamen's Church Institute of New York, a great church for sailors which overlooks the sea! The chaplain there informs us that many sailors stop and gaze raptly at this picture, moved by its message.

## Jesus Walking on the Sea

And when even was now come, his disciples went down into the sea, and entered into a ship, and went over the sea toward Capernaum. And it was now dark, and Jesus was not come to them. And the sea arose by reason of a great wind that blew. So when they had rowed about five and twenty or thirty furlongs, they see Jesus walking on the sea, and drawing nigh unto the ship: and they were afraid.

But he saith unto them, "It is I; be not afraid." Then they willingly received him into the ship: and immediately the ship was at the land whither they went.

— John 6:16–21.

## The Teaching of Jesus Beside the Sea

The day following, when the people which stood on the other side of the sea saw that there was none other boat there, save that one whereinto his disciples were entered, and that Jesus went not with his disciples into the boat, but that his disciples were gone away alone; howbeit there came other boats from Tiberias nigh unto the place where they did eat bread, after that the Lord had given thanks: when the people therefore saw that Jesus was not there, neither his disciples, they also took shipping, and came to Capernaum, seeking for Jesus.

And when they had found him on the other side of the sea, they said unto him, "Rabbi, when camest thou hither?"

Jesus answered them and said, "Verily, verily, I say unto you, ye seek me, not because ye saw the miracles, but because ye did eat of the loaves, and were filled. Labour not for the meat which perisheth, but for that meat which endureth unto everlasting life, which the

Son of man shall give unto you: for him hath God the Father sealed."

Then said they unto him, "What shall we do, that we might work the works of God?"

Jesus answered and said unto them, "This is the work of God, that ye believe on him whom he hath sent."

They said therefore unto him, "What sign showest thou then, that we may see, and believe thee? What dost thou work? Our fathers did eat manna in the desert; as it is written, 'He gave them bread from heaven to eat.'"

Then Jesus said unto them, "Verily, verily, I say unto you, Moses gave you not that bread from heaven; but my Father giveth you the true bread from heaven. For the bread of God is he which cometh down from heaven, and giveth life unto the world."

### "LORD, EVERMORE GIVE US THIS BREAD"

Then said they unto him, "Lord, evermore give us this bread."

And Jesus said unto them, "I am the bread of life: he that cometh to me shall never hunger; and he that believeth on me shall never thirst. But I said unto you that ye also have seen me, and believe not. All that the Father giveth me shall come to me; and him that cometh to me I will in no wise cast out. For I came down from heaven, not to do mine own will, but the will of him that sent me. And this is the Father's will which hath sent me, that of all which he hath given me I should lose nothing, but should raise it up again at the last day. And this is the will of him that sent me, that every one which seeth the Son, and believeth on him, may have everlasting life: and I will raise him up at the last day."

The Jews then murmured at him, because he said,

## "By the Sheep Market a Pool"

Photograph by W. A. Pottenger
expressly for The Book of Life

In the Gospel of John 5:2, we read in the account of Jesus' visit to Jerusalem at the Feast of Dedication:

"Now there is at Jerusalem by the sheep market a pool which is called in the Hebrew tongue 'Bethesda' having five porches."

There have been various identifications of the pool of Bethesda, the one now most commonly accepted being to the northwest of St. Stephen's Gate. This most interesting picture shows a modern sheep market near a pool. It shows that still, as in the ancient days, the sheep market of Jerusalem is by a pool, perhaps transferred from the old pool of Bethesda to this larger pool, Birket Suttan, the Pool of the Sultan in the Valley of Hinnom.

"I am the bread which came down from heaven." And they said, "Is not this Jesus, the son of Joseph, whose father and mother we know? How is it then that he saith, 'I came down from heaven'?"

Jesus therefore answered and said unto them, "Murmur not among yourselves. No man can come to me, except the Father which hath sent me draw him: and I will raise him up at the last day. It is written in the prophets, 'And they shall be all taught of God.' Every man therefore that hath heard, and hath learned of the Father, cometh unto me. Not that any man hath seen the Father, save he which is of God, he hath seen the Father. Verily, verily, I say unto you, he that believeth on me hath everlasting life.

### "I AM THAT BREAD OF LIFE"

"I am that bread of life. Your fathers did eat manna in the wilderness, and are dead. This is the bread which cometh down from heaven, that a man may eat thereof, and not die. I am the living bread which came down from heaven: if any man eat of this bread, he shall live forever: and the bread that I will give is my flesh, which I will give for the life of the world."

The Jews therefore strove among themselves, saying, "How can this man give us his flesh to eat?"

Then Jesus said unto them, "Verily, verily, I say unto you, except ye eat the flesh of the Son of man, and drink his blood, ye have no life in you. Whoso eateth my flesh, and drinketh my blood, hath eternal life; and I will raise him up at the last day. For my flesh is meat indeed, and my blood is drink indeed. He that eateth my flesh, and drinketh my blood, dwelleth in me, and I in him. As the living Father hath sent me, and I live by the Father: so he that eateth me, even he shall live by me.  This is that bread which came down from heaven: not as your fathers did eat manna, and are dead: he that eateth of this bread shall live forever."

These things said he in the synagogue, as he taught in Capernaum.          — John 6:22–59.

## MANY TURN BACK FROM FOLLOWING JESUS

Many therefore of his disciples, when they had heard this, said, "This is an hard saying; who can hear it?"

When Jesus knew in himself that his disciples murmured at it, he said unto them, "Doth this offend you? What then if ye shall see the Son of man ascend up where he was before?  It is the spirit that quickeneth; the flesh profiteth nothing: the words that I speak unto you, they are spirit, and they are life.  But there are some of you that believe not."  For Jesus knew from the beginning who they were that believed not, and who should betray him.

And he said, "Therefore said I unto you, that no man can come unto me, except it were given unto him of my Father."

From that time many of his disciples went back, and walked no more with him.

Then said Jesus unto the twelve, "Will ye also go away?"

Then Simon Peter answered him, "Lord, to whom shall we go?  Thou hast the words of eternal life.  And we believe and are sure that thou art that Christ, the Son of the living God."

Jesus answered them, "Have not I chosen you twelve, and one of you is a devil?"  He spake of Judas Iscariot the son of Simon: for he it was that should betray him, being one of the twelve.          — John 6:60–71.

# Angel Bearing a Lily

By Melozzo da Forli (1438-1494)
In the Uffizi Gallery, Florence, Italy
Color Photograph by Alinari Brothers, Florence

THIS beautiful figure in motion is the angel Gabriel greeting Mary as he brings her God's message that she is to be the mother of the Messiah. With what speed he has come to make this all important announcement! "Hail, thou that art highly favoured, the Lord is with thee; blessed art thou among women." The rest of his message is given on page 17.

Two other paintings of this scene are given on pages 14 and 16. In those Mary is shown receiving the announcement, but in this picture we have just a detail of the representation showing the announcing angel. The lily which he carries is a symbol of purity and is often seen in pictures of the Annunciation. We are told that this figure of Gabriel and the one of Mary which belongs with it were painted originally on organ doors. They may both be seen today in the Uffizi Gallery in Florence.

Melozzo da Forli, the painter of this figure, was born in the town of Forli and died there. His family name was Ambrosi. Not much is known of him except that he worked in Rome, Loreto, Forli and Urbino. His work was evidently known to Giovanni Santi of Urbino, father of the great Raphael, for we have Giovanni's rhymed chronicle in which he praised Melozzo's skill in perspective. Other artists and critics of that day were also impressed with Melozzo's successful use of perspective and foreshortening in the representation of buildings and human figures. This knowledge Melozzo gained from his master, Piero della Francesca, who spent his life working out solutions to these problems. This figure of Gabriel in Florence and the Music-making Angels at Rome are the best loved pictures of Melozzo. They show him to be a painter of talent, vivid and skillful.

# The Story of the Master

## From the Gospel of John

## An Autumn Visit to Jerusalem

### JESUS AT THE FEAST OF TABERNACLES

#### "MY TIME IS NOT YET COME"

AFTER these things Jesus walked in Galilee: for he would not walk in Jewry, because the Jews sought to kill him. Now the Jews' feast of tabernacles was at hand. His brethren therefore said unto him, "Depart hence, and go into Judæa, that thy disciples also may see the works that thou doest. For there is no man that doeth anything in secret, and he himself seeketh to be known openly. If thou do these things, shew thyself to the world." For neither did his brethren believe in him.

Then Jesus said unto them, "My time is not yet come: but your time is alway ready. The world cannot hate you; but me it hateth, because I testify of it, that the works thereof are evil. Go ye up unto this feast: I go not up yet unto this feast; for my time is not yet full come."

#### JESUS GOES TO THE FEAST SECRETLY

When he had said these words unto them, he abode still in Galilee. But when his brethren were gone up, then went he also up unto the feast, not openly, but as it were in secret.

Then the Jews sought him at the feast, and said, "Where is he?"

And there was much murmuring among the people concerning him: for some said, "He is a good man": others said "Nay; but he deceiveth the people." Howbeit no man spake openly of him for fear of the Jews.

### JESUS APPEARS IN THE TEMPLE

Now about the midst of the feast Jesus went up into the temple, and taught. And the Jews marveled, saying, "How knoweth this man letters, having never learned?"

Jesus answered them, and said, "My doctrine is not mine, but his that sent me. If any man will do his will, he shall know of the doctrine, whether it be of God, or whether I speak of myself. He that speaketh of himself seeketh his own glory: but he that seeketh his glory that sent him, the same is true, and no unrighteousness is in him. Did not Moses give you the law, and yet none of you keepeth the law? Why go ye about to kill me?"

The people answered and said, "Thou hast a devil: who goeth about to kill thee?"

Jesus answered and said unto them, "I have done one work, and ye all marvel. Moses therefore gave unto you circumcision; (not because it is of Moses, but of the fathers;) and ye on the sabbath day circumcise a man. If a man on the sabbath day receive circumcision, that the law of Moses should not be broken; are ye angry at me, because I have made a man every whit whole on the sabbath day? Judge not according to the appearance but judge righteous judgment."

Then said some of them of Jerusalem, "Is not this he whom they seek to kill? But, lo, he speaketh boldly, and they say nothing unto him. Do the rulers know indeed that this is the very Christ? Howbeit we know this man whence he is: but when Christ cometh, no man knoweth whence he is."

Then cried Jesus in the temple as he taught, saying, "Ye both know me, and ye know whence I am: and I am not come of myself, but he that sent me is true, whom ye know not. But I know him: for I am from him, and he hath sent me."

Then they sought to take him: but no man laid hands on him, because his hour was not yet come. And many of the people believed on him, and said, "When Christ cometh, will he do more miracles than these which this man hath done?"

The Pharisees heard that the people murmured such things concerning him; and the Pharisees and the chief priests sent officers to take him.

Then said Jesus unto them, "Yet a little while am I with you, and then I go unto him that sent me. Ye shall seek me, and shall not find me: and where I am, thither ye cannot come."

Then said the Jews among themselves, "Whither will he go, that we shall not find him? Will he go unto the dispersed among the Gentiles, and teach the Gentiles? What manner of saying is this that he said, 'Ye shall seek me, and shall not find me: and where I am, thither ye cannot come'?"

JESUS TEACHES AT THE GREAT DAY OF THE FEAST

In the last day, that great day of the feast, Jesus stood and cried, saying, "If any man thirst, let him come unto me, and drink. He that believeth on me, as the scripture hath said, out of his belly shall flow rivers of living water." But this spake he of the Spirit, which they that believe on him should receive: for the Holy Ghost was not yet given; because that Jesus was not yet glorified.

Many of the people therefore, when they heard this saying, said, "Of a truth this is the Prophet."

Others said, "This is the Christ." But some said, "Shall Christ come out of Galilee? Hath not the scripture said, that Christ cometh of the seed of David, and out of the town of Bethlehem, where David was?"

So there was a division among the people because of him. And some of them would have taken him; but no man laid hands on him.

Then came the officers to the chief priests and Pharisees; and they said unto them, "Why have ye not brought him?"

The officers answered, "Never man spake like this man."

Then answered them the Pharisees, "Are ye also deceived? Have any of the rulers or of the Pharisees believed on him? But this people who knoweth not the law are cursed."

### NICODEMUS SPEAKS FOR JESUS

Nicodemus saith unto them, he that came to Jesus by night, being one of them: "Doth our law judge any man, before it hear him, and know what he doeth?"

They answered and said unto him, "Art thou also of Galilee? Search, and look: for out of Galilee ariseth no prophet."        — John 7:1-52.

### THE WOMAN TAKEN IN ADULTERY

And every man went unto his own house, but Jesus went unto the Mount of Olives.

And early in the morning he came again into the temple, and all the people came unto him; and he sat down, and taught them. And the scribes and Pharisees brought unto him a woman taken in adultery; and when they had set her in the midst, they say unto him, "Master, this woman was taken in adultery, in the very act. Now Moses in the law commanded us that such should be stoned: but what sayest thou?"

This they said, tempting him, that they might have to accuse him. But Jesus stooped down, and with his finger wrote on the ground, as though he heard them not. So when they continued asking him, he lifted up himself, and said unto them, "He that is without sin among you, let him first cast a stone at her." And again he stooped down, and wrote on the ground. And they which heard it, being convicted by their own conscience, went out one by one, beginning at the eldest, even unto the last: and Jesus was left alone, and the woman standing in the midst.

When Jesus had lifted up himself, and saw none but the woman, he said unto her, "Woman, where are those thine accusers? Hath no man condemned thee?"

She said, "No man, Lord."

And Jesus said unto her, "Neither do I condemn thee: go, and sin no more."

### "I AM THE LIGHT OF THE WORLD"

I heard the voice of Jesus say,
"I am this dark world's light;
Look unto Me, thy morn shall rise,
And all thy day be bright."
I looked to Jesus, and I found
In Him my star, my sun;
And in that light of life I'll walk
Till travelling days are done.
—*Horatius Bonar.*

Then spake Jesus again unto them, saying, "I am the light of the world: he that followeth me shall not walk in darkness, but shall have the light of life."

The Pharisees therefore said unto him, "Thou bearest record of thyself; thy record is not true."

Jesus answered and said unto them, "Though I bear record of myself, yet my record is true: for I know whence I came, and whither I go; but ye cannot tell whence I come, and whither I go. Ye judge after the flesh; I judge no man. And yet if I judge, my judgment is true: for I am not alone, but I and the Father that sent me. It is also written in your law, that the testimony of two men is true. I am one that bear witness of myself, and the Father that sent me beareth witness of me."

Then said they unto him, "Where is thy Father?"

Jesus answered, "Ye neither know me, nor my Father: if ye had known me, ye should have known my Father also."

These words spake Jesus in the treasury, as he taught in the temple: and no man laid hands on him; for his hour was not yet come. Then said Jesus again unto them, "I go my way, and ye shall seek me, and shall die in your sins: whither I go, ye cannot come."

Then said the Jews, "Will he kill himself?" because he saith, "Whither I go, ye cannot come."

And he said unto them, "Ye are from beneath; I am from above: ye are of this world; I am not of this world. I said therefore unto you, that ye shall die in your sins: for if ye believe not that I am he, ye shall die in your sins."

Then said they unto him, "Who art thou?"

And Jesus saith unto them, "Even the same that I said unto you from the beginning. I have many things to say and to judge of you: but he that sent me is true; and I speak to the world those things which I have heard of him." They understood not that he spake to them of the Father.

Then said Jesus unto them, "When ye have lifted up the Son of man, then shall ye know that I am he, and that I do nothing of myself; but as my Father hath taught me, I speak these things. And he that sent me is with me: the Father hath not left me alone; for I do always those things that please him." As he spake these words, many believed on him. — John 7:53—8:30.

## "The Truth Shall Make You Free"

Then said Jesus to those Jews which believed on him, "If ye continue in my word, then are ye my disciples indeed; and ye shall know the truth, and the truth shall make you free."

They answered him, "We be Abraham's seed, and were never in bondage to any man: how sayest thou, 'Ye shall be made free'?"

Jesus answered them, "Verily, verily, I say unto you, whosoever committeth sin is the servant of sin. And the servant abideth not in the house forever: but the Son abideth ever. If the Son therefore shall make you free, ye shall be free indeed. I know that ye are Abraham's seed; but ye seek to kill me, because my word hath no place in you. I speak that which I have seen with my Father: and ye do that which ye have seen with your father."

They answered and said unto him, "Abraham is our father."

Jesus saith unto them, "If ye were Abraham's children, ye would do the works of Abraham. But now ye seek to kill me, a man that hath told you the truth, which I have heard of God: this did not Abraham. Ye do the deeds of your father."

Then said they to him, "We be not born of fornication, we have one Father, even God."

Jesus said unto them, "If God were your Father, ye would love me: for I proceeded forth and came from God; neither came I of myself, but he sent me. Why do ye not understand my speech? Even because ye cannot hear my word. Ye are of your father the devil, and the lusts of your father ye will do. He was a murderer from the beginning, and abode not in the truth, because there is no truth in him. When he speaketh a lie, he speaketh of his own: for he is a liar, and the father of it. And because I tell you the truth, ye believe me not. Which of you convinceth me of sin? And if I say the truth, why do ye not believe me? He that is of God heareth God's words: ye therefore hear them not, because ye are not of God."

Then answered the Jews, and said unto him, "Say we not well that thou art a Samaritan, and hast a devil?"

Jesus answered, "I have not a devil; but I honour my Father, and ye do dishonour me. And I seek not mine own glory: there is one that seeketh and judgeth. Verily, verily, I say unto you, if a man keep my saying, he shall never see death."

Then said the Jews unto him, "Now we know that thou hast a devil. Abraham is dead, and the prophets; and thou sayest, 'If a man keep my saying, he shall never taste of death.' Art thou greater than our father Abraham, which is dead? And the prophets are dead. Whom makest thou thyself?"

Jesus answered, "If I honour myself, my honour is nothing: it is my Father that honoureth me; of whom ye say, that he is your God: yet ye have not known him; but I know him: and if I should say, I know him not, I shall be a liar like unto you: but I know him, and keep his saying. Your father Abraham rejoiced to see my day: and he saw it, and was glad."

Then said the Jews unto him, "Thou art not yet fifty years old, and hast thou seen Abraham?"

Jesus said unto them, "Verily, verily, I say unto you, before Abraham was, I am."

Then took they up stones to cast at him: but Jesus hid himself, and went out of the temple, going through the midst of them, and so passed by.    — John 8:31–59.

THE NEEDLE'S EYE

*Photograph by Frances Jenkins Olcott*

This little door through which an American missionary is passing cut in a bigger door, in Palestine, is called a needle's eye. It is too small for a loaded beast to pass through. It keeps pack animals out.

This may be what the Saviour referred to in his saying, "It is easier for a camel to go through the eye of a needle, than for a rich man to enter into the Kingdom of God."

Can you tell what more he said to the very rich young man? Read Matthew 19:16–30, pages 169–170.

# The Story of the Master

### From the Gospel of John

## Days in the Northern Country

### THE MAN BORN BLIND

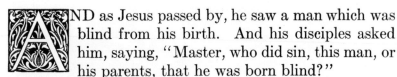ND as Jesus passed by, he saw a man which was blind from his birth. And his disciples asked him, saying, "Master, who did sin, this man, or his parents, that he was born blind?"

Jesus answered, "Neither hath this man sinned, nor his parents: but that the works of God should be made manifest in him. I must work the works of him that sent me, while it is day: the night cometh, when no man can work. As long as I am in the world, I am the light of the world."

When he had thus spoken, he spat on the ground, and made clay of the spittle, and he anointed the eyes of the blind man with the clay, and said unto him, "Go, wash in the pool of Siloam," (which is by interpretation, Sent.) He went his way therefore, and washed, and came seeing.

The neighbours therefore, and they which before had seen him that he was blind, said, "Is not this he that sat and begged?"

Some said, "This is he": others said, "He is like him": but he said, "I am he."

Therefore said they unto him, "How were thine eyes opened?"

He answered and said "A man that is called Jesus made clay, and anointed mine eyes, and said unto me,

'Go to the pool of Siloam, and wash': and I went and washed, and I received sight."

Then said they unto him, "Where is he?"

He said, "I know not."

They brought to the Pharisees him that aforetime was blind. And it was the sabbath day when Jesus made the clay, and opened his eyes. Then again the Pharisees also asked him how he had received his sight. He said unto them, "He put clay upon mine eyes, and I washed, and do see."

Therefore said some of the Pharisees, "This man is not of God, because he keepeth not the sabbath day."

Others said, "How can a man that is a sinner do such miracles?" and there was a division among them.

They say unto the blind man again, "What sayest thou of him, that he hath opened thine eyes?"

He said, "He is a prophet."

But the Jews did not believe concerning him, that he had been blind, and received his sight, until they called the parents of him that had received his sight. And they asked them, saying, "Is this your son, who ye say was born blind? How then doth he now see?"

His parents answered them and said, "We know that this is our son, and that he was born blind: but by what means he now seeth, we know not; or who hath opened his eyes, we know not: he is of age; ask him: he shall speak for himself." These words spake his parents, because they feared the Jews: for the Jews had agreed already, that if any man did confess that he was Christ, he should be put out of the synagogue. Therefore said his parents, "He is of age; ask him."

Then again called they the man that was blind, and said unto him, "Give God the praise: we know that this man is a sinner."

"ONCE I WAS BLIND; NOW I SEE"

He answered and said, "Whether he be a sinner or no, I know not: one thing I know, that, whereas I was blind, now I see."

Then said they to him again, "What did he to thee? How opened he thine eyes?"

He answered them, "I have told you already, and ye did not hear. Wherefore would ye hear it again? Will ye also be his disciples?"

Then they reviled him, and said, "Thou art his disciple; but we are Moses' disciples. We know that God spake unto Moses: as for this fellow, we know not from whence he is."

The man answered and said unto them, "Why, herein is a marvelous thing, that ye know not from whence he is, and yet he hath opened mine eyes. Now we know that God heareth not sinners: but if any man be a worshiper of God, and doeth his will, him he heareth. Since the world began was it not heard that any man opened the eyes of one that was born blind. If this man were not of God, he could do nothing."

They answered and said unto him, "Thou wast altogether born in sins, and dost thou teach us?" And they cast him out.

Jesus heard that they had cast him out; and when he had found him, he said unto him, "Dost thou believe on the Son of God?"

He answered and said, "Who is he, Lord, that I might believe on him?"

And Jesus said unto him, "Thou hast both seen him, and it is he that talketh with thee."

And he said, "Lord, I believe." And he worshiped him.

And Jesus said, "For judgment I am come into this

world, that they which see not might see; and that they which see might be made blind."

And some of the Pharisees which were with him heard these words, and said unto him, "Are we blind also?"

Jesus said unto them, "If ye were blind, ye should have no sin: but now ye say, 'We see'; therefore your sin remaineth."
— John 9.

### "THE KING OF LOVE MY SHEPHERD IS"

The King of love my Shepherd is,
  Whose goodness faileth never;
I nothing lack if I am His,
  And He is mine forever.

Where streams of living water flow
  My ransomed soul He leadeth,
And where the verdant pastures grow,
  With food celestial feedeth.

Perverse and foolish oft I strayed,
  But yet in love He sought me,
And on His shoulder gently laid,
  And home, rejoicing, brought me.

In death's dark vale I fear no ill
  With Thee, dear Lord, beside me;
Thy rod and staff my comfort still,
  Thy cross before to guide me.

And so, through all the length of days
  Thy goodness faileth never;
Good Shepherd, may I sing Thy praise
  Within Thy house forever.
— *Sir H. W. Baker.*

"Verily, verily, I say unto you, he that entereth not by the door into the fold of the sheep, but climbeth up some other way, the same is a thief and a robber. But he that entereth in by the door is the shepherd of the sheep. To him the porter openeth; and the sheep hear his voice: and he calleth his own sheep by name, and leadeth them out. And when he putteth forth his own sheep, he goeth before them, and the sheep follow him: for they know his voice. And a stranger will they not follow, but will flee from him: for they know not the voice of strangers."

This parable spake Jesus unto them: but they understood not what things they were which he spake unto them.

Then said Jesus unto them again, "Verily, verily, I say unto you, I am the door of the sheep. All that ever came before me are thieves and robbers: but the sheep did not hear them. I am the door: by me if any man enter in, he shall be saved, and shall go in and out, and find pasture. The thief cometh not, but for to steal, and to kill, and to destroy: I am come that they might have life, and that they might have it more abundantly. I am the good shepherd: the good shepherd giveth his life for the sheep. But he that is an hireling, and not the shepherd, whose own the sheep are not, seeth the wolf coming, and leaveth the sheep, and fleeth: and the wolf catcheth them and scattereth the sheep. The hireling fleeth, because he is an hireling, and careth not for the sheep. I am the good shepherd, and know my sheep, and am known of mine. As the Father knoweth me, even so know I the Father: and I lay down my life for the sheep. And other sheep I have, which are not of this fold: them also I must bring, and they shall hear my voice; and there shall be one fold, and one shepherd. Therefore doth my Father love me, because I lay down my life, that I might take it again. No man taketh it from me, but I lay it down of myself. I have power to lay it down,

and I have power to take it again. This commandment
have I received of my Father." There was a division
therefore again among the Jews for these sayings. And
many of them said, "He hath a devil, and is mad; why
hear ye him?"

Others said, "These are not the words of him that
hath a devil. Can a devil open the eyes of the blind?"

— John 10:1–21.

## JESUS AT THE FEAST OF DEDICATION

And it was at Jerusalem the feast of the dedication,
and it was winter. And Jesus walked in the temple in
Solomon's porch. Then came the Jews round about him,
and said unto him, "How long dost thou make us to
doubt? If thou be the Christ, tell us plainly."

Jesus answered them, "I told you, and ye believed
not: the works that I do in my Father's name, they bear
witness of me. But ye believe not, because ye are not
of my sheep, as I said unto you. My sheep hear my voice,
and I know them, and they follow me: and I give unto
them eternal life; and they shall never perish, neither
shall any man pluck them out of my hand. My Father,
which gave them me, is greater than all; and no man is
able to pluck them out of my Father's hand. I and my
Father are one."

Then the Jews took up stones again to stone him.

Jesus answered them, "Many good works have I
showed you from my Father; for which of those works do
ye stone me?"

The Jews answered him, saying, "For a good work
we stone thee not; but for blasphemy; and because that
thou, being a man, makest thyself God."

Jesus answered them, "Is it not written in your law,
'I said, Ye are gods'? If he called them gods, unto whom

the word of God came, and the scripture cannot be broken; say ye of him, whom the Father hath sanctified, and sent into the world, 'Thou blasphemest'; because I said, 'I am the Son of God'? If I do not the works of my Father, believe me not. But if I do, though ye believe not me, believe the works: that ye may know, and believe, that the Father is in me, and I in him."

Therefore they sought again to take him: but he escaped out of their hand, and went away again beyond Jordan into the place where John at first baptized; and there he abode. And many resorted unto him, and said, "John did no miracle: but all things that John spake of this man were true." And many believed on him there.

— John 10:22–42.

IF THE BLIND
LEAD THE BLIND

*Photograph by*
*Frances Jenkins Olcott*

Blind men are often seen in Jerusalem, for diseases of the eye are a scourge in Palestine. We often see one blind man leading another, like these Arab Moslem Sheikhs. The white band they wear around the fez, signifies that they have made the Pilgrimage to Mecca, the Moslem's most sacred city.

This scene illustrates the Lord Jesus' words, "Can the blind lead the blind? Shall they not both fall into the ditch?"

Can you tell the real meaning of his words? For the answer read Luke 6, pages 89–90.

# The Raising of Lazarus

By Fra Angelico da Fiesole (1387-1455)
In the Museum of the Monastery of San Marco, Florence
Photograph by Alinari Brothers, Florence, Italy

THE story of the raising of Lazarus begins on page 301.

THE story of the raising of Lazarus begins on page 301.

Fra Angelico's picture shows us the moment when Lazarus comes forth from the tomb at the command of the Saviour. Lazarus stands wrapped in the grave-clothes behind his sisters, Mary and Martha, who are kneeling in gratitude and worship before the Master. What a beautiful gesture of welcome and friendship is Jesus' outstretched hand! His whole figure as well as the deed speaks of compassion and love for this family of Bethany whom our Lord loved to visit. At the left two figures start away from Lazarus as if in fear, while on the right the disciples and others crowd around in reverent amazement.

It is a dramatic scene delicately rendered. A study of the faces and heads and hands reveals much sensitive characterization. Jesus here is the perfection of a type created by Giotto, as you will see when you compare this with Giotto's picture on page 308. But Fra Angelico has painted a less austere, less remote Saviour who seems more human and yet all divine.

This little picture is another of the series on the Life of Christ ornamenting originally a cabinet which held the silver treasures of a chapel in the Church of the Annunciation in Florence. These paintings may now be seen in the Museum connected with the Monastery of San Marco, one of the Dominican convents where Fra Angelico lived.

Fra Angelico joined the Dominican order of monks at the age of twenty. He was admitted at the convent of Fiesole, near his home in Vicchio, was given the name of Fra (brother) Giovanni, and because of his sweet and devout character was soon called Fra Angelico (angel). His work and his life earned for him the name, "the artist saint."

# The Story of the Master

## From the Gospel of John

## Jesus and His Friends

### THE RAISING OF LAZARUS

NOW a certain man was sick, named Lazarus, of Bethany, the town of Mary and her sister Martha. (It was that Mary which anointed the Lord with ointment, and wiped his feet with her hair, whose brother Lazarus was sick.) Therefore his sisters sent unto him, saying, "Lord, behold, he whom thou lovest is sick."

When Jesus heard that, he said, "This sickness is not unto death, but for the glory of God, that the Son of God might be glorified thereby."

Now Jesus loved Martha, and her sister, and Lazarus. When he had heard therefore that he was sick, he abode two days still in the same place where he was. Then after that saith he to his disciples, "Let us go into Judæa again."

His disciples say unto him, "Master, the Jews of late sought to stone thee; and goest thou thither again?"

Jesus answered, "Are there not twelve hours in the day? If any man walk in the day, he stumbleth not, because he seeth the light of this world. But if a man walk in the night, he stumbleth, because there is no light in him." These things said he: and after that he saith unto them, "Our friend Lazarus sleepeth; but I go, that I may awake him out of sleep."

Then said his disciples, "Lord, if he sleep, he shall do well."

Howbeit Jesus spake of his death: but they thought that he had spoken of taking of rest in sleep. Then said Jesus unto them plainly, "Lazarus is dead. And I am glad for your sakes that I was not there, to the intent ye may believe; nevertheless let us go unto him."

Then said Thomas, which is called Didymus, unto his fellow disciples, "Let us also go, that we may die with him."

Then when Jesus came, he found that he had lain in the grave four days already. Now Bethany was nigh unto Jerusalem, about fifteen furlongs off: and many of the Jews came to Martha and Mary to comfort them concerning their brother. Then Martha, as soon as she heard that Jesus was coming, went and met him: but Mary sat still in the house. Then said Martha unto Jesus, "Lord, if thou hadst been here, my brother had not died. But I know, that even now, whatsoever thou wilt ask of God, God will give it thee."

Jesus saith unto her, "Thy brother shall rise again."

Martha saith unto him, "I know that he shall rise again in the resurrection at the last day."

Jesus said unto her, "I am the resurrection and the life: he that believeth in me, though he were dead, yet shall he live: and whosoever liveth and believeth in me shall never die. Believest thou this?"

She saith unto him, "Yea, Lord: I believe that thou art the Christ, the Son of God, which should come into the world." And when she had so said, she went her way, and called Mary, her sister, secretly, saying, "The Master is come, and calleth for thee."

As soon as she heard that, she arose quickly, and came unto him. Now Jesus was not yet come into the town, but was in that place where Martha met him.

## THE LIGHT OF THE WORLD

By William Holman Hunt (1827–1910)
Used by special permission of the Warden and Council
of Keble College, Oxford, England

THE ORIGINAL of this famous picture is owned by Keble
College, Oxford, and is hung in a small room adjoining
the chapel.

"The legend beneath it is the beautiful verse—'Behold I
stand at the door and knock. If any man hear my voice,
and open the door, I will come in to him, and will sup with
him, and he with me.' Rev. 3:20. On the left-hand side
of the picture is seen this door of the human soul. It is
fast barred; its bars and nails are rusty; it is knitted
and bound to its stanchions by creeping tendrils of ivy,
showing that it has never been opened. A bat hovers
about it; its threshold is overgrown with brambles, net-
tles, and fruitless corn,—the wild grass,'whereof the mower
filleth not his hand, nor he that bindeth the sheaves his
bosom.' Christ approaches it in the night-time,—Christ
in his everlasting offices, of Prophet, Priest, and King. He
wears the white robe, representing the power of the Spirit
upon him; the jeweled robe and breastplate, representing
the sacerdotal investiture; the rayed crown of gold, in-
woven with the crown of thorns; not dead thorns, but now
bearing soft leaves, for the healing of the nations.

"Now, when Christ enters any human heart, he bears
with him a twofold light: first, the light of conscience,
which displays past sin, and afterwards the light of peace,
the hope of salvation. The lantern, carried in Christ's
left hand, is this light of conscience. Its fire is red and
fierce; it falls only on the closed door, on the weeds which
encumber it, and on an apple shaken from one of the trees
of the orchard, thus marking that the entire awakening of
the conscience is not merely to committed, but to heredi-
tary guilt.

"The light is suspended by a chain wrapt about the
wrist of the figure, shewing that the light which reveals
sin appears to the sinner also to chain the hand of Christ.
The light which proceeds from the head of the Saviour,
on the contrary, is that of the hope of salvation; it springs
from the crown of thorns, and, though itself sad, subdued,
and full of softness, is yet so powerful that it entirely
melts into the glow of it the forms of the leaves and boughs,
which it crosses, shewing that every earthly object must
be hidden by this light, where its sphere extends."—Ruskin,
"Arrows of the Chase."

BETHANY

*Photograph by W. A. Pottenger expressly for The Book of Life*

This town was the residence of Mary and Martha whose home Jesus so loved to visit.

TOMB OF LAZARUS—
BETHANY

*Photograph by W. A. Pottenger expressly for The Book of Life*

This is the reputed tomb in which Lazarus was buried and from which he came forth at the call of Jesus.

The Jews then which were with her in the house, and comforted her, when they saw Mary, that she rose up hastily and went out, followed her, saying, "She goeth unto the grave to weep there."

Then when Mary was come where Jesus was, and saw him, she fell down at his feet, saying unto him, "Lord, if thou hadst been here, my brother had not died."

When Jesus therefore saw her weeping, and the Jews also weeping which came with her, he groaned in the spirit, and was troubled, and said, "Where have ye laid him?"

They said unto him, "Lord, come and see." Jesus wept.

Then said the Jews, "Behold how he loved him!"

And some of them said, "Could not this man, which opened the eyes of the blind, have caused that even this man should not have died?" Jesus therefore again groaning in himself cometh to the grave. It was a cave, and a stone lay upon it.

Jesus said, "Take ye away the stone."

Martha, the sister of him that was dead, saith unto him, "Lord, by this time he stinketh: for he hath been dead four days."

Jesus saith unto her, "Said I not unto thee, that, if thou wouldest believe, thou shouldest see the glory of God?"

Then they took away the stone from the place where the dead was laid. And Jesus lifted up his eyes, and said, "Father, I thank thee that thou hast heard me. And I knew that thou hearest me always: but because of the people which stand by I said it, that they may believe that thou hast sent me."

And when he thus had spoken, he cried with a loud voice, "Lazarus, come forth."

And he that was dead came forth, bound hand and foot with graveclothes: and his face was bound about with a napkin.

Jesus saith unto them, "Loose him, and let him go."

Then many of the Jews which came to Mary, and had seen the things which Jesus did, believed on him. But some of them went their ways to the Pharisees, and told them what things Jesus had done. — John 11:1–46.

# The Raising of Lazarus

By Giotto di Bondone (1266-1336)
In the Chapel of the Arena, Padua, Italy
Photograph by Alinari Brothers, Florence

THE Bible story pictured here begins on page 301. It is the moment when Jesus "cried with a loud voice, 'Lazarus come forth.' And he that was dead came forth bound hand and foot with graveclothes."

We see Jesus with Mary and Martha kneeling at his feet. Two boys are carrying away the stone which lay upon the tomb. Our eyes are drawn to the pallor of Lazarus' face, the incredulous amazement of the bystanders, the sublime gesture of Christ and the tense interest of the disciples. The two sisters do not greet their brother Lazarus. The moment is too awful, the occasion too tremendous for expressions of joy. They are lost in wonder and gratitude. What reality is here given to this beautiful act of divine friendship!

Do you find, in Fra Angelico's picture on page 300, a similar restrained emotion expressed by the figures and echoed by the severe landscape? It is hard to believe that these two pictures were painted one hundred and fifty years apart. But look closely. Has not Fra Angelico created a more life-like and individual type of person and a more natural landscape than Giotto? These differences tell us that Fra Angelico lived close enough to the oncoming Renaissance period to share its enthusiastic interest in man and nature and its greater skill in representation. Giotto's age, however, was interested in other things.

Giotto's painting is from a series of frescoes which adorn the interior walls of the Arena Chapel at Padua. The colors Giotto has used are of the loveliest. The whites of the classical draperies dominate yet reflect the rose, pale blue or gray green nearby. It is a bright and original color scheme balancing crimsons and azures with violets and greens.

For other pictures by Giotto see pages 36, 230 and 332.

## The Pharisees Are Alarmed Because of the Popularity of Jesus

Then gathered the chief priests and the Pharisees a council, and said, "What do we? For this man doeth many miracles. If we let him thus alone, all men will believe on him: and the Romans shall come and take away both our place and nation."

And one of them, named Caiaphas, being the high priest that same year, said unto them, "Ye know nothing at all, nor consider that it is expedient for us, that one man should die for the people, and that the whole nation perish not." And this spake he not of himself: but being high priest that year, he prophesied that Jesus should die for that nation; and not for that nation only, but that also he should gather together in one the children of God that were scattered abroad.

Then from that day forth they took counsel together for to put him to death. Jesus therefore walked no more openly among the Jews; but went thence unto a country near to the wilderness, into a city called Ephraim, and there continued with his disciples.　　　— John 11:47-54.

HOME OF MARY AND MARTHA
*Photograph by the Rev. Frederick J. Moore*
Ruins of the house of Mary and Martha, Bethany. See page **305.**

# The Story of the Master

From the Gospel of John

## The Last Days at Jerusalem

Beginning with the words, "These things spake Jesus and departed, and did hide himself from them," a new and most important crisis came in Jesus' life. The section which follows is the Gospel's summary of his public ministry. He had not won all the people. Plots were being formed against his life, but many believed on him secretly. Then the author gives the words of Jesus, summing up his own teaching. After this Jesus turns from the public to his own disciples to prepare them for the future.

### THE PASSOVER IS AT HAND

ND the Jews' passover was nigh at hand: and many went out of the country up to Jerusalem before the passover, to purify themselves. Then sought they for Jesus, and spake among themselves, as they stood in the temple, "What think ye, that he will not come to the feast?"

Now both the chief priests and the Pharisees had given a commandment, that, if any man knew where he were, he should show it, that they might take him. —John 11:55-57.

### JESUS IS ANOINTED BY MARY OF BETHANY

The gospels tell the story of two anointings of Jesus: one by the woman who was a sinner; and one by Mary of Bethany, who had been for a long time a friend of Jesus. Perhaps Mary of Bethany had heard of the gracious act of the other Mary, and she was glad to show the Master the same courtesy and distinction. It was a royal honor, for so kings were anointed.

310

# Jesus at the House of Mary and Martha

### By Hendrik Siemiradski (1843-1902)
### In the Alexandre III Museum, Leningrad, Russia

THIS scene is laid in a beautiful Eastern garden where brilliant sunlight filters through vine trellises and olive branches to the figures and ground below. In the foreground are two people quietly talking. The rest of the scene is full of the movement of the dancing light, the fluttering pigeons and the woman approaching carrying a water jar on her shoulder. Even the distant landscape seems to quiver with life.

Can you name the persons represented here? Have you read the stories of what happened at this home while Jesus was there? The account as given in Luke will be found on page 143. Another incident recorded by John begins on page 312. It is easy to understand why our Lord loved to stop with these friends in Bethany whenever He passed that way.

The Polish artist, Hendrik Siemiradski, was born in Charkof, Russia, in 1843. He began his education at the St. Petersburg Academy but laid the foundation of his art in Munich, Germany, under the noted teacher, Piloty. From Munich, Siemiradski went to Rome where he remained until his death in 1902. During his life he received many medals and honors.

Siemiradski belonged to the new realistic European school which in the 1880's was exercising a vast influence in every province of art. Older painters of sacred subjects looked upon anything like a naturalistic treatment as irreverent. But younger artists believed that sacred personages should be treated from the same point of view as ordinary mortals, and that surroundings and actions should be natural. Here, Siemiradski has, without detracting from the beauty and dignity of the Bible characters, shown us the human quality of Jesus' relations with His followers. We owe much to artists like Siemiradski for they have helped to bring the Saviour's life and teachings nearer to us.

Then Jesus six days before the passover came to Bethany, where Lazarus was which had been dead, whom he raised from the dead. There they made him a supper; and Martha served: but Lazarus was one of them that sat at the table with him. Then took Mary a pound of ointment of spikenard, very costly, and anointed the feet of Jesus, and wiped his feet with her hair: and the house was filled with the odour of the ointment.

Then saith one of his disciples, Judas Iscariot, Simon's son, which should betray him, "Why was not this ointment sold for three hundred pence, and given to the poor?"

This he said, not that he cared for the poor; but because he was a thief, and had the bag, and bare what was put therein.

Then said Jesus, "Let her alone: against the day of my burying hath she kept this. For the poor always ye have with you; but me ye have not always." Much people of the Jews therefore knew that he was there: and they came not for Jesus' sake only, but that they might see Lazarus also, whom he had raised from the dead.

But the chief priests consulted that they might put Lazarus also to death; because that by reason of him many of the Jews went away, and believed on Jesus.

—John 12:1–11.

### THE TRIUMPHAL ENTRY

On the next day much people that were come to the feast, when they heard that Jesus was coming to Jerusalem, took branches of palm-trees, and went forth to meet him, and cried, "Hosanna: Blessed is the King of Israel that cometh in the name of the Lord."

And Jesus, when he had found a young ass, sat thereon; as it is written. "Fear not, daughter of Sion: behold, thy King cometh, sitting on an ass's colt."

These things understood not his disciples at the first: but when Jesus was glorified, then remembered they that these things were written of him, and that they had done these things unto him.  The people therefore that was with him when he called Lazarus out of his grave, and raised him from the dead, bare record.  For this cause the people also met him, for that they heard that he had done this miracle.  The Pharisees therefore said among themselves, "Perceive ye how ye prevail nothing? Behold, the world is gone after him."          — John 11:55—12:19.

## The Greeks Desire to See Jesus

"AND I, IF I BE LIFTED UP FROM THE EARTH, WILL DRAW ALL MEN UNTO ME."

And there were certain Greeks among them that came up to worship at the feast.  The same came therefore to Philip, which was of Bethsaida of Galilee, and desired him, saying, "Sir, we would see Jesus."

Philip cometh and telleth Andrew: and again Andrew and Philip tell Jesus.  And Jesus answered them, saying, "The hour is come, that the Son of man should be glorified.  Verily, verily, I say unto you, except a corn of wheat fall into the ground and die, it abideth alone: but if it die, it bringeth forth much fruit.  He that loveth his life shall lose it; and he that hateth his life in this world shall keep it unto life eternal.  If any man serve me, let him follow me; and where I am, there shall also my servant be: if any man serve me, him will my Father honour.  Now is my soul troubled; and what shall I say?  Father, save me from this hour: but for this cause came I unto this hour.  Father, glorify thy name."

Then came there a voice from heaven, saying, "I have both glorified it, and will glorify it again."

VIA DOLOROSA

*Photograph by W. A. Pottenger expressly for The Book of Life*

This is the Sixth Station of the Cross.

THE VIA DOLOROSA

*Photograph by W. A. Pottenger expressly for The Book of Life*

The Via Dolorosa, the way of Jesus to the Cross, contains fourteen tablets which mark the fourteen stations of the Cross. The tablet in the picture is at the spot where the street is crossed by the "Ecce Homo Arch" marking the spot where according to tradition Pilate uttered the words "Behold the Man."

THE FIFTH STATION OF THE CROSS, JERUSALEM

*Photograph by W. A. Pottenger expressly for The Book of Life*

The point at which Simon of Cyrene is said to have taken up the cross. Over the windows are the words: "Simoni Cyrenae crux imponitur" (The cross is taken by Simon of Cyrene.) The Via Dolorosa is one of the most solemnly impressive streets in the world.

The people therefore, that stocd by, and heard it, said that it thundered: others said, "An angel spake to him."

Jesus answered and said, "This voice came not because of me, but for your sakes. Now is the judgment of this world: now shall the prince of this world be cast out. And I, if I be lifted up from the earth, will draw all men unto me." This he said, signifying what death he should die.

The people answered him, "We have heard out of the law that Christ abideth forever: and how sayest thou, 'The Son of man must be lifted up'? Who is this Son of man?"

Then Jesus said unto them, "Yet a little while is the light with you. Walk while ye have the light, lest darkness come upon you: for he that walketh in darkness knoweth not whither he goeth. While ye have light, believe in the light, that ye may be the children of light."

These things spake Jesus, and departed, and did hide himself from them. — John 12:20-36.

## MANY SECRETLY BELIEVE ON JESUS

But though he had done so many miracles before them, yet they believed not on him: that the saying of Esaias, the prophet, might be fulfilled, which he spake,

"LORD, who hath believed our report?
And to whom hath the arm of the LORD been revealed?"

Therefore they could not believe because that Esaias said again,

"He hath blinded their eyes, and hardened their heart;
That they should not see with their eyes, nor understand with their heart,

# Jesus Washing the Disciples' Feet

By Fra Angelico da Fiesole (1387-1455)
In the Museum of the Monastery of San Marco, Florence
Photograph by Alinari Brothers, Florence, Italy

THE Bible account of the scene pictured here begins on page 320. From it we learn that this event took place in the Upper Room in Jerusalem immediately after the Last Supper.

Pictured here is the moment when Jesus kneels before Peter preparing to wash the disciple's feet and Peter protests. What does Peter, after the Master has replied to his protest, ask Jesus to do? On the right, a disciple stands holding the pitcher of water. The rest are seated in a circle reverently watching, some preparing for their turns. It is a group of faithful, earnest men deeply moved by this great lesson in humility and love.

The artist has placed the scene at one end of a cloistered quadrangle. Through the pillars trees are seen growing in the open court. It seems to be afternoon from the way the cloister is lighted, which reminds us that artists did not know how to paint night-time effects in Fra Angelico's time. As we noticed on page 206, artists were still learning how to draw objects in perspective, that is as they recede from the eye into distance, such as the courtyard here.

After studying this picture, let us turn to page 324 and see how a nineteenth century English artist has treated the theme, and then to page 332 to a fourteenth century Italian artist's representation. Nearly one hundred and fifty years come between Giotto's painting and Fra Angelico's and four hundred years between Fra Angelico's painting and Ford Maddox Brown's. Thus, we have in these three pictures an expression of the artistic knowledge, talent and religious feeling of different generations, nationalities and personalities. Yet each still lives for us today as truly as it lived for its own age bearing witness to the timelessness of God-given talents and spiritual truths.

And be converted,
And I should heal them."

These things said Esaias, when he saw the glory, and spake of him.

Nevertheless among the chief rulers also many believed on him; but because of the Pharisees they did not confess him, lest they should be put out of the synagogue: for they loved the praise of men more than the praise of God.

Jesus cried and said, "He that believeth on me, believeth not on me, but on him that sent me. And he that seeth me seeth him that sent me. I am come a light into the world, that whosoever believeth on me should not abide in darkness. And if any man hear my words, and believe not, I judge him not: for I came not to judge the world, but to save the world. He that rejecteth me, and receiveth not my words, hath one that judgeth him: the word that I have spoken, the same shall judge him in the last day. For I have not spoken of myself; but the Father which sent me. He gave me a commandment, what I should say, and what I should speak. And I know that this commandment is life everlasting: whatsoever I speak therefore, even as the Father said unto me, so I speak."

— John 12:37–50.

## THE LAST SUPPER

Now before the feast of the passover, when Jesus knew that his hour was come that he should depart out of this world unto the Father, having loved his own which were in the world, he loved them unto the end. And supper being ended, the devil having now put into the heart of Judas Iscariot, Simon's son, to betray him, Jesus knowing that the Father had given all things into his hands, and that he was come from God, and went to

God, he riseth from supper, and laid aside his garments; and took a towel, and girded himself.

JESUS WASHES THE DISCIPLES' FEET

After that he poureth water into a bason, and began to wash the disciples' feet, and to wipe them with the towel wherewith he was girded.

Then cometh he to Simon Peter: and Peter saith unto him, "Lord, dost thou wash my feet?"

Jesus answered and said unto him, "What I do thou knowest not now; but thou shalt know hereafter."

Peter saith unto him, "Thou shalt never wash my feet."

Jesus answered him, "If I wash thee not, thou hast no part with me."

Simon Peter saith unto him, "Lord, not my feet only, but also my hands and my head."

Jesus saith to him, "He that is washed needeth not save to wash his feet, but is clean every whit: and ye are clean, but not all."

For he knew who should betray him; therefore said he, "Ye are not all clean."

So after he had washed their feet, and had taken his garments, and was set down again, he said unto them, "Know ye what I have done to you? Ye call me Master and Lord: and ye say well; for so I am. If I then, your Lord and Master, have washed your feet; ye also ought to wash one another's feet. For I have given you an example, that ye should do as I have done to you. Verily, verily, I say unto you, the servant is not greater than his lord; neither he that is sent greater than he that sent him. If ye know these things, happy are ye if ye do them."

JUDAS GOES OUT AND IT
IS NIGHT

"I speak not of you all:
I know whom I have
chosen: but that the scripture may be fulfilled, 'He
that eateth bread with me
hath lifted up his heel
against me.' Now I tell
you before it come, that,

CHURCH AT CALVARY

*Photograph by W. A. Pottenger expressly
for The Book of Life*

This modern Lutheran Church is
built near the supposed site of Calvary.

ENTRANCE TO THE CHURCH OF
THE HOLY SEPULCHER

*Photograph by W. A. Pottenger expressly
for The Book of Life*

This church is supposed to have
been built on the site of the sepulcher
of Jesus.

when it is come to pass, ye
may believe that I am he.
Verily, verily, I say unto
you, he that receiveth
whomsoever I send receiv-
eth me; and he that re-
ceiveth me receiveth him
that sent me."

When Jesus had thus
said, he was troubled in
spirit, and testified, and

said, "Verily, verily, I say unto you, that one of you shall betray me."

Then the disciples looked one on another, doubting of whom he spake. Now there was leaning on Jesus' bosom one of his disciples, whom Jesus loved. Simon Peter therefore beckoned to him, that he should ask who it should be of whom he spake. He then lying on Jesus' breast saith unto him, "Lord, who is it?"

Jesus answered, "He it is, to whom I shall give a sop, when I have dipped it." And when he had dipped the sop, he gave it to Judas Iscariot, the son of Simon. And after the sop Satan entered into him. Then said Jesus unto him, "That thou doest, do quickly." Now no man at the table knew for what intent he spake this unto him. For some of them thought, because Judas had the bag, that Jesus had said unto him, "Buy those things that we have need of against the feast;" or, that he should give something to the poor. He then having received the sop went immediately out: and it was night. — John 13:1–30.

### The Last, Tender Discourses of Jesus

Therefore, when he was gone out, Jesus said, "Now is the Son of man glorified, and God is glorified in him. If God be glorified in him, God shall also glorify him in himself, and shall straightway glorify him. Little children, yet a little while I am with you. Ye shall seek me: and as I said unto the Jews, 'Whither I go, ye cannot come'; so now I say to you. A new commandment I give unto you, that ye love one another; as I have loved you, that ye also love one another. By this shall all men know that ye are my disciples, if ye have love one to another."

Simon Peter said unto him, "Lord, whither goest thou?"

### JESUS WASHING PETER'S FEET

By Ford Madox Brown (1821–1893)
In the National (Tate) Gallery, London

THE ARTIST treats the incident of the
Last Supper with great spiritual power.
Nothing could show more plainly the
humility of the Master.

"He riseth from supper, and laid aside
his garments; and took a towel, and girded
himself.

"After that he poureth water into a basin,
and began to wash the disciples' feet, and
to wipe them with the towel wherewith he
was girded."—John 13:4, 5.

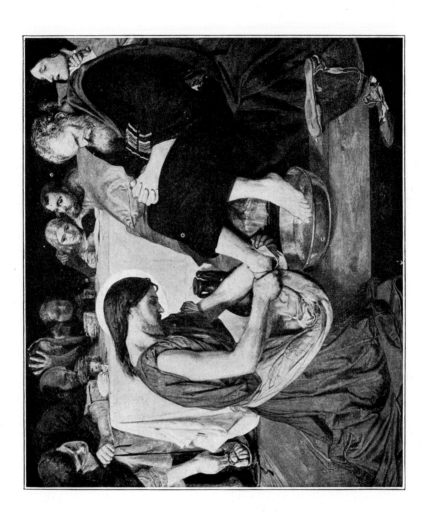

Jesus answered him, "Whither I go, thou canst not follow me now; but thou shalt follow me afterwards."

Peter said unto him, "LORD, why cannot I follow thee now? I will lay down my life for thy sake."

Jesus answered him, "Wilt thou lay down thy life for my sake? Verily, verily, I say unto thee, the cock shall not crow, till thou hast denied me thrice."

—John 13:31–38.

## "IN MY FATHER'S HOUSE ARE MANY MANSIONS"

"Let not your heart be troubled: ye believe in God, believe also in me. In my Father's house are many mansions: if it were not so, I would have told you. I go to prepare a place for you. And if I go and prepare a place for you, I will come again, and receive you unto myself; that where I am, there ye may be also. And whither I go ye know, and the way ye know."

Thomas saith unto him, "Lord, we know not whither thou goest; and how can we know the way?"

Jesus saith unto him, "I am the way, the truth, and the life: no man cometh unto the Father, but by me. If ye had known me, ye should have known my Father also: and from henceforth ye know him, and have seen him."

Philip saith unto him, "Lord, show us the Father, and it sufficeth us."

Jesus saith unto him, "Have I been so long time with you, and yet hast thou not known me, Philip? He that hath seen me hath seen the Father; and how sayest thou then, 'Show us the Father'? Believest thou not that I am in the Father, and the Father in me? The words that I speak unto you I speak not of myself: but the Father that dwelleth in me, he doeth the works. Believe me that I am in the Father, and the Father in me: or else believe me for the very works' sake. Verily, verily, I say unto you, he that believeth on me, the works that I do shall he do also; and greater works than these shall he do; because I go unto my Father. And whatsoever ye shall ask in my name, that will I do, that the Father may be glorified in the Son. If ye shall ask anything in my name, I will do it.

"If ye love me, keep my commandments. And I will pray the Father, and he shall give you another Comforter, that he may abide with you forever; even the Spirit of truth; whom the world cannot receive, because it seeth him not, neither knoweth him: but ye know him; for he dwelleth with you, and shall be in you. I will not leave you comfortless: I will come to you. Yet a little while, and the world seeth me no more; but ye see me: because I live, ye shall live also. At that day ye shall know that I am in my Father, and ye in me, and I in you. He that hath my commandments, and keepeth them, he it is that loveth me: and he that loveth me shall be loved of my Father, and I will love him, and will manifest myself to him."

Judas saith unto him, not Iscariot, "Lord, how is it that thou wilt manifest thyself unto us, and not unto the world?"

Jesus answered and said unto him, "If a man love me, he will keep my words: and my Father will love him, and we will come unto him, and make our abode with him. He that loveth me not keepeth not my sayings: and the word which ye hear is not mine, but the Father's which sent me.

"These things have I spoken unto you, being yet present with you. But the Comforter, which is the Holy Ghost, whom the Father will send in my name, he shall teach you all things, and bring all things to your remembrance, whatsoever I have said unto you. Peace I

# The Descent from the Cross

By Peter-Paul Rubens (1577-1640)
In the Cathedral, Antwerp, Belgium

THIS painting, one of the most greatly admired in the world, depicts several of Jesus' closest followers lowering his precious body from the cross with a winding-sheet. The account of this scene as told in John's gospel begins on page 353.

Jesus' friends are engaged in the age-old human drama of caring for the dead, here so supremely significant because it is the beloved Master to whom they minister. What an impression of inert weight expressed in the body of Jesus! His drooping figure, heroic even in death, is the center of interest toward which the others turn, framing it in.

The lifelessness of Jesus' body is emphasized by the living vigor of the other figures. Deep reverence and fear lest the sacred burden fall unify and animate the action. John strains backward to receive the weight of the body. Halfway up the ladders, Nicodemus, on the left, and Joseph of Arimathaea, help sustain the heavy burden, pausing momentarily to gaze upon Jesus, thus emphasizing the vivid exertion of the men at the top of the cross, one of whom is just releasing his hold, the other, bracing himself against the downward pull. The women draw sympathetically toward the helpless body. Mary Magdalene receives the feet, an action symbolizing her passionate sorrow and sense of unworthiness.

The love and the despair of these faithful friends are intense yet restrained, confined deep within the heart, where true sorrow keeps its vigil. This reserved emotion gives the painting its profound religious feeling. The painter has caught and powerfully expressed the eternal meaning of this event in the life of our Lord. We cannot forget this representation of it. Here elevated interpretation and skillful execution meet and produce a masterpiece. Another of Rubens' great paintings is in Volume VIII, page 249.

leave with you, my peace I give unto you: not as the world giveth, give I unto you. Let not your heart be troubled, neither let it be afraid. Ye have heard how I said unto you, I go away, and come again unto you. If ye loved me, ye would rejoice, because I said, I go unto the Father: for my Father is greater than I. And now I have told you before it come to pass, that, when it is come to pass, ye might believe. Hereafter I will not talk much with you: for the prince of this world cometh, and hath nothing in me. But that the world may know that I love the Father; and as the Father gave me commandment, even so I do. Arise, let us go hence." —John 14.

### "I AM THE VINE; YE ARE THE BRANCHES"

"I am the true vine, and my Father is the husbandman. Every branch in me that beareth not fruit he taketh away: and every branch that beareth fruit, he purgeth it, that it may bring forth more fruit. Now ye are clean through the word which I have spoken unto you. Abide in me, and I in you. As the branch cannot bear fruit of itself, except it abide in the vine; no more can ye, except ye abide in me. I am the vine, ye are the branches: he that abideth in me, and I in him, the same bringeth forth much fruit: for without me ye can do nothing. If a man abide not in me, he is cast forth as a branch, and is withered; and men gather them, and cast them into the fire, and they are burned. If ye abide in me, and my words abide in you, ye shall ask what ye will, and it shall be done unto you. Herein is my Father glorified, that ye bear much fruit; so shall ye be my disciples. As the Father hath loved me, so have I loved you: continue ye in my love. If ye keep my commandments, ye shall abide in my love; even as I have kept my Father's commandments, and abide in his love.

"These things have I spoken unto you, that my joy might remain in you, and that your joy might be full. This is my commandment, That ye love one another, as I have loved you. Greater love hath no man than this, that a man lay down his life for his friends. Ye are my friends, if ye do whatsoever I command you. Henceforth I call you not servants; for the servant knoweth not what his lord doeth: but I have called you friends; for all things that I have heard of my Father I have made known unto you. Ye have not chosen me, but I have chosen you, and ordained you, that ye should go and bring forth fruit, and that your fruit should remain: that whatsoever ye shall ask of the Father in my name, he may give it you.

"These things I command you, that ye love one another. If the world hate you, ye know that it hated me before it hated you. If ye were of the world, the world would love his own: but because ye are not of the world, but I have chosen you out of the world, therefore the world hateth you. Remember the word that I said unto you, 'The servant is not greater than his lord.' If they have persecuted me, they will also persecute you; if they have kept my saying, they will keep yours also. But all these things will they do unto you for my name's sake, because they know not him that sent me. If I had not come and spoken unto them, they had not had sin: but now they have no cloke for their sin. He that hateth me hateth my Father also. If I had not done among them the works which none other man did, they had not had sin: but now have they both seen and hated both me and my Father. But this cometh to pass, that the word might be fulfilled that is written in their law, 'They hated me without a cause.' But when the Comforter is come, whom I will send unto you from the

# Jesus Washing the Disciples' Feet

By Giotto di Bondone (1266-1337)
In the Chapel of the Arena, Padua, Italy
Photograph by Alinari Brothers, Florence

HERE we have a solemnly beautiful presentation of that moving scene in the Upper Room in Jerusalem immediately following the Last Supper wherein Jesus teaches his disciples the meaning of brotherly love. "If I then, your Lord and Master, have washed your feet; ye also ought to wash one another's feet." What character and devotion in this group of men! Study the heads of the disciples and see if you can name them. Which one's face is not shown? As you turn back to page 320 to read the Bible account, notice the pictures on pages 318 and 324.

In contrast with the work of a modern artist, such as Ford Maddox Brown whose powerful treatment of this theme appears on page 324, Giotto's figures seem too stiff and massive. But when compared with the work of a preceding artist of the 13th century, such as Cimabue whose hampered yet interesting style is shown on page 124 of Volume VIII, Giotto's figures are completely expressive.

This is one of six paintings by Giotto which we have studied. The two depicting the Adoration of the Wise Men and The Triumphal Entry are in Volume I on pages 268 and 350. The other four are in this Volume on pages 36, 230, 308 and here. All of these are from the series of frescoes on the life of Christ in the Arena Chapel at Padua, Italy.

Time has shown that Giotto was one of the greatest artists who ever lived. It was he who turned from artistic tradition to observation of nature and thereby infused into the art of painting a spirit of experimentation which led to the artistic triumphs of the Renaissance. You will find more about Giotto in Volume VIII beginning on page 125.

Father, even the Spirit of truth, which proceedeth from the Father, he shall testify of me: and ye also shall bear witness, because ye have been with me from the beginning."                                                —John 15.

## "THE HOUR COMETH"

"These things have I spoken unto you, that ye should not be offended. They shall put you out of the synagogues: yea, the time cometh, that whosoever killeth you will think that he doeth God service. And these things will they do unto you, because they have not known the Father, nor me. But these things have I told you, that when the time shall come, ye may remember that I told you of them. And these things I said not unto you at the beginning, because I was with you. But now I go my way to him that sent me; and none of you asketh me, 'Whither goest thou?' But because I have said these things unto you, sorrow hath filled your heart.

"Nevertheless I tell you the truth. It is expedient for you that I go away; for if I go not away, the Comforter will not come unto you; but if I depart, I will send him unto you. And when he is come, he will reprove the world of sin, and of righteousness, and of judgment: of sin, because they believe not on me; of righteousness, because I go to my Father, and ye see me no more; of judgment, because the prince of this world is judged.

"I have yet many things to say unto you, but ye cannot bear them now. Howbeit when he, the Spirit of truth, is come, he will guide you into all truth: for he shall not speak of himself; but whatsoever he shall hear, that shall he speak: and he will show you things to come. He shall glorify me: for he shall receive of mine, and shall show it unto you. All things that the Father hath are mine: therefore said I, that he shall take of mine, and shall show it unto you. A little while, and ye shall not see me: and again, a little while, and ye shall see me, because I go to the Father."

Then said some of his disciples among themselves, "What is this that he saith unto us, 'A little while, and ye shall not see me: and again, a little while, and ye shall see me': and, 'Because I go to the Father'?"

They said therefore, "What is this that he saith, 'A little while'? We cannot tell what he saith."

Now Jesus knew that they were desirous to ask him, and said unto them, "Do ye enquire among yourselves of that I said, 'A little while, and ye shall not see me: and again, a little while, and ye shall see me'? Verily, verily, I say unto you, that ye shall weep and lament, but the world shall rejoice: and ye shall be sorrowful, but your sorrow shall be turned into joy. A woman when she is in travail hath sorrow, because her hour is come: but as soon as she is delivered of the child, she remembereth no more the anguish, for joy that a man is born into the world. And ye now therefore have sorrow: but I will see you again, and your heart shall rejoice, and your joy no man taketh from you.

"And in that day ye shall ask me nothing. Verily, verily, I say unto you, whatsoever ye shall ask the Father in my name, he will give it you. Hitherto have ye asked nothing in my name: ask, and ye shall receive, that your joy may be full. These things have I spoken unto you in proverbs: but the time cometh, when I shall no more speak unto you in proverbs, but I shall show you plainly of the Father. At that day ye shall ask in my name: and I say not unto you, that I will pray the Father for you: for the Father himself loveth you, because ye have loved me, and have believed that I came out from God. I came forth from the Father, and am

# Jesus in Gethsemane

By Heinrich Hofmann (1824-1911)
In the Riverside Church, New York City

AFTER Jesus' last prayer with his disciples, see page 338, he took Peter, James and John and went into the garden to gather strength for the supreme ordeal that was at hand. Matthew's account of this momentous hour begins on page 208. The agony of spirit that Jesus suffered, just before his betrayal, is described by Luke: "Being in an agony, he prayed more earnestly: and his sweat was as it were great drops of blood falling down to the ground."

Sidney Lanier in his *Ballad of the Trees and the Master*, gives the inner meaning of this lonely struggle.

"Into the woods my Master went
Clean forspent, forspent.
Into the woods my Master came,
Forspent with love and shame.
But the olives they were not blind to Him;
The little gray leaves were kind to Him;
The thorn-tree had a mind to Him
When into the woods He came.

Out of the woods my Master went,
And He was well content.
Out of the woods my Master came,
Content with death and shame.
When Death and Shame would woo Him last,
From under the trees they drew Him last:
'Twas on a tree they slew Him—last
When out of the woods He came."

The artist has chosen that exalted moment when, the conflict past, Jesus says, "Not my will but thine be done." In the dim background rises the city and on a nearby slope are the reclining figures of the three disciples. The "garden" of bare rock symbolizes the relentless fate ahead of Jesus and the thornbush, tomorrow's crown. The light about the Saviour's head is the outward sign of the glory of his spiritual victory, and the light streaming from heaven is the smile of the approving Father. Faith is the victory!

come into the world: again, I leave the world, and go to the Father."

His disciples said unto him, "Lo, now speakest thou plainly, and speakest no proverb. Now are we sure that thou knowest all things, and needest not that any man should ask thee: by this we believe that thou camest forth from God."

Jesus answered them, "Do ye now believe? Behold, the hour cometh, yea, is now come, that ye shall be scattered, every man to his own, and shall leave me alone: and yet I am not alone, because the Father is with me. These things I have spoken unto you, that in me ye might have peace. In the world ye shall have tribulation: but be of good cheer; I have overcome the world."

—John 16.

## ROCK OF AGES

Rock of Ages, cleft for me!
Let me hide myself in Thee;
Let the water and the blood,
From Thy riven side which flowed
Be of sin the double cure,
Cleanse me from its guilt and power.

Not the labors of my hands
Can fulfil Thy law's demands;
Could my zeal no respite know,
Could my tears forever flow,
All for sin could not atone;
Thou must save, and Thou alone.

Nothing in my hand I bring;
Simply to Thy cross I cling;
Naked, come to Thee for dress;
Helpless, look to Thee for grace;
Foul, I to the fountain fly;
Wash me, Saviour, or I die.

—*Augustus Montague Topiady.*

## The Prayer of Jesus

**These** words spake Jesus, and lifted up his eyes to heaven, and said, "Father, the hour is come; glorify thy Son, that thy Son also may glorify thee: as thou hast given him power over all flesh, that he should give eternal life to as many as thou hast given him. And this is life eternal, that they might know thee the only true God, and Jesus Christ, whom thou hast sent. I have glorified thee on the earth: I have finished the work which thou gavest me to do. And now, O Father, glorify thou me with thine own self with the glory which I had with thee before the world was. I have manifested thy name unto the men which thou gavest me out of the world: thine they were, and thou gavest them me; and they have kept thy word. Now they have known that all things whatsoever thou hast given me are of thee.

"For I have given unto them the words which thou gavest me; and they have received them, and have known surely that I came out from thee, and they have believed that thou didst send me. I pray for them: I pray not for the world, but for them which thou hast given me; for they are thine. And all mine are thine, and thine are mine; and I am glorified in them. And now I am no more in the world, but these are in the world, and I come to thee. Holy Father, keep through thine own name those whom thou hast given me, that they may be one, as we are. While I was with them in the world, I kept them in thy name: those that thou gavest me I have kept, and none of them is lost, but the son of perdition, that the scripture might be fulfilled. And now come I to thee; and these things I speak in the world, that they might have my joy fulfilled in themselves. I have given them thy word; and the world hath hated them, because they are not of the world, even as I am not of the world.

# Jesus in the Garden of Gethsemane

By Fra Angelico da Fiesole (1387-1455)
In the Museum of the Monastery of San Marco, Florence
Photograph by Alinari Brothers, Florence, Italy

THE Bible tells us that after the Last Supper and the washing of the disciples' feet, the company went out "unto a place called Gethsemane" where there was a garden. Jesus selected Peter, James and John to watch with Him. But while He prayed, the disciples fell asleep. It was that dark hour just before the betrayal and arrest. The story may be read beginning on pages 208 and 342.

The artist has shown the figure of Jesus in the distance with an angel above him. The three disciples are in the foreground, too weary to stay awake, little dreaming of what is to come. The scene is laid in a hilly place where trees and flowers are growing.

Once again we notice that Fra Angelico has not been able to give us a night-time effect. But his interest in the individual and his sympathy with nature, characteristics of the coming Renaissance era, are given in Fra Angelico's own delightful way with all the knowledge and skill at his command. It is interesting to compare this early master with a nineteenth century artist, Heinrich Hofmann, whose well-known picture is given on page 336.

Fra Angelico's picture is another of the series of thirty-five on the Life of Christ, several of which we have already studied in this Volume on pages 178, 206, 210, 214, 250, 300 and 318. They were all painted on the doors of a silver-press belonging to one of the chapels in the Church of the Annunciation in Florence and may now be seen in the Museum of San Marco in Florence. On pages 130 and 389 we can get an idea of the delicate colors that Fra Angelico used.

I pray not that thou shouldest take them out of the world, but that thou shouldest keep them from the evil. They are not of the world, even as I am not of the world. Sanctify them through thy truth: thy word is truth. As thou hast sent me into the world, even so have I also sent them into the world. And for their sakes I sanctify myself, that they also might be sanctified through the truth. Neither pray I for these alone, but for them also which shall believe on me through their word; that they all may be one; as thou, Father, art in me, and I in thee, that they also may be one in us: that the world may believe that thou hast sent me. And the glory which thou gavest me I have given them; that they may be one, even as we are one: I in them, and thou in me, that they may be made perfect in one; and that the world may know that thou hast sent me, and hast loved them, as thou hast loved me. Father, I will that they also, whom thou hast given me, be with me where I am; that they may behold my glory, which thou hast given me: for thou lovedst me before the foundation of the world. O righteous Father, the world hath not known thee: but I have known thee, and these have known that thou hast sent me. And I have declared unto them thy name and will declare it: that the love wherewith thou hast loved me may be in them, and I in them." —John 17.

### O FOR A CLOSER WALK WITH GOD

O for a closer walk with God,
  A calm and heavenly frame,
A light to shine upon the road
  That leads me to the Lamb!

Return, O Holy Dove, return,
  Sweet messenger of rest!
I hate the sins that made Thee mourn,
  And drove Thee from my breast.

The dearest idol I have known,
  Whate'er that idol be,
Help me to tear it from Thy throne,
  And worship only Thee.

So shall my walk be close with God,
  Calm and serene my frame;
So purer light shall mark the road
  That leads me to the Lamb.
                        —*William Cowper.*

## In the Garden of Gethsemane

When Jesus had spoken these words, he went forth with his disciples over the brook Cedron, where was a garden, into the which he entered and his disciples. And Judas also, which betrayed him, knew the place: for Jesus ofttimes resorted thither with his disciples. Judas then, having received a band of men and officers from the chief priests and Pharisees, cometh thither with lanterns and torches and weapons. Jesus therefore, knowing all things that should come upon him, went forth, and said unto them, "Whom seek ye?"

They answered him, "Jesus of Nazareth."

Jesus saith unto them, "I am he." And Judas also, which betrayed him, stood with them. As soon then as he had said unto them, "I am he," they went backward, and fell to the ground.

Then asked he them again, "Whom seek ye?"

And they said, "Jesus of Nazareth."

Jesus answered, "I have told you that I am he: if therefore ye seek me, let these go their way": that the saying might be fulfilled, which he spake, "Of them which thou gavest me have I lost none."

Then Simon Peter having a sword drew it, and smote the high priest's servant, and cut off his right ear. The

# Jesus Before Caiaphas

By Fra Angelico da Fiesole (1387-1455)
In the Museum of the Monastery of San Marco, Florence
Photograph by Alinari Brothers, Florence, Italy

THE Bible story of the various authorities, both Jewish and Roman, before whom Jesus was brought by his accusers may be read beginning on page 345. Here the scene is in the council chamber of Caiaphas. Jesus, bound and guarded, stands silently before the high priest. The accusers are on either side of Caiaphas. Two of the soldiers carry spears and one a torch. The torch is meant perhaps to indicate that it is night. How skillfully the artist has portrayed the silent strength of Jesus, the weak uncertainty of Caiaphas, the unscrupulous suavity of the accusers!

On page 218 is a painting of Jesus before Pilate done by a nineteenth century Hungarian painter, Mihály Munkácsy. It is interesting to note the difference in conception. The early Renaissance artist paints a scene of unaffected simplicity, the modern artist one of dramatic complexity.

Fra Angelico's painting is one of thirty-five exquisite little panels originally ornamenting a cupboard in which were kept the silver treasures for a chapel in the Church of the Annunciation in Florence. These pictures are now carefully preserved in the Museum connected with the Monastery of San Marco in that same city. San Marco is one of the Dominican monasteries where Fra Angelico lived and painted. Fra Giovanni was called Angelico (angel) by his fellow Dominicans and it is this name that the world knows best. This holy monk devoted his life and special talent to portraying his charming medieval conception of the joys of belief in the Christian faith.

For other paintings by Fra Angelico from this same series see pages 340, 352, and Volume I, pages 264, 362. Other of his works are given in Volume VII, pages 211, 448 and in Volume VIII, page 261.

PERCVTIENT MAXILLAM IVDICIS ISRℓ. MICHEE . V . C

ASSISTES MINISTRORV DEDIT ALAPA VHM DICES SIC REPODES PONTIFICI. IO. XVIII

servant's name was Malchus. Then said Jesus unto Peter, "Put up thy sword into the sheath: the cup which my Father hath given me, shall I not drink it?"

— John 18:1-11.

## The Hearing Before Annas

Then the band and the captain and officers of the Jews took Jesus and bound him, and led him away to Annas first; for he was father-in-law to Caiaphas, which was the high priest that same year. Now Caiaphas was he which gave counsel to the Jews, that it was expedient that one man should die for the people.

And Simon Peter followed Jesus, and so did another disciple: that disciple was known unto the high priest, and went in with Jesus into the palace of the high priest. But Peter stood at the door without. Then went out that other disciple, which was known unto the high priest, and spake unto her that kept the door, and brought in Peter. Then saith the damsel that kept the door unto Peter, "Art not thou also one of this man's disciples?"

He saith, "I am not."

And the servants and officers stood there, who had made a fire of coals; for it was cold: and they warmed themselves: and Peter stood with them, and warmed himself.

The high priest then asked Jesus of his disciples, and of his doctrine. Jesus answered him, "I spake openly to the world; I ever taught in the synagogue, and in the temple, whither the Jews always resort; and in secret have I said nothing. Why askest thou me? Ask them which heard me what I have said unto them. Behold, they know what I said."

And when he had thus spoken, one of the officers which stood by struck Jesus with the palm of his hand, saying, "Answerest thou the high priest so?"

Jesus answered him, "If I have spoken evil, bear witness of the evil: but if well, why smitest thou me?"

Now Annas had sent him bound unto Caiaphas the high priest. And Simon Peter stood and warmed himself. They said therefore unto him, "Art not thou also one of his disciples?"

He denied it, and said, "I am not."

One of the servants of the high priest, being his kinsman whose ear Peter cut off, saith, "Did not I see thee in the garden with him?" Peter then denied again: and immediately the cock crew. — John 18:12–27.

## BEFORE PILATE

Then led they Jesus from Caiaphas into the hall of judgment: and it was early; and they themselves went not into the judgment hall, lest they should be defiled; but that they might eat the passover. Pilate then went out unto them, and said, "What accusation bring ye against this man?"

They answered and said unto him, "If he were not a malefactor, we would not have delivered him up unto thee."

Then said Pilate unto them, "Take ye him, and judge him according to your law."

The Jews therefore said unto him, "It is not lawful for us to put any man to death": that the saying of Jesus might be fulfilled, which he spake, signifying what death he should die.

Then Pilate entered into the judgment hall again, and called Jesus, and said unto him, "Art thou the King of the Jews?"

Jesus answered him, "Sayest thou this thing of thyself, or did others tell it thee of me?"

Pilate answered, "Am I a Jew? Thine own nation and the chief priests have delivered thee unto me. What hast thou done?"

Jesus answered, "My kingdom is not of this world: if my kingdom were of this world, then would my servants fight, that I should not be delivered to the Jews: but now is my kingdom not from hence."

Pilate therefore said unto him, "Art thou a king then?"

Jesus answered, "Thou sayest that I am a king. To this end was I born, and for this cause came I into the world, that I should bear witness unto the truth. Every one that is of the truth heareth my voice."

### PILATE WOULD RELEASE JESUS

Pilate saith unto him, "What is truth?" And when he had said this, he went out again unto the Jews, and saith unto them, "I find in him no fault at all. But ye have a custom, that I should release unto you one at the passover. Will ye therefore that I release unto you the King of the Jews?"

Then cried they all again, saying, "Not this man, but Barabbas." Now Barabbas was a robber.

### THE SCOURGING AND THE CROWN OF THORNS

Then Pilate therefore took Jesus, and scourged him. And the soldiers platted a crown of thorns, and put it on his head, and they put on him a purple robe, and said, "Hail, King of the Jews!" And they smote him with their hands.

Pilate therefore went forth again, and saith unto them, "Behold, I bring him forth to you, that ye may know that I find no fault in him."

Then came Jesus forth, wearing the crown of thorns,

and the purple robe. And Pilate saith unto them, "Behold the man!"

"CRUCIFY HIM! CRUCIFY HIM!"

When the chief priests therefore and officers saw him, they cried out, saying, "Crucify him! crucify him!"

Pilate saith unto them, "Take ye him, and crucify him: for I find no fault in him."

The Jews answered him, "We have a law, and by our law he ought to die, because he made himself the Son of God."

When Pilate therefore heard that saying, he was the more afraid; and went again into the judgment hall, and saith unto Jesus, "Whence art thou?" But Jesus gave him no answer.

Then saith Pilate unto him, "Speakest thou not unto me? Knowest thou not that I have power to crucify thee, and have power to release thee?"

Jesus answered, "Thou couldest have no power at all against me, except it were given thee from above: therefore he that delivered me unto thee hath the greater sin." And from thenceforth Pilate sought to release him: but the Jews cried out, saying, "If thou let this man go, thou art not Cæsar's friend: whosoever maketh himself a king speaketh against Cæsar."

When Pilate therefore heard that saying, he brought Jesus forth, and sat down in the judgment seat in a place that is called the Pavement, but in the Hebrew, Gabbatha. And it was the preparation of the passover, and about the sixth hour: and he saith unto the Jews, "Behold your King!"

But they cried out, "Away with him! away with him! crucify him!"

Pilate saith unto them, "Shall I crucify your king?"

The chief priests answered, "We have no king but Cæsar." Then delivered he him therefore unto them to be crucified. And they took Jesus, and led him away.

— John 18:28, 19:16.

## JESUS, LOVER OF MY SOUL

Jesus, lover of my soul,
  Let me to Thy bosom fly,
While the billows near me roll,
  While the tempest still is high:
Hide me, O my Saviour hide,
  Till the storm of life is past;
Safe into the haven guide;
  O receive my soul at last.

Other refuge have I none,
  Hangs my helpless soul on Thee;
Leave, ah! leave me not alone,
  Still support and comfort me;
All my trust on Thee is stayed,
  All my help from Thee I bring;
Cover my defenceless head
  With the shadow of Thy wing.

Thou, O Christ, art all I want,
  Boundless love in Thee I find.
Raise the fallen, cheer the faint,
  Heal the sick, and lead the blind.
Just and holy is Thy name,
  I am all unrighteousness;
Vile and full of sin I am,
  Thou art full of truth and grace.

Plenteous grace with Thee is found,
  Grace to pardon all my sin;
Let the healing streams abound,
  Make and keep me pure within;
  Thou of life the fountain art,
  Freely let me take of Thee;
Spring Thou up within my heart,
  Rise to all eternity.        — *Charles Wesley.*

## The Crucifixion at Golgotha

And he bearing his cross went forth into a place called the place of a skull, which is called in the Hebrew Golgotha: where they crucified him, and two other with him, on either side one, and Jesus in the midst.

And Pilate wrote a title, and put it on the cross. And the writing was, "JESUS OF NAZARETH THE KING OF THE JEWS." This title then read many of the Jews: for the place where Jesus was crucified was nigh to the city: and it was written in Hebrew, and Greek, and Latin.

Then said the chief priests of the Jews to Pilate, "Write not, 'The King of the Jews'; but that he said, 'I am King of the Jews.'"

Pilate answered, "What I have written I have written."

Then the soldiers, when they had crucified Jesus, took his garments, and made four parts, to every soldier a part; and also his coat: now the coat was without seam, woven from the top throughout. They said therefore among themselves, "Let us not rend it, but cast lots for it, whose it shall be": that the scripture might be fulfilled, which saith, "They parted my raiment among them, and for my vesture they did cast lots." These things therefore the soldiers did.

### THE WOMEN AT THE CROSS

Now there stood by the cross of Jesus his mother, and his mother's sister, Mary the wife of Cleophas, and Mary Magdalene. When Jesus therefore saw his mother, and the disciple standing by, whom he loved, he saith unto his mother, "Woman, behold thy son!"

Then saith he to the disciple, "Behold thy mother!" And from that hour that disciple took her unto his own home.

# The Entombment of Jesus

By Fra Angelico da Fiesole (1387-1455)
In the Museum of the Monastery of San Marco, Florence
Photograph by Alinari Brothers, Florence, Italy

THE Bible story of the burial of Jesus begins on page 353.

The picture represents the final ministrations being given the body of Jesus preparatory to laying him in the tomb. The face of the Master shows a bodily emaciation but a spiritual serenity. Mary Magdalene kisses the wounded hand while Mary the mother and John, the beloved disciple, kneel on either side grieving. Five other women are shown in sad contemplation and two men are silently preparing to wrap the body for burial. It is a desolate hour for those who knew him and loved him while He lived and taught on earth. Little do they realize that this is not the end but rather the beginning of his ministry to all mankind.

Fra Angelico has here given us a revelation of human thought and feeling and a delicate representation of the beauties of nature. It is a work, born of love and contemplation, from the hand of a devoutly religious and innately artistic man. When we study the life of this painter, we are struck by the two qualities of artist and saint which characterize his work and life. Fra Angelico was admitted as a young man of twenty to the Dominican order of monks and by his character and actions soon won the name of Beato Angelico. He lived during the early Renaissance, a period of rapid change, and in him the Medieval faith in authority and the Renaissance belief in the individual met and were in perfect harmony. All his lifetime he studied constantly in order to find some more perfect way of giving material form to the religious subjects he loved to paint. Thus we may understand something of the great energy and fine spirit that went into his artistic creations.

PM GETES DEPRE·ABUT R 7 ERIT SEPULCRUM EIVS GLORIOSVM. YS. XI.

IOSEPH DEPOSITV CORPVS IHV IVOLVIT IN SINDONE 7 POSVIT IN MONVMĒTO. LV. XXIII.

After this, Jesus knowing that all things were now accomplished, that the scripture might be fulfilled, saith, "I thirst." Now there was set a vessel full of vinegar: and they filled a sponge with vinegar, and put it upon hyssop, and put it to his mouth. When Jesus therefore had received the vinegar, he said, "It is finished": and he bowed his head, and gave up the ghost.

The Jews therefore, because it was the preparation, that the bodies should not remain upon the cross on the sabbath day, (for that sabbath day was an high day,) besought Pilate that their legs might be broken, and that they might be taken away. Then came the soldiers, and brake the legs of the first, and of the other which was crucified with him. But when they came to Jesus, and saw that he was dead already, they brake not his legs: but one of the soldiers with a spear pierced his side, and forthwith came there out blood and water. And he that saw it bare record, and his record is true: and he knoweth that he saith true, that ye might believe. For these things were done, that the scripture should be fulfilled, "A bone of him shall not be broken." And again another scripture saith, "They shall look on him whom they pierced." — John 19:17–37.

### Jesus Is Laid in the Sepulcher of Joseph of Arimathæa

And after this Joseph of Arimathæa, being a disciple of Jesus, but secretly for fear of the Jews, besought Pilate that he might take away the body of Jesus: and Pilate gave him leave. He came therefore, and took the body of Jesus. And there came also Nicodemus, which at the first came to Jesus by night, and brought a mixture of myrrh and aloes, about an hundred pound weight. Then took they the body of Jesus, and wound it in linen clothes with the spices, as the manner of the Jews is to bury. Now in the place where he was crucified there was a garden; and in the garden a new sepulcher, wherein was never man yet laid. There laid they Jesus therefore because of the Jews' preparation day; for the sepulcher was nigh at hand. —John 19:38–42.

## The Seven Last Words of Jesus

The words of Jesus on the cross have always been regarded with especial reverence, they are so full of beauty, of tenderness, of pathos, of power. A French musician, Dubois, has written a cantata called "The Seven Last Words of Christ." These sublime words are here collected from the Gospels.

"Father, forgive them; for they know not what they do."

"Verily I say unto thee, to-day shalt thou be with me in paradise."

"Woman, behold thy son!" "Behold thy mother!"

"Eloi, Eloi, lama sabachthani?" which is being interpreted, "My God, my God, why hast thou forsaken me?"

"I thirst."

"It is finished."

"Father, into thy hands I commend my spirit."

# Peter and John on the Way to the Tomb

By Eugène Burnand (1850-1921)
In the Museum of the Luxembourg, Paris, France

THIS painting depicts Peter and John in those tense moments when they are hurrying to the tomb after Mary Magdalene's announcement that the tomb is empty. The Bible tells us: "Peter therefore went forth, and that other disciple, and came to the sepulcher. So they ran both together; and the other disciple did outrun Peter."

What a fearful weight of anxiety in the faces of these two faithful ones at the thought of Mary's message: "They have taken away the Lord, and we know not where they have laid him!" Little have they understood the Master's forewarnings that this was to happen. We sense here only their feeling of painful loss and uncertainty as they hasten along the way.

The artist has portrayed this scene with such spirit that the spectator feels himself pushing along against the wind beside these two men sharing their anxiety. How striking the contrast in personalities! Here we see Peter, the oldest of the disciples, the impulsive one, "the rock;" and John, the youngest, "that other disciple whom Jesus loved," in all the force and beauty of character which distinguished them among men.

Eugène Burnand, a modern Swiss painter, was born at Moudon, Switzerland. He was a deeply religious man, and sought through his art to teach understanding of the humanity of Christ. The remarkable similarity between the Provençal landscape about his winter home at Fontfroide, France, and that of Palestine helped him to visualize the Master in a modern setting. The Provençal shepherd, outlined against the sinking sun, became the Good Shepherd; the French peasants became the disciples. Thus through the sensitive eye and devout spirit of the painter, we are shown the inner meanings of the life about us. This painting, the first of many Scriptural subjects treated by Burnand, is considered by many to be his masterpiece.

# The Story of the Master
## From the Gospel of John

## The Resurrection and the Last Appearances of the Master

CHRIST, THE LORD, IS RISEN TO-DAY

Christ, the Lord, is risen to-day,
Sons of men and angels say.
Raise your joys and triumphs high;
Sing, ye heavens, and earth, reply.

Love's redeeming work is done,
Fought the fight, the battle won.
Lo, our Sun's eclipse is o'er;
Lo, He sets in blood no more.

Vain the stone, the watch, the seal;
Christ has burst the gates of hell;
Death in vain forbids His rise:
Christ has opened Paradise

Lives again our glorious King:
Where, O death, is now thy sting?
Once He died our souls to save:
Where thy victory, O grave?

Soar we now where Christ has led,
Following our exalted Head:
Made like Him, like Him we rise;
Ours the cross, the grave, the skies.

Hail, the Lord of earth and Heaven!
Praise to Thee by both be given:
Thee we greet triumphant now;
Hail, the Resurrection Thou!

*—Charles Wesley.*

357

### The Resurrection Morning

THE first day of the week cometh Mary Magdalene early, when it was yet dark, unto the sepulcher and seeth the stone taken away from the sepulcher. Then she runneth, and cometh to Simon Peter, and to the other disciple, whom Jesus loved, and saith unto them, "They have taken away the Lord out of the sepulcher, and we know not where they have laid him."

Peter therefore went forth, and that other disciple, and came to the sepulcher. So they ran both together: and the other disciple did outrun Peter, and came first to the sepulcher. And he stooping down, and looking in, saw the linen clothes lying; yet went he not in. Then cometh Simon Peter following him, and went into the sepulcher, and seeth the linen clothes lie, and the napkin, that was about his head, not lying with the linen clothes, but wrapped together in a place by itself. Then went in also that other disciple, which came first to the sepulcher, and he saw, and believed. For as yet they knew not the scripture, that he must rise again from the dead. Then the disciples went away again unto their own home.

#### MARY SEES JESUS IN THE GARDEN

But Mary stood without at the sepulcher weeping: and as she wept, she stooped down, and looked into the sepulcher, and seeth two angels in white sitting, the one at the head, and the other at the feet, where the body of Jesus had lain. And they say unto her, "Woman, why weepest thou?"

She saith unto them, "Because they have taken away my Lord, and I know not where they have laid him."

And when she had thus said, she turned herself back, and saw Jesus standing, and knew not that it was Jesus.

# The Miraculous Draught of Fishes

By Raphael Sanzio (1483-1520)
In the Victoria and Albert Museum, London, England
Photograph by Anderson, Rome, Italy

HERE we see a richly dramatic portrayal of the miraculous draught of fishes. You will find the Bible story on page 362.

In the picture we see the two boats laden with fish, one containing Jesus with Peter and Andrew, the other containing the partners hauling in the net. The lake stretches away in the distance until it seems to meet the sky in a line of light at the horizon. On the opposite shore are the people to whom Jesus was speaking before the fishermen launched out. Fish hawks wheel above and herons are watching from the shore to catch the fish which escape the net.

This picture, like the one in Volume VII, page 57, is from a series of patterns made by Raphael for tapestries to be hung in the Sistine Chapel of the Vatican. Raphael made the designs and helped his assistants paint them in colors on a coarse kind of paper. These drawings, called cartoons, were then sent from Rome to the weavers in Brussels to be copied in tapestry. There they were cut in strips for the convenience of the artisans, and were pricked with holes, the method used in transferring a design. The tapestry copies were executed with wonderful skill and were first exhibited in the Sistine Chapel in December, 1519.

The original ten tapestries are now preserved in the Vatican, and seven of the original drawings are in England, the other three having been lost. The extraordinary popularity and influence of these cartoons are due to their artistic merit and Biblical accuracy. They seem to reflect the new spirit of inquiry and Bible-reading which was then just beginning. Thus Raphael, in these drawings, unconsciously foreshadowed the teaching of Luther and the coming Reformation.

On pages 243, 246 and 428 are other paintings by Raphael.

Jesus saith unto her, "Woman, why weepest thou? Whom seekest thou?"

She, supposing him to be the gardener, saith unto him, "Sir, if thou have borne him hence, tell me where thou hast laid him, and I will take him away."

Jesus saith unto her, "Mary."

She turned herself, and saith unto him, "Rabboni"; which is to say, "Master."

Jesus saith unto her, "Touch me not; for I am not yet ascended to my Father: but go to my brethren, and say unto them, I ascend unto my Father, and your Father; and to my God, and your God." Mary Magdalene came and told the disciples that she had seen the Lord, and that he had spoken these things unto her.

— John 20:1–18.

### JESUS MEETS THE DISCIPLES

Then the same day at evening, being the first day of the week, when the doors were shut where the disciples were assembled for fear of the Jews, came Jesus and stood in the midst, and saith unto them, "Peace be unto you." And when he had so said, he showed unto them his hands and his side. Then were the disciples glad, when they saw the Lord.

Then said Jesus to them again, "Peace be unto you: as my Father hath sent me, even so send I you." And when he had said this, he breathed on them, and saith unto them, "Receive ye the Holy Ghost: whose soever sins ye remit, they are remitted unto them; and whose soever sins ye retain, they are retained."     — John 20:19–23.

### DOUBTING THOMAS

But Thomas, one of the twelve, called Didymus, was not with them when Jesus came. The other disciples therefore said unto him, "We have seen the Lord."

But he said unto them, "Except I shall see in his hands the print of the nails, and put my finger into the print of the nails, and thrust my hand into his side, I will not believe."

And after eight days again his disciples were within, and Thomas with them: then came Jesus, the doors being shut, and stood in the midst, and said, "Peace be unto you." Then saith he to Thomas, "Reach hither thy finger, and behold my hands; and reach hither thy hand, and thrust it into my side: and be not faithless, but believing."

And Thomas answered and said unto him, "My Lord and my God."

Jesus saith unto him, "Thomas, because thou hast seen me, thou hast believed: blessed are they that have not seen, and yet have believed."  — John 20:24-29.

### Jesus Appears to the Disciples While They Are Fishing

After these things Jesus showed himself again to the disciples at the sea of Tiberias; and on this wise showed he himself. There were together Simon Peter, and Thomas called Didymus, and Nathanael of Cana in Galilee, and the sons of Zebedee, and two other of his disciples. Simon Peter saith unto them, "I go a fishing."

They say unto him, "We also go with thee." They went forth, and entered into a ship immediately; and that night they caught nothing.

But when the morning was now come, Jesus stood on the shore: but the disciples knew not that it was Jesus. Then Jesus saith unto them, "Children, have ye any meat?" They answered him, "No."

And he said unto them, "Cast the net on the right side of the ship, and ye shall find." They cast therefore, and now they were not able to draw it for the multitude of fishes.

Therefore that disciple whom Jesus loved saith unto Peter, "It is the Lord."

Now when Simon Peter heard that it was the Lord, he girt his fisher's coat unto him, for he was naked, and did cast himself into the sea.

And the other disciples came in a little ship; for they were not far from land, but as it were two hundred cubits, dragging the net with fishes. As soon then as they were come to land, they saw a fire of coals there, and fish laid thereon, and bread.

Jesus saith unto them, "Bring of the fish which ye have now caught."

Simon Peter went up, and drew the net to land full of great fishes, an hundred and fifty and three: and for all there were so many, yet was not the net broken.

Jesus saith unto them, "Come and dine."

And none of the disciples durst ask him, "Who art thou?" knowing that it was the Lord.

Jesus then cometh, and taketh bread, and giveth them, and fish likewise. This is now the third time that Jesus showed himself to his disciples, after that he was risen from the dead.

### "LOVEST THOU ME?"

So when they had dined, Jesus saith to Simon Peter, "Simon, son of Jonas, lovest thou me more than these?"

He saith unto him, "Yea, Lord; thou knowest that I love thee."

He saith unto him, "Feed my lambs."

He saith to him again the second time, "Simon, son of Jonas, lovest thou me?"

He saith unto him, "Yea, Lord; thou knowest that I love thee."

He saith unto him, "Feed my sheep."

He saith unto him the third time, "Simon, son of Jonas, lovest thou me?"

Peter was grieved because he said unto him the third time, "Lovest thou me?" And he said unto him, "Lord, thou knowest all things; thou knowest that I love thee."

Jesus saith unto him, "Feed my sheep.

"Verily, verily, I say unto thee, when thou wast young, thou girdedst thyself, and walkedst whither thou wouldest: but when thou shalt be old, thou shalt stretch forth thy hands, and another shall gird thee, and carry thee whither thou wouldest not." This spake he, signifying by what death he should glorify God. And when he had spoken this, he saith unto him, "Follow me."

Then Peter, turning about, seeth the disciple whom Jesus loved following; which also leaned on his breast at supper, and said, "Lord, which is he that betrayeth thee?" Peter seeing him saith to Jesus, "Lord, and what shall this man do?"

Jesus saith unto him, "If I will that he tarry till I come, what is that to thee? Follow thou me." Then went this saying abroad among the brethren, that that disciple should not die: yet Jesus said not unto him, "He shall not die"; but, "If I will that he tarry till I come, what is that to thee?" This is the disciple which testifieth of these things, and wrote these things: and we know that his testimony is true.                — John 21:1-24.

### "Many Other Signs"

And many other signs truly did Jesus in the presence of his disciples, which are not written in this book: but these are written, that ye might believe that Jesus is the Christ, the Son of God; and that believing ye might have life through his name. And there are also

many other things which Jesus did, the which, if they
should be written every one, I suppose that even the world
itself could not contain the books that should be written.
Amen.

— John 20:30–31; 21:25.

## ALL HAIL THE POWER OF JESUS' NAME

All hail the power of Jesus' name!
Let angels prostrate fall,
Bring forth the royal diadem,
And crown Him Lord of all.

Crown Him, ye martyrs of your God,
Who from His altar call;
Extol the stem of Jesse's rod,
And crown Him Lord of all.

Ye seed of Israel's chosen race,
Ye ransomed from the fall,
Hail Him, who saves you by His grace,
And crown Him Lord of all.

Sinners, whose love can ne'er forget
The wormwood and the gall,
Go, spread your trophies at His feet,
And crown Him Lord of all.

Let every kindred, every tribe,
On this terrestrial ball,
To him all majesty ascribe,
And crown Him Lord of all.

— *Edward Perronet*

## NOTES ON THE GOSPELS

**Theophilus,** to whom the Gospel of Luke was dedicated, is also mentioned at the beginning of Acts. Nothing else is known of him, but as he is called "most excellent," he was perhaps an official, and doubtless was a Christian.

**The Course of Abia.** The priests were divided into 24 groups, which served in the temple by turn, a week at a time. One of these groups bore the name of Abia.

**Mary's Song** is known in the church as the Magnificat, and from early ages has been used as part of the service of the church.

**Holpen,** Old English for helped, which the Revised Version here used.

**Taxed,** rather, enrolled. An enrollment of the whole empire was determined on by the emperor. This enrollment was a sort of census.

**His own city.** Rome usually enrolled a man at his place of residence, but the Jews wished to be enrolled as of the town of their ancestors, especially when they came from royal ancestry.

**Bethlehem.** A very ancient town, a few miles south of Jerusalem. It had long been famous among the Jews as the native town of King David; and Joseph traced his ancestry to David.

**Christ.** The Greek translation of the Hebrew word Messiah, the Great King who was to come. In the Gospels it is usually used as a title; in the letters of Paul, sometimes as a title but often as a proper name.

**Purification.** The Jewish law required sacrifices to be offered after the birth of a child. As Bethlehem is only five or six miles from Jerusalem, the child Jesus was brought there.

**Raiment of camel's hair and a leathern girdle.** So it was said the old prophets dressed (2 Kings 1:8). This clothing suggested to the people that John was a prophet like those of ancient time.

**Capernaum.** A town mentioned only in the Gospels. A flourishing town on the northwest border of the Sea of Galilee. The exact site has been much disputed, two ruined places not far apart having each some claims to be regarded as Capernaum.

**As his custom was.** Jesus had been a regular attendant at the place of worship in his home town of Nazareth.

**Stood up to read.** After the reading of the law, the reading of the prophets was open to any competent person, with the permission of the elders.

**Unclean devil.** Rather, "demon." The Bible tells us of many strange and obscure diseases, especially mental ailments, which were caused by demons.

**Leprosy.** This disease was contagious, loathsome, and seldom cured. Lev. 14:1–32 gives elaborate directions for making sure of a cure before the person was restored to society. Quarantine was very strict. The disease has always been common in parts of the East.

**Uncovered the roof.** The houses of the common people were made of mud walls and a roof of poles covered with brushwood and overlaid with earth, easily broken and as easily repaired.

**Levi son of Alphaeus.** The man better known as "Matthew the publican."

**Place of toll.** In the East custom houses were frequent, and goods often paid duty at the entrance of a town.

**Publican.** Not, as in English, an innkeeper, but a taxgatherer. Jews who would consent to enter this occupation and collect taxes for the Romans were despised as traitors to their nation. They were often dishonest and oppressive. The government demanded of a town or district a certain sum. The taxgatherer agreed to pay that sum, and had as his pay whatever he could collect above it. The system encouraged overcharges, and publicans had the worst name for dishonesty of any class in the community. And yet from them Jesus chose a disciple. Nothing perhaps shows more clearly the universality of our Lord's mission.

**Pharisees.** A Jewish religious party, strongly opposed to the Roman rule, very strict in keeping the Jewish law and applying it to the minutest matters of life. They contained many sincerely religious persons, but the tendency was to pay more attention to keeping the religious laws than to purifying the heart. Jesus said they cleaned the outside of the cup, but the inside was not clean.

**Herodians.** Adherents of the evil family of Herod, friendly to the Roman rule. In most things direct opponents of the Pharisees.

**Fast.** Fasting was a part of the worship of the Jews; one day a week for the strict Jews, while the Pharisee in the parable boasts that he fasts twice a week.

**Centurion.** An officer in the Roman army, literally the captain of a hundred. The Roman officers were not Jews, so this is a case of Gentile faith in Jesus' power.

**Go your way and tell John.**  John in prison had begun to wonder if Jesus was really the deliverer of Israel.  Jesus in his answer practically says, "My work is to help the needy, not to make war on Rome."

**Beelzebub.**  Correctly, Beelzebul.  The king of demons, lord of the pit where the demons dwell.

**Tares.**  That is, darnel; somewhat resembling growing grain, but with a poisonous seed.

**Becometh a tree.**  The mustard of Palestine grows large enough so that birds may rest on it, and is sometimes from 8 to 12 feet high.

**Gergesenes.**  Better, Gadarenes, as Revised Version.  Gadara was several miles from the Sea of Galilee, on the eastern side.  The event described was on the shore.  The Gospels therefore say, "the country of the Gadarenes," not "Gadara."

**"Talitha cumi."**  Mark alone gives the very words which Jesus used, in Aramaic, the language spoken in Palestine.  Mark gives his very words several times, as 7:11, 34; 15:34.  It is one of the ways in which he makes his picture of Jesus marvelously vivid.

**Herodias.**  She was herself of the family of the Herods, and had abandoned her first husband Philip to marry his brother Herod Antipas.  This marriage was against the Jewish law, and John had publicly denounced it; hence the bitterness of her enmity.

**Charger.**  A platter.

**Fourth watch.**  Between 3 and 6 A.M.

**Corban.**  "Given" to God.  If a man declared that his property was devoted to God he need not use it in support of his parents.

**Purging all meats.**  Revised Version, "This he said, making all meats clean."  Jesus here indicates that the eating of unclean food is not inherently harmful and that clean food does not necessarily make one pure.

**Parts of Tyre and Sidon.**  Jesus had gone far north, outside of Palestine proper, into a region more than half Gentile, perhaps in search of quiet and a chance to teach his disciples; but his reputation as a healer went with him.

**Dogs.**  Not the usual contemptuous word, but "little dogs," the household pets; so Jesus modifies the seeming harshness of his saying.  The woman does not resent it, but says, "Then let the little dogs have their share too."

**Sadducees.** A party in nearly all respects the opposite of the Pharisees. They held to the old Jewish theology and rejected the belief in a future life; they were not careful to keep the law; they cared more for political power than for religion. They were a small aristocratic party, led by the family of the high priests. They were afraid Jesus would announce himself as the Messiah and lead a revolt against the Romans.

**Caesarea Philippi.** A prosperous town, beautifully situated high on the slopes of Hermon, at the source of the Jordan. The northern limit of Israel, at or near the site of ancient Dan.

DENARIUS

Obverse, profile of Tiberius, "Tiberius Caesar, the Son of the Deified Augustus."

Reverse, priest seated, "High Priest."

This is the coin often mentioned in the New Testament, called "penny" in the Authorized Version, "shilling" in the Revised Version. It was for several hundred years the unit of money in the Roman world, and was struck in great numbers.

**High mountain.** The mount of transfiguration is not known; probably one of the shoulder of Hermon, near Caesarea Philippi. Hermon is about 10,000 feet high, snow-capped and visible from many parts of Palestine.

**Elias.** The Greek form of Elijah.

**Tribute money.** Half-shekel paid by all Jews in all parts of the world to the temple treasury.

**Piece of money.** Literally, "stater," equal to a shekel.

**Ten thousand talents.** Not less than ten million dollars.

**Hundred pence.** Literally, "hundred denarii," about twenty dollars, about three months' wages of a working man.

**Leave the dead to bury their own dead.** Perhaps a proverb meaning, "Do not be absorbed in the past."

THE STATER OR SHEKEL

Obverse, profile of Augustus, "Augustus the Emperor."

Reverse, symbolic figure of Antioch seated, compare page 438. "Of Antioch, the Metropolis."

The Roman empire gave certain cities the right to coin money. This is a coin of Antioch, such as circulated freely in Palestine. In the New Testament time the coins of ordinary business were those of some city of the Roman empire. In Matt. 17:27, "stater" is translated "piece of money" in the Authorized Version, "shekel" in the Revised Version.

**Lawyer.**  A student of the Hebrew religious law: used much in the same meaning as "scribe."

**Chorazin, Bethsaida.**  Towns near together on the lake of Galilee, north of Capernaum.  All these lake towns knew much of the work of Jesus, for he had taught and healed in their streets.

**Going down from Jerusalem to Jericho.**  The road wound steeply down between cliffs and mountain sides, and was always a haunt of robbers, even to recent times.

**Samaritan.**  The Jews and Samaritans hated each other, and therein lay the sting of the parable.

**The better part.**  Literally, "the good part," as in Revised Version.  Jesus does not make a comparison between different kinds of service.

**My children are with me in bed.**  In a peasant's cottage the family slept on the floor, and all would be wakened if the father arose.

**Not first washed.**  Not for cleanliness.  The reference is to the elaborate ceremonial washing which the Pharisees had developed. Jesus thought they paid more attention to ceremonies than to morals.

**Take no thought.**  This does not mean, "Be careless about the future," but as in Revised Version, "Be not anxious."

**What will I, if it is already kindled.**  Rather, "How I would that it had been already kindled!"

**Eat bread in the Kingdom of God.**  One of the common Jewish figures of the glorious Messianic time was of a great supper at which the people of God should feast.

**Commended the steward.**  Not for his dishonesty, but for his cleverness.  Even his master said, "Shrewd fellow!"  Jesus advises men to be as clever in doing right as this man was in doing wrong.

**Mammon** means simply riches, which may be used for good or for evil.  Mammon is not necessarily "unrighteous."

**Abraham's bosom.**  A Jewish figure for the place of abode of righteous Jews between death and the resurrection.

**Shall not God avenge his elect?**  This is a parable of contrast. If an unjust judge listens to a prayer, how much more will the just and loving God!

**Find faith on the earth?**  Literally, "the faith"; that is, the faith needed for this persistent prayer.

**Little children.**  Luke says, "their babes."

**A penny a day.** A denarius, the usual daily wage.

**Jericho.** The ancient city in the valley of the Jordan was in the time of Jesus a prosperous town with rich gardens. Jesus had been traveling in the country east of the Jordan, and now crossed the river and passed through Jericho on his way to the passover at Jerusalem.

**The chief among the publicans;** rather, "chief publican," as in the Revised Version. The Romans sold the privilege of collecting taxes—and as much more as could be extorted—to men who in turn sold the local taxes to others. The "head contractors" often became very rich, but paid for their wealth with the bitter hatred and contempt of the people. The people are astounded that Jesus should stoop to dine with such an unpatriotic Jew as a taxgatherer for the Romans.

**Pound.** Literally, mina, about nineteen dollars.

**Bethany.** Bethany was just over the brow of the Mount of Olives. Many of the pilgrims to the passover lodged in the villages outside Jerusalem, for the city was crowded at that time. Jesus probably stayed in the home of Lazarus, Mary and Martha. Who Simon was is unknown; perhaps a man whose leprosy had been healed by Jesus.

**A woman having an alabaster box.** John says she was Mary, presumably the sister of Martha and Lazarus. It was customary to anoint honored guests, and Mary used costly oil in reverent gratitude for her brother's resurrection to life. This Mary is not to be confused with either Mary Magdalene or the woman who was a sinner, who wept at Jesus' feet in the house of Simon the Pharisee.

**An ass.** This animal was used by kings and persons of dignity. The horse was used in war; the ass was ridden in times of peace.

**Blessed is he that cometh.** The Galilean pilgrims thought that now at last their countryman was to announce himself the Messiah, as they had long believed he was.

**Fig-tree having leaves.** Since the fruit appears on the fig-tree before the leaves, this tree, in leaf even earlier than usual, should have had fruit.

**Cast out them that sold.** It was convenient to have near the temple a market for animals to be sacrificed and an exchange for the coins which must be used in the temple offering; but the trade had invaded the very courts of the temple. An eastern market is noisy, for business proceeds with long and loud bargaining in which passersby like to stop and take part. The temple was not the place for business, even if it had been conducted honestly.

**Is it lawful to give tribute to Cæsar?** If Jesus said, "Yes," it would discredit him with loyal Jews; if he said "No," they could complain of him to the Romans as a dangerous revolutionist. He said "Yes," but added, "and also pay God what you owe him."

**Penny.** Denarius, the ordinary coin of commerce with which taxes were paid. On one side was the emperor's figure and name.

**Sadducees.** (See page 369). Although this small, but powerful party appear to have given little consideration to the Messianic claims and ministry of Christ and was noted for its antagonism toward the Pharisees, certain leaders among them joined the Pharisees in seeking to entrap Jesus. By an exaggerated question on the future resurrection life, they sought to discredit Christ and His teachings.

**What is the great commandment?** Jesus replies by quoting the passage from Deuteronomy 6:5 which was used more familiarly in the synagogue service than any other.

**The treasury.** Near the door of the temple were boxes with trumpet-shaped openings for the gifts of the people. Some put money in with ostentation. Perhaps the poor widow hoped none would see her, the gift was so small.

**Two mites.** Literally, two lepta, making about half a cent. The lepton was the smallest copper coin used, and two was the smallest gift allowed to be given to the temple. For the widow, however, it was large, for her purse was now empty.

**Tribulation.** The last months of the siege of Jerusalem by the Romans in A.D. 66 and 67 were full of great miseries and terrible suffering. The Christians, perhaps because of Jesus' warning, all fled early in the siege to Pella, beyond the Jordan.

**Talent.** A weight of silver or gold. In Greek money, a talent of silver was over a thousand dollars.

**Palace.** Rather, "court," as Revised Version. The open court of an eastern house is a common place of assembly.

**Caiaphas.** High priest from A.D. 26 to 38. A less able man than his father-in-law, Annas, who had been high priest before him.

**Thirty pieces of silver.** About nineteen dollars, the legal price for the death of a slave.

**Go into the city.** Jesus had evidently arranged for the place of the supper so privately that not even the disciples knew where it was to be. Those who went to complete the arrangements met a man with a water jar who led them to the house. The result was that Judas, already plotting to betray Jesus, did not know where he was to be till they actually entered the door. The privacy of the last few sacred hours was safe.

**Eat the passover.** The passover was a family feast. Jesus and the twelve, all away from home, ate it together as a family; but their hearts must have turned to the home circles eating that night without them. Somewhere in the city was Jesus' mother, eating with friends, for the next day she was at the cross.

**Gethsemane.** A garden in the valley east of the city, at the beginning of the road to Bethany. This is an inclosure with ancient olive-trees, though the olives do not reach back to that time. In the siege of Jerusalem the Roman army cut down all the olive-trees about the city, though the tradition is that one survived.

**A certain young man followed.** This incident is told only in Mark, and some have surmised that the young man was Mark.

**The trials of Jesus** were three: 1. An inquiry into the case in the house of the high priest; 2. A formal trial before the council, or sanhedrin; 3. A trial before the Roman governor, Pilate. The examination before Herod, which resulted in nothing, was an attempt of Pilate to shift responsibility from himself.

**The whole council.** The sanhedrin, the "supreme court" of the Jewish nation. This court represented the best learning of Judaism. Its rules were carefully drawn up to insure exact justice, but these rules were not followed in Jesus' case. Most of the court believed that Jesus was a dangerous character, to be put out of the way by any means, legal or illegal. "Mob law" is always dangerous. They condemned him for blasphemy, but only the Roman governor could pass a death sentence, and they must have some other charge to bring to Pilate. So they change the charge to plotting rebellion against Rome. The Jewish sanhedrin concerned about the safety of Roman rule was fine irony!

**Thou sayest** means, "You are right. I am." But even with Jesus acknowledging that he claimed kingship, Pilate is sure he is not a dangerous revolutionist.

**Golgotha.** Literally, "the skull." The Latin "Calvary" is a translation of it. The famous Church of the Holy Sepulcher has stood for many hundred years on the traditional site. Whether the true site or not, the church has a wonderful historic interest to any intelligent Christian. Some have urged another site north of the present city wall, on a low hill which has now—although not proof that it had in ancient time—a fancied resemblance to a skull. There is a possibility that either site may be right, but no one knows certainly. Perhaps it is as well; we might care too much about the place itself. The name, "the skull," may have come not from any appearance, but from its being a place of execution. Even about this there is at present no certainty.

**Wine mingled with gall.** Mark says with myrrh. An opiate furnished in pity for the intense suffering of crucifixion; so much of mercy was shown even to criminals. Jesus refused. He would meet suffering and death with a clear mind.

**Eli, Eli, lama sabacthani.** The first words of Psalm 22. Does Jesus mean to suggest that this Psalm, with its expression of splendid faith, speaks his own feeling on the cross? If so, his words are not a cry of despair.

**Vinegar.** Sour wine, the drink of the common soldiers. It was an act of kindness in these rough men, who would quench the thirst that suffering brought; and Jesus accepted it from them.

**Gave up the ghost.** Better, "spirit," as in the Revised Version. In old English, ghost was not merely used for the spirits of the dead, but for a living spirit. Compare the Holy Ghost for the Holy Spirit.

**Joseph of Arimathaea.** A member of the sanhedrin which had judged Jesus worthy of death that morning.

**Rolled a great stone.** Ancient tombs with huge round stone doors, rolling in great grooves, are still to be seen near Jerusalem. The Jewish rock tombs varied all the way from cavities for a single body to rooms in the walls of which were recesses for the bodies of a whole family. Some of the rock about Jerusalem is easily cut lime stone.

**Emmaus.** Perhaps a little village now called Kuloniyeh, northwest of Jerusalem.

**Cephas.** Everywhere else in the gospels he is called Peter, the Greek word meaning "rock." Jesus saw that Peter was as stable as a rock—and so he was usually, in spite of the fact that once he denied Jesus.

## NOTES ON THE GOSPEL OF JOHN

**Dwelt.** Literally, "tented" for a time.

**That prophet.** The prophet whom some expected as further preparation for the Messiah.

**Esaias.** Greek for Isaiah.

**Bethabara.** Properly, Bethany, as in the Revised Version. The change to Bethabara was made because no Bethany beyond Jordan was known a few hundred years after Jesus.

**We have found him.** "The Messiah has come at last. We have found him. He is Jesus of Nazareth."

**Can any good thing come out of Nazareth?** Nothing against Nazareth is known, but it was an obscure hill town from which nothing could be expected.

**Cana.** A town about six miles north of Nazareth.

**Firkins.** A "firkin" was about nine gallons.

**Capernaum.** This was a flourishing town by the Sea of Galilee, the scene of much of Jesus' teaching in his early ministry. For some reason Jesus and his family moved there from Nazareth.

**Went up to Jerusalem.** This visit to Jerusalem is told only in John.

**He that cometh.** This paragraph is probably not a quotation, but the writer's comment.

**Sychar.** A village now called Askar, near Nablous, the ancient Shechem.

**Jacob gave to his son Joseph.** See Genesis 33:19, 48:22, Joshua 24:32 for the history of this plot of ground.

**Jacob's well** is still there, about half a mile south of Askar. It is now about 70 feet deep, and was formerly much deeper. The low, broad curb of stone is worn where ropes have lowered water jars into it.

**Sat on the well.** Better "by the well," as in the Revised Version.

**Sixth hour.** About noon. Not the usual time for women to bring water from the wells. The story implies that the well was deserted except for the woman and Jesus.

**No dealings with Samaritans.** The enmity between the races went back at least five hundred years. The Samaritans were descended in part from foreigners brought in by conquerors of Northern Israel. When, more than 500 years before Jesus, the Jews started to build the temple after the return from the exile, the Samaritans wished to join and were repulsed as not being Jews of pure blood. Later the Samaritans built a temple of their own, and the break between the races widened. The Samaritans are still a small community at Shechem, with their own priesthood and worship.

**Bethesda.** The pool has been identified. It was near the temple and now lies below the surface of the city. The story implies that the water in it was from an intermittent spring.

**Five barley loaves.** The loaves were thin, flat cakes, like large pancakes. Five would make a good lunch for one, with perhaps something left over for supper.

**Many of his disciples went back.** This marks a crisis in Jesus' ministry, as this gospel presents it. Up to this time Jesus had been trying to draw hearers, to spread the good news as widely as possible. Now he began to sift his hearers, giving hard sayings which drove away those not genuinely his followers. From this time the Jews began to plot his death, and Jesus devoted more time to the teaching of his apostles. The apostles themselves understood him hardly more than the others, but were held to him because they believed that he had "the words of life."

**Jewry** means Judæa, as in the Revised Version.

**Feast of tabernacles, or of booths.** One of the three yearly feasts. In it the people lived for seven days in booths, in memory of the ancient life in the wilderness after their fathers left Egypt. It was also a harvest feast. It was a joyous festival, and as many as could kept it at Jerusalem.

**The dispersed.** The technical name for the Jews living in foreign countries.

**Let him come unto me and drink.** On each of the days of the feast except the last it seems to have been the custom to bring water from the pool of Siloam, with a great procession, and pour it over the altar. On the last day Jesus directs them to abiding sources of living water, in allusion to the customs of the feast.

**In the treasury.** Better, "at the treasury," that is, in the court near the boxes for gifts, where later he saw the poor widow give her two mites. (Luke 21:1–4.)

**Thou art a Samaritan.** The most contemptuous term they could apply.

**Thou hast a devil.** Better, "demon," as in the Revised Version. Mental disorders especially were ascribed to demons. The meaning is "You are crazy," with the additional sneer, "a demon is in you."

**Law,** here used for the Old Testament.

**Ye are gods.** Psalms 82:6, where rulers are called "gods" as acting with divine authority.

**Bethany.** A village near Jerusalem, just over the brow of the Mount of Olives. How Jesus came to be so friendly with Lazarus and his sisters we do not know.

**Die with him.** Jesus was going to Jerusalem, into the enemies' country. Thomas feared that Jesus would lose his life, but he was willing to die with him. Such was the splendid loyalty with which Jesus had inspired his disciples.

**Fifteen furlongs.** Somewhat less than two miles.

**The Romans will come.** Caiaphas regarded it as a matter of course that if Jesus obtained a popular following he would proclaim himself the Messiah, lead an army against Rome, and bring defeat and disaster upon the nation. This being the case, he reasoned that Jesus should be put out of the way to save the nation. Both Jesus' friends and his enemies misunderstood his mission, supposing it to be political rather than spiritual.

**He prophesied.** The writer says that God so guided the utterance of Caiaphas that it expressed more truth than he supposed.

**Three hundred pence.** Literally, three hundred denarii; about seventy-five dollars. As a denarius was a day's wage, the value of the ointment was equal to the wages of a workman for about ten months.

**Greeks.** The same word as "Gentile" in 7:35. These were proselytes, Gentiles who had adopted the Jewish religion.

**But though he had done so many miracles.** This paragraph is the writer's summary of the ministry of Jesus. As in the days of the old prophets, the people did not see the truth; or if they did, feared to confess it.

**Jesus cried and said.** This paragraph is the writer's summary of the teaching of Jesus. Compare it with the first paragraph of the gospel.

**Wash his disciples' feet.** At a feast it was the place of a slave or servant to wash the dust-covered feet of the guests as they came in. Here there was no servant, and perhaps none of the disciples, with his dreams of a place in the court of the Messiah's kingdom, would demean himself to do the slave's task; so Jesus did it.

**He that is washed.** Literally, "bathed," a different word from "washed" in the rest of the passage.

**The disciple whom Jesus loved.** This is John, the author of the gospel, to whom at the cross Jesus gave over the care of his mother. (John 19:26, 27.)

**The world hateth you.** This gospel uses "world" as the name of all the forces which are opposed to God and his kingdom.

**In proverbs.** The same word is translated "parables" in 10:6. It means allegories, figures, a way of speaking outside the plain path. A little further on the disciples make the contrast between speaking plainly and in "proverbs."

**Father, the hour is come.** The prayer with which this begins is the most wonderful prayer in the Bible. It is (1) for himself, (2) for the disciples, (3) for the church that is to be. The last is for all Christians to-day as well as in the past. Read and see what Jesus wished for us.

**Cedron.** Kidron is the Old Testament form. A steep, narrow valley just east of the walls of Jerusalem.

**Preparation.** The day before the Sabbath of the feast.

**Lest they should be defiled.** Entering a house not ceremonially cleansed of leaven would defile a Jew during passover.

**What is truth?** Asked with a sneer.

**Sixth hour.** About noon.

**What I have written I have written.** Pilate was in no mood to make further concessions to the Jews; he was angry and doubtless chagrined that he had felt obliged to crucify Jesus at their demands.

**Rabboni.** The very word Mary used is preserved. Literally, "My Master."

**My Lord and my God.** It is significant that the last incident of the gospel is this acknowledgment of Jesus; then follows the statement of the writer's purpose, which is to win belief in Jesus as the Messiah and the Son of God.

**Lovest thou me?** In Greek there are two words for love. One is dignified, expressing a devotion resting on reason and a moral obligation. The other is more intimate and personal, a word to use between friends and members of a family. In the first two questions Jesus uses the first; in Peter's answers and in Jesus' third question, the latter and more intimate term is used. This conversation is the restoration of Peter, who has denied his Lord, in the position of a trusted follower of Jesus.

**The date of the birth of Christ.** On the margin of your Bibles, at the beginning of the Gospels of Matthew and Luke, you will find the date of the birth of Christ given as 4 B.C., or possibly, 5 B.C. That means that the birth of Christ is set several years before Christ, for the christian era is supposed to begin with the birth of Christ. The explanation is that when, in 533 A.D., the christian era first began to be used as a means of dating events, the adjustment of it to the Roman era which was used before was carelessly made. Later, when the mistake was known, it was easier to set the birth of Christ earlier than to change the whole system of dating which all the people were using.

**The wide world of Jesus' time** was the Roman Empire. Outside its boundaries, as everybody knew, were other lands and other peoples, but the Roman Empire was the civilized world. It stretched all along the shores of the great Mediterranean Sea, from Spain on the north shore to Morocco on the south. It reached to Britain on the north, and London was for centuries a Roman town. It stretched through France and parts of Germany, and along the south shore of the Black Sea to the borders of Persia. In the New Testament times this great empire, the greatest the world had ever seen, was in the full vigor of its early power. Its rulers were sometimes unjust and often selfish, but many of them were as able and as good as any government of that day was likely to furnish. They made the world safe for travel and trade. Ships could sail the length of the Mediterranean and find in any port Roman law and order. Travelers could go across the empire, from the Euphrates to the Atlantic Ocean on Roman roads protected by Roman soldiers. It was a wonderful empire, and for four hundred years held its power and most of its territory.

# Sayings Ascribed to Jesus, Outside the Gospels

HE New Testament itself contains one saying of Jesus outside the Gospels.

It is more blessed to give than to receive. (Acts 20:35.)

Some of the early manuscripts of the Gospels contain sayings not in the other manuscripts. In an early copy of the Gospels, at Luke 6:4, are these words:

"On the same day, seeing one working on the Sabbath, he said to him, 'Man, if thou knowest what thou doest, blessed art thou; but if thou knowest not, thou art accursed, and a transgressor of the law.'"

In an early Christian writing of the second century, known as the Second Epistle of Clement of Rome, we have:

"The Lord said, 'Though ye be gathered together in my bosom, and do not my commandments, I will cast you away, and will say, "Depart from me, I know not whence ye are, ye workers of iniquity."'"

Justin Martyr, living in the latter part of the second century, quotes Jesus as saying,

"In whatsoever things I apprehend you, in those I shall judge you."

Hippolytus, writing about 200 A.D., quotes:

"So when the Lord told the disciples about the coming kingdom of the saints, how it was glorious and marvelous, Judas, amazed at what was spoken, said, 'And who then shall see these things?' And the Lord replied, 'These things they shall see who become worthy.'"

Clement of Alexandria, about 200 A.D., quotes as sayings of Jesus:

"That which is weak shall be saved through that which is strong."

"Be ye trustworthy moneychangers, disapproving some things, but holding fast that which is good."

"He that seeketh shall not stop until he find; and when he hath found, he shall wonder; and when he hath wondered he shall reign; and when he hath reigned he shall rest."

"Good things must come, but blessed," saith he, "is he through whom they come; in like manner, it must needs be that evils come, but woe to him through whom they come."

"Ask for the great things, and the small shall be added to you; and ask for the heavenly things and the earthly shall be added to you."

"My mystery is for me and the sons of my house."

Origen, who wrote a little later than Clement of Alexandria, quotes a saying of Jesus, but says he does not know whether it should be taken as genuine:

"He that is near me is near the fire. He that is far from me is far from the kingdom."

He also quotes:

"Ye see me in yourselves, as one of you sees himself in water or a mirror."

Jerome, about 400 A.D., quotes from a book called the Gospel of the Hebrews:

"Among the greatest sinners is he who hath grieved the spirit of his brother."

"'And never,' said he, 'rejoice, except when ye have looked upon your brother in love.'"

"But when the Lord had given the linen cloth to the priest's servant, he went to James and appeared to him.

For James had taken an oath that he would not eat bread from that hour in which he had drunk the cup of the Lord, until he should see him rising from them that sleep. . . . 'Bring me,' saith the Lord, 'a table and bread.' He took the bread, and blessed, and brake, and gave to James the Just, and said to him, 'My brother, eat thy bread, inasmuch as the Son of man hath risen from them that sleep.'"

All these are quoted incidentally. Some of them may be genuine, others may be memories of Gospel sayings of Jesus. No collection of sayings of Jesus has come to us. But in 1897 a leaf of a papyrus book was published by two English explorers in Egypt, Grenfell and Hunt. The leaf came from the ruins of an ancient town, Oxyrhynchus, in the oasis of the Fayum. Here was part of a collection of short quotations from Jesus, some from the Gospels, others before unknown, and each beginning with "Jesus said." The leaf was found in a pile of rubbish and old papyri, like the dumpings of waste baskets. Sand had drifted over the piles and the dry climate had preserved the papyrus. The leaf was mutilated, so that only fragments are left of some lines. The Sayings are usually called the Oxyrhynchus Logia, the term "Logia" being the Greek word for "Sayings."

1. " . . . And then shalt thou see clearly to cast out the mote that is in thy brother's eye."

2. "Jesus saith, 'Except ye fast to the world, ye shall in no wise find the kingdom of God; and except ye make the sabbath a real sabbath, ye shall not see the Father.'"

3. "Jesus saith, 'I stood in the midst of the world, and in the flesh was I seen of them, and I found all men drunken, and none found I athirst among them, and my soul grieveth over the sons of men, because they are blind in their heart, and see not.'"

4. ". . . poverty."

5. "Jesus saith, 'Wherever there are two they are not without God; and wherever there is one alone, I say, I am with him. Raise the stone and there shalt thou find me; cleave the wood and there am I.'"

6. "Jesus saith, 'A prophet is not acceptable in his own country, neither doth a physician work cures upon them that know him.'"

7. "Jesus saith, 'A city built upon the top of a high hill and stablished, can neither fall nor be hid.'"

8. "Jesus saith, 'Thou hearest with one ear. . . . "

The second saying needs some explanation. One would not expect to find Jesus emphasizing fasts and the strict keeping of the Sabbath. To "fast to the world" was a phrase used by the early Christians in the meaning of abstaining from sins, and to "sabbatize the sabbath," the phrase here used, was to keep the heart pure and the life clean.

In 1903 Grenfell and Hunt found among the rubbish heaps of old Oxyrhynchus another fragment from a collection of sayings of Jesus. These were not on a leaf of a book, but copied out on the back of a survey list of plots of land in Oxyrhynchus. It may be a part of the same collection from which the first came, though most think that it represents another book. Perhaps some Christian, wishing to have a copy of the sayings, copied them on the back of a cast-off business paper.

The following are the second Oxyrhynchus Logia of Jesus:

"These are the (wonderful) words which Jesus the living (Lord) spake to . . . and Thomas; and he said unto (them), 'everyone that hearkens to these words shall never taste of death.'"

1. "Jesus saith, 'Let not him who seeks . . . cease

until he finds, and when he finds he shall be astonished; astonished he shall reach the kingdom, and having reached the kingdom, he shall rest.'"

2. "Jesus saith, '(Ye ask who are those) that draw us (to the kingdom if) the kingdom is in heaven? . . . the fowls of the air and all beasts that are under the earth or upon the earth and the fishes of the sea, (these are they which draw) you; and the kingdom of heaven is within you, and whosoever shall know himself shall find it. (Strive therefore) to know yourselves, and ye shall be aware that ye are the sons of the (Almighty) Father; (and) ye shall know that ye are in (the city of God) and ye are (the city).'"

3. "Jesus saith, 'A man shall not hesitate . . . to ask concerning his place (in the kingdom. Ye shall know) that many that are first shall be last, and the last first, and (they shall have eternal life).'"

4. "Jesus saith, 'Everything that is not before thy face and that is hidden from thee shall be revealed to thee. For there is nothing hidden which shall not be made manifest; nor buried, which shall not be raised.'"

5. "His disciples question him and say, 'How shall we fast and how shall we (pray) . . . and what (commandment) shall we keep . . . ?' Jesus saith . . . 'do not . . . of truth . . . blessed is he.'"

There has been much discussion as to whether these sayings of Jesus, so far as they are not found in the Gospels, are genuine. Possibly they represent real sayings, passed down through the generations, but their genuineness can hardly be guaranteed. The manuscripts are not later than 300 A.D. They are most interesting, for they represent what the early church in Egypt considered to be words of Jesus.

# OUTLINE CHART OF THE MINISTRY OF JESUS

(Any arrangement of this kind is necessarily approximate.)

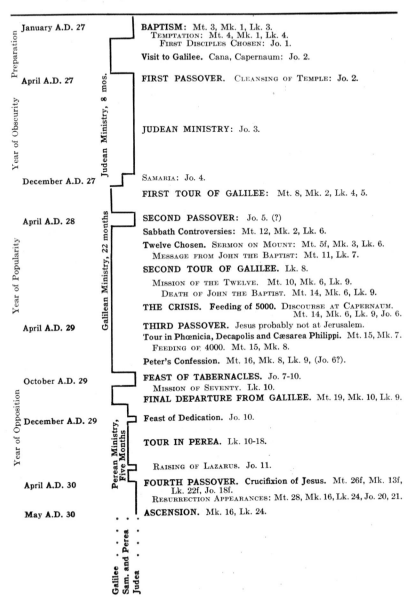

| | | |
|---|---|---|
| **Preparation** | January A.D. 27 | **BAPTISM:** Mt. 3, Mk. 1, Lk. 3.<br>TEMPTATION: Mt. 4, Mk. 1, Lk. 4.<br>FIRST DISCIPLES CHOSEN: Jo. 1.<br>Visit to Galilee. Cana, Capernaum: Jo. 2. |
| | April A.D. 27 | **FIRST PASSOVER.** CLEANSING OF TEMPLE: Jo. 2. |
| **Year of Obscurity** / Judean Ministry, 8 mos. | | **JUDEAN MINISTRY:** Jo. 3. |
| | December A.D. 27 | SAMARIA: Jo. 4.<br>**FIRST TOUR OF GALILEE:** Mt. 8, Mk. 2, Lk. 4, 5. |
| **Year of Popularity** / Galilean Ministry, 22 months | April A.D. 28 | **SECOND PASSOVER:** Jo. 5. (?)<br>Sabbath Controversies: Mt. 12, Mk. 2, Lk. 6.<br>**Twelve Chosen.** SERMON ON MOUNT: Mt. 5f, Mk. 3, Lk. 6.<br>MESSAGE FROM JOHN THE BAPTIST: Mt. 11, Lk. 7.<br>**SECOND TOUR OF GALILEE.** Lk. 8.<br>MISSION OF THE TWELVE. Mt. 10, Mk. 6, Lk. 9.<br>DEATH OF JOHN THE BAPTIST. Mt. 14, Mk. 6, Lk. 9.<br>**THE CRISIS. Feeding of 5000.** DISCOURSE AT CAPERNAUM.<br>Mt. 14, Mk. 6, Lk. 9, Jo. 6. |
| | April A.D. 29 | **THIRD PASSOVER.** Jesus probably not at Jerusalem.<br>Tour in Phœnicia, Decapolis and Cæsarea Philippi. Mt. 15, Mk. 7.<br>FEEDING OF 4000. Mt. 15, Mk. 8.<br>**Peter's Confession.** Mt. 16, Mk. 8, Lk. 9, (Jo. 6?). |
| | October A.D. 29 | **FEAST OF TABERNACLES.** Jo. 7-10.<br>MISSION OF SEVENTY. Lk. 10.<br>**FINAL DEPARTURE FROM GALILEE.** Mt. 19, Mk. 10, Lk. 9. |
| **Year of Opposition** / Perean Ministry, Five Months | December A.D. 29 | Feast of Dedication. Jo. 10.<br>**TOUR IN PEREA.** Lk. 10-18. |
| | April A.D. 30 | RAISING OF LAZARUS. Jo. 11.<br>**FOURTH PASSOVER. Crucifixion of Jesus.** Mt. 26f, Mk. 13f,<br>Lk. 22f, Jo. 18f.<br>RESURRECTION APPEARANCES: Mt. 28, Mk. 16, Lk. 24, Jo. 20, 21. |
| | May A.D. 30 | **ASCENSION.** Mk. 16, Lk. 24. |

Galilee · Sam. and Perea · Judea

## QUESTIONS

How was the coming birth of John the Baptist announced? Who were his parents? How was the coming birth of Jesus announced? What was the "Magnificat"? What were the circumstances of Jesus' birth? Who visited Jesus at Nazareth? Why did the wise men "turn back another way"? Why did Herod slaughter the babies of Bethlehem? How did Jesus escape? Where did his parents make their home afterwards? Describe the visit of Jesus to Jerusalem. How long was he at home at Nazareth? Describe the ministry of John the Baptist. How did he describe the relation of his career to that of Jesus?

How did the ministry of Jesus begin? Name the temptations in the wilderness. How was each conquered? What was John's testimony before the priests and Levites? What title did John give to Jesus? Who were the first three disciples? What was the first miracle? What events happened on the first visit to Capernaum? Where was John the Baptist imprisoned and what was his fate? What four disciples were called in the early Galilean ministry? What was the treatment of Jesus at his own home? What passage of Scripture did he read in the synagogue?

Give an outline of the Sabbath day's ministry at Capernaum. When did Jesus preach on a ship? How was a paralytic brought to Jesus? What taxgatherer was called to service? What was Jesus' teaching about fasting? the Sabbath? What man was healed on the Sabbath? What were the names of the twelve disciples? What were the beatitudes? Give an outline of the Sermon on the Mount.

What did Jesus do for a Roman captain? What happened at Nain? What was John the Baptist's last message? Who anointed Jesus at the house of Simon? Who were Jesus' companions on his second preaching tour? What warnings did he give the scribes and Pharisees? Who are Jesus' true kindred? What stories did Jesus tell beside the sea? How did Jesus still the storm? What happened to the swine of Gadara? What happened to Jesus on his second visit to his old home? Who asked for the head of John the Baptist? What did the Syro-Phoenician woman say to Jesus about dogs? How many people did Jesus feed beside the sea? What sign did the Pharisees and Sadducees ask? What man did Jesus heal near Bethsaida? To what mountain did Jesus go? Whom did he take with him? What was Peter's confession? What name did Jesus give to

Peter? Who appeared at the transfiguration? What happened when Jesus came down from the mountain? What did Jesus say would happen to him at Jerusalem? What was the mission of the seventy? Tell the story of the Good Shepherd; of the Good Samaritan.

What did Jesus teach of prayer? What did Jesus say while being entertained by a Pharisee? What did he say of counting the cost? What were the three parables of grace? those of warning? What did Jesus tell the ten lepers whom he healed? What did he say of the Pharisee and the publican in the Temple? What did Jesus say about his love for little children? How did he treat them? What did Jesus tell the rich young ruler he must do? What ambition had the mother of James and John? Who was healed by Jesus near Jericho? What man climbed a tree to see Jesus? What did Jesus say to him?

How did Jesus enter Jerusalem? Give the events of each day of the last week of his life. What was his teaching and where did he stay at night? What directions did he give for the Passover? What did he do at the Lord's Supper? Who arrested Jesus? Before what tribunals was he brought? What was his treatment by the Roman soldiers? Who bore his cross? Where was he crucified? What were his words on the cross? In whose tomb was he laid? Who came to the tomb on the Sabbath morning? What did they find? How many times did Jesus appear to his disciples? What was his final message?

What are the characteristics of the Book of John? Does it give any account of the birth of Jesus? What was John the Baptist's testimony before the priests and Levites? What did he call Jesus at his baptism? Who were the first three disciples? Who brought them to Jesus? What was the first miracle?

What did Jesus do in the Temple at the beginning of his ministry? Whom did Jesus visit at night? Whom did Jesus meet at Jacob's well? What part did a little boy take in the feeding of five thousand people? What did Jesus say of the bread of life? To what feast did Jesus go in winter? What did Jesus teach of truth and freedom?

Who were Jesus' friends at Bethany? What did he do for them? Where did Jesus go after his visit to Mary and Martha? Compare John's account of the last days at Jerusalem with that of the other gospels. How many appearances of Jesus does John record?

STAIRCASE TO THE HIGH PRIEST'S HOUSE

*Photograph by Frances Jenkins Olcott*

Only a section of the handsome and long stone flight of steps leading up a hill from the brook Kidron, Jerusalem, to the traditional site of the House of Caiaphas, the High Priest.

Up and down these stairs the Saviour probably walked. It may be that the blind man whom he commanded, "Go, wash in the pool of Siloam," walked down these steps to the pool in the valley.

And we wonder, did the officers and soldiers of the high priest, who arrested the Lord Jesus in the Garden of Gethsemane, lead him up these stairs to the house of Caiaphas?

Read John 9:7, page 293; Mark 14:51-72, pages 212-16.

# Christ as a Pilgrim

By Fra Angelico da Fiesole (1387-1455)
Fresco in the Cloister of the Monastery of
San Marco, Florence
Photograph by Alinari Brothers, Florence, Italy

THIS picture, which decorates the semi-circular wall space over the door to the guest quarters of the Monastery of San Marco, represents the virtue of brotherly love. In the stranger we entertain the Lord himself is the simple lesson.

We see two Dominican monks welcoming the Saviour's arrival, unaware of course, of the visitor's identity. The traveler is clad in the skin garment of a pilgrim, holding a staff, and his hat hanging down over his shoulders. The scene is concisely yet exquisitely rendered. The brethren truly rejoice to meet the pilgrim, while the glance of the Saviour displays the truest sense of gratitude. Handsome, youthful, noble, with a slight beard on the chin and long locks flowing over the shoulders, this is the perfection of a type created by Giotto, the exact semblance of one without human dross and all divine. Illustrations of Giotto's work are on pages 308 and 332. Thus does Fra Angelico remind men not only of their obligation toward strangers, but also of the duty of practicing continually brotherly kindness to all.

Fra Angelico was occupied for the greater part of the eleven years that he spent in residence at San Marco with decorating the corridors and cells of the monastery. He was here painting for deeply religious men who knew the Scriptures thoroughly. Perhaps for this reason the painter left out all the smaller realisms presenting the concept directly in the sparse, effective method we see here. These compositions, at their best, such as this one and the one on page 130, reach a simple sublimity which was new to Italian art. It has been said that of all the many beautiful works of Fra Angelico which have come down to us, the one imperishable monument is his frescoed home of San Marco.

# The Beginnings of the New Faith

**W**HEN Jesus finally left the little company of the disciples and appeared to them no more, they were at first greatly dismayed. They determined, however, to wait together at Jerusalem, as he had commanded them. And as they waited, they were all filled with the Holy Spirit, the "other Comforter" whom Christ had promised.

Thus the disciples were empowered for the great missionary task to which Christ had commissioned them. The Book of Acts tells how this was gloriously accomplished, first in the founding of the church at Jerusalem, then in the carrying forth of the gospel from there unto Judea, Samaria, and the uttermost parts of the world.

CHURCH OF THE HOLY SEPULCHRE AT EASTERTIME
*Photograph by Ewing Galloway*

## THE ARCH OF DRUSUS, ROME

Photograph by Anderson, Rome, Italy

BENEATH this arch walked Peter and Paul. The arch of Drusus was decreed by the senate in honor of the second son of the Empress Livia, by her first husband, Tiberius Nero. He died during a campaign on the Rhine in the year 9 B.C. This arch is one of the most perfect existing monuments of Augustan architecture. "It is heavy, plain, and narrow, with all the dignified but stern simplicity which belongs to the character of its age." The masses of masonry on the top are the remains of an aqueduct which formerly crossed the arch.

# Beginnings of the New Faith

## The Early Days of the Church
## at Jerusalem

### Persons of the Story

*The Disciples, especially Peter and Philip.*
*Stephen, the Martyr.*
*A lame man.*
*Ananias.*
*Sapphira.*
*Stephen.*
*Simon, the Sorcerer.*
*Rhoda.*
*Dorcas.*
*Æneas.*
*Cornelius, a Roman Captain.*
*Herod.*
*Annas, Caiaphas.*
*Priests, Officers, Messengers.*

### Places of the Story

*Jerusalem.*
*The country of Palestine and surrounding regions.*
*Joppa.*
*Cæsarea.*
*Lydda.*

### The Command to Service

The disciples were comforted for forty days by the occasional appearances of Jesus. When he met them for the last time, he told them that they should receive power from on high, and that their mission was not only to Judæa and Samaria, but to the uttermost parts of the earth.

HE former treatise have I made, O Theophilus, of all that Jesus began both to do and teach, until the day in which he was taken up, after that he through the Holy Ghost had given commandments unto the apostles whom he had chosen: to whom also he showed himself alive after his passion by many infallible proofs, being seen of them forty days, and speaking of the things pertaining to the kingdom of God: and, being assembled together with them, commanded them that they should not depart from Jerusalem, but wait for the promise of the Father, which, saith he, "Ye have heard of me, for John truly baptized with water; but ye shall be baptized with the Holy Ghost not many days hence."

When they therefore were come together, they asked of him, saying, "Lord, wilt thou at this time restore again the kingdom to Israel?"

And he said unto them, "It is not for you to know the times or the seasons, which the Father hath put in his own power. But ye shall receive power, after that the Holy Ghost is come upon you: and ye shall be witnesses unto me both in Jerusalem, and in all Judæa, and in Samaria, and unto the uttermost part of the earth."

And when he had spoken these things, while they beheld, he was taken up; and a cloud received him out of their sight. And while they looked steadfastly toward heaven as he went up, behold, two men stood by them in white apparel; which also said, "Ye men of Galilee, why stand ye gazing up into heaven? This same Jesus, which is taken up from you into heaven, shall so come in like manner as ye have seen him go into heaven."

— Acts 1:1–11.

## A New Apostle Is Chosen

The disciples began to meet for prayer and consultation. Judas went to his terrible fate and a new member of the company was appointed.

Then returned they unto Jerusalem from the mount called Olivet, which is from Jerusalem a sabbath day's journey. And when they were come in, they went up into an upper room, where abode both Peter, and James, and John, and Andrew, Philip, and Thomas, Bartholomew, and Matthew, James, the son of Alphæus, and Simon Zelotes, and Judas, the brother of James. These all continued with one accord in prayer and supplication, with the women, and Mary, the mother of Jesus, and with his brethren.

THE TREE OF JUDAS

*Photograph by W. A. Pottenger expressly for The Book of Life*

An impossible tradition makes this the tree upon which Judas hanged himself. The site of the country home of Caiaphas is nearby.

And in those days Peter stood up in the midst of the disciples, and said (the number of names together were about an hundred and twenty,)

"Men and brethren, this scripture must needs have been fulfilled, which the Holy Ghost by the mouth of David spake before concerning Judas, which was guide to them that took Jesus. For he was numbered with us, and had obtained part of this ministry." (Now this man purchased a field with the reward of iniquity; and falling headlong, he burst asunder in the midst, and all his bowels gushed out. And it was known unto all the dwellers at Jerusalem; insomuch as that field is called in their proper tongue, "Aceldama," that is to say, "The field of blood.") "For it is written in the book of Psalms,

'Let his habitation be desolate,
And let no man dwell therein':
And his bishopric let another take.'

"Wherefore of these men which have companied with us all the time that the Lord Jesus went in and out among us, beginning from the baptism of John, unto that same day that he was taken up from us, must one be ordained to be a witness with us of his resurrection."

And they appointed two, Joseph called Barsabas, who was surnamed Justus, and Matthias. And they prayed, and said, "Thou, Lord, which knowest the hearts of all men, show whether of these two thou hast chosen, that he may take part of this ministry and apostleship, from which Judas by transgression fell, that he might go to his own place. And they gave forth their lots; and the lot fell upon Matthias; and he was numbered with the eleven apostles.                               — Acts 1:12–26.

### THE DAY OF PENTECOST

And when the day of Pentecost was fully come, they were all with one accord in one place. And suddenly there came a sound from heaven as of a rushing mighty wind, and it filled all the house where they were sitting. And there appeared unto them cloven tongues like as of fire, and it sat upon each of them. And they were all filled with the Holy Ghost, and began to speak with other tongues, as the Spirit gave them utterance.

And there were dwelling at Jerusalem Jews, devout men, out of every nation under heaven. Now when this was noised abroad, the multitude came together, and were confounded, because that every man heard them speak in his own language. And they were all amazed and marvelled, saying one to another, "Behold, are not all these which speak Galilæans? And how hear we every man in our own tongue, wherein we were born? Parthians and Medes and Elamites, and the dwellers in Mesopotamia, in Judæa and Cappadocia, in Pontus and Asia, Phrygia and Pamphylia, in Egypt, and in the parts of Libya about Cyrene, and strangers of Rome, Jews and proselytes, Cretes and Arabians, we do hear them speak in our tongues the wonderful works of God."

And they were all amazed, and were in doubt, saying one to another, "What meaneth this?"

Others mocking said, "These men are full of new wine."

But Peter, standing up with the eleven, lifted up his voice, and said unto them, "Ye men of Judæa, and all ye that dwell at Jerusalem, be this known unto you, and hearken to my words: for these are not drunken, as ye suppose, seeing it is but the third hour of the day  But this is that which was spoken by the prophet Joel;

'And it shall come to pass in the last days, saith God,
I will pour out of my Spirit upon all flesh:
And your sons and your daughters shall prophesy,
And your young men shall see visions,
And your old men shall dream dreams:
And on my servants and on my handmaidens
I will pour out in those days of my Spirit;
And they shall prophesy:
And I will shew wonders in heaven above,

And signs in the earth beneath;
Blood, and fire, and vapour of smoke:
The sun shall be turned into darkness.
And the moon into blood,
Before that great and notable day of the Lord come:
And it shall come to pass, that whosoever shall call
    on the name of the Lord shall be saved.'

"Ye men of Israel, hear these words; Jesus of Nazareth, a man approved of God among you by miracles and
wonders and signs, which God did by him in the midst of
you, as ye yourselves also know: him, being delivered by
the determinate counsel and foreknowledge of God, ye
have taken, and by wicked hands have crucified and slain:
whom God hath raised up, having loosed the pains of
death: because it was not possible that he should be
holden of it.   For David speaketh concerning him,

'I foresaw the Lord always before my face,
For he is on my right hand, that I should not be
    moved:
Therefore did my heart rejoice, and my tongue was
    glad;
Moreover also my flesh shall rest in hope:
Because thou wilt not leave my soul in hell,
Neither wilt thou suffer thine Holy One to see corrup-
    tion.
Thou hast made known to me the ways of life:
Thou shalt make me full of joy with thy countenance.'

"Men and brethren, let me freely speak unto you of
the patriarch David, that he is both dead and buried,
and his sepulcher is with us unto this day.   Therefore
being a prophet, and knowing that God had sworn
with an oath to him, that of the fruit of his loins, according to the flesh, he would raise up Christ to sit on

his throne; he seeing this before spake of the resurrection of Christ, that his soul was not left in hell, neither his flesh did see corruption. This Jesus hath God raised up, whereof we all are witnesses. Therefore being by the right hand of God exalted, and having received of the Father the promise of the Holy Ghost, he hath shed forth this, which ye now see and hear. For David is not ascended into the heavens: but he saith himself,

'The LORD said unto my Lord, "Sit thou on my right hand,
Until I make thy foes thy footstool."'

"Therefore let all the house of Israel know assuredly that God hath made that same Jesus, whom ye have crucified, both Lord and Christ."

Now when they heard this, they were pricked in their heart, and said unto Peter and to the rest of the apostles, "Men and brethren, what shall we do?"

Then Peter said unto them, "Repent, and be baptized every one of you in the name of Jesus Christ for the remission of sins, and ye shall receive the gift of the Holy Ghost. For the promise is unto you, and to your children, and to all that are afar off, even as many as the Lord our God shall call."

And with many other words did he testify and exhort, saying, "Save yourselves from this untoward generation."

Then they that gladly received his word were baptized: and the same day there were added unto them about three thousand souls. And they continued steadfastly in the apostles' doctrine and fellowship, and in breaking of bread, and in prayers. And fear came upon every soul: and many wonders and signs were done by the apostles. And all that believed were together, and had all things common; and sold their possessions and goods, and parted them to all men, as every man had need. And they, continuing daily with one accord in the temple, and breaking bread from house to house, did eat their meat with gladness and singleness of heart, praising God, and having favour with all the people. And the Lord added to the church daily such as should be saved.                    — Acts 2.

### The Miracle at the Gate Beautiful

Peter and John began at once the ministry of healing. A great throng gathered in Solomon's Porch, and Peter, speaking in the power of the Holy Spirit, led more than five thousand converts to Christ. The new teaching soon became known as "The Way."

Now Peter and John went up together into the temple at the hour of prayer, being the ninth hour. And a certain man lame from his birth, was carried, whom they laid daily at the gate of the temple which is called Beautiful, to ask alms of them that entered into the temple; who seeing Peter and John about to go into the temple asked an alms. And Peter, fastening his eyes upon him with John, said, "Look on us." And he gave heed unto them, expecting to receive something of them.

Then Peter said, "Silver and gold have I none; but such as I have give I thee: in the name of Jesus Christ of Nazareth rise up and walk." And he took him by the right hand, and lifted him up: and immediately his feet and ankle bones received strength. And he leaping up stood, and walked, and entered with them into the temple, walking, and leaping, and praising God. And all the people saw him walking and praising God: and they knew that it was he which sat for alms at the Beautiful gate of the temple: and they were filled with wonder and amazement at that which had happened unto him. And as the lame man which was healed held Peter and John, all the people ran together unto them in the porch that is called Solomon's, greatly wondering.

And when Peter saw it, he answered unto the people, "Ye men of Israel, why marvel ye at this? Or why look ye so earnestly on us, as though by our own power or holiness we had made this man to walk? The God of Abraham, and of Isaac, and of Jacob, the God of our fathers, hath glorified his Son Jesus; whom ye delivered up, and denied him in the presence of Pilate, when he was determined to let him go. But ye denied the Holy One and the Just, and desired a murderer to be granted unto you; and killed the Prince of life, whom God hath raised from the dead; whereof we are witnesses. And his name through faith in his name hath made this man strong, whom ye see and know: yea, the faith which is by him hath given him this perfect soundness in the presence of you all. And now, brethren, I wot that through ignorance ye did it, as did also your rulers. But those things, which God before had showed by the mouth of all his prophets, that Christ should suffer, he hath so fulfilled.

"Repent ye therefore, and be converted, that your sins may be blotted out, when the times of refreshing shall come from the presence of the Lord; and he shall send Jesus Christ, which before was preached unto you: whom the heaven must receive until the times of restitution of all things, which God hath spoken by the mouth of all his holy prophets since the world began. For Moses truly said unto the fathers, 'A prophet shall the LORD your God raise up unto you of your brethren, like unto me; him shall ye hear in all things whatsoever he shall say unto you. And it shall come to pass, that every soul, which will not hear that prophet, shall be destroyed from among the people.'

"Yea, and all the prophets from Samuel and those that follow after, as many as have spoken, have likewise foretold of these days.  Ye are the children of the prophets, and of the covenant which God made with our fathers, saying unto Abraham, 'And in thy seed shall all the kindreds of the earth be blessed.'  Unto you first God, having raised up his Son Jesus, sent him to bless you, in turning away every one of you from his iniquities."

— Acts 3.

## The Alarm of the Rulers

The authorities had put Jesus to death.  They were soon to find that he had risen from the dead.  They charged the disciples to keep silence, but they could not silence the truth.

And as they spake unto the people, the priests, and the captain of the temple, and the Sadducees, came upon them, being grieved that they taught the people, and preached through Jesus the resurrection from the dead. And they laid hands on them, and put them in hold unto the next day:  for it was now eventide.  Howbeit many of them which heard the word believed;  and the number of the men was about five thousand.

And it came to pass on the morrow, that their rulers, and elders, and scribes, and Annas, the high priest, and Caiaphas, and John, and Alexander, and as many as were of the kindred of the high priest, were gathered together at Jerusalem.  And when they had set them in the midst, they asked, "By what power, or by what name, have ye done this?"

Then Peter, filled with the Holy Ghost, said unto them, "Ye rulers of the people, and elders of Israel, if we this day be examined of the good deed done to the impotent man, by what means he is made whole;  be it known unto you all, and to all the people of Israel, that by the name of Jesus Christ of Nazareth, whom ye crucified, whom God raised from the dead, even by him doth this man stand here before you whole. This is the stone which was set at naught of you builders, which is become the head of the corner. Neither is there salvation in any other: for there is none other name under heaven given among men, whereby we must be saved."

Now when they saw the boldness of Peter and John, and perceived that they were unlearned and ignorant men, they marveled; and they took knowledge of them, that they had been with Jesus. And beholding the man which was healed standing with them, they could say nothing against it. But when they had commanded them to go aside out of the council, they conferred among themselves, saying, "What shall we do to these men? For that indeed a notable miracle hath been done by them is manifest to all them that dwell in Jerusalem; and we cannot deny it. But that it spread no further among the people, let us straitly threaten them, that they speak henceforth to no man in this name."

And they called them, and commanded them not to speak at all nor teach in the name of Jesus. But Peter and John answered and said unto them, "Whether it be right in the sight of God to hearken unto you more than unto God, judge ye. For we cannot but speak the things which we have seen and heard."

So when they had further threatened them, they let them go, finding nothing how they might punish them, because of the people: for all men glorified God for that which was done. For the man was above forty years old, on whom this miracle of healing was showed.

And being let go, they went to their own company, and reported all that the chief priests and elders had said unto them. And when they heard that, they lifted up their voice to God with one accord, and said, "Lord, thou art God, which hast made heaven, and earth, and the sea, and all that in them is: who by the mouth of thy servant David hast said,

'Why did the heathen rage,
And the people imagine vain things?
The kings of the earth stood up
And the rulers were gathered together
Against the Lord, and against his Christ.'

For of a truth against thy holy child Jesus, whom thou hast anointed, both Herod, and Pontius Pilate, with the Gentiles, and the people of Israel, were gathered together, for to do whatsoever thy hand and thy counsel determined before to be done. And now, Lord, behold their threatenings: and grant unto thy servants, that with all boldness they may speak thy word, by stretching forth thine hand to heal; and that signs and wonders may be done by the name of thy holy child Jesus."

And when they had prayed, the place was shaken where they were assembled together; and they were all filled with the Holy Ghost, and they spake the word of God with boldness.

And the multitude of them that believed were of one heart and of one soul: neither said any of them that ought of the things which he possessed was his own; but they had all things common. And with great power gave the apostles witness of the resurrection of the Lord Jesus: and great grace was upon them all. Neither was there any among them that lacked: for as many as were possessors of lands or houses sold them, and brought the prices of the things that were sold, and laid them down at the apostles' feet: and distribution was made unto every man according as he had need. And Joses, who

JOPPA

*Photograph by W. A. Pottenger expressly for The Book of Life*

A view of the ancient city where Peter lodged at the house of Simon the Tanner.

by the apostles was surnamed Barnabas, (which is, being interpreted, "The son of consolation") a Levite, and of the country of Cyprus, having land, sold it, and brought the money, and laid it at the apostles' feet.        — Acts 4.

## A LIE AND ITS CONSEQUENCES

At first, the new converts had all things in common. The avarice and deceit of Ananias and Sapphira brought down upon them a dreadful punishment.

But a certain man named Ananias, with Sapphira his wife, sold a possession, and kept back part of the price, his wife also being privy to it, and brought a certain part, and laid it at the apostles' feet. But Peter said, "Ananias, why hath Satan filled thine heart to lie to the Holy Ghost, and to keep back part of the price of the land? Whiles it remained, was it not thine own? And after it was sold, was it not in thine own power? Why hast thou conceived this thing in thine heart? Thou hast not lied unto men, but unto God."

And Ananias hearing these words fell down, and gave up the ghost: and great fear came on all them that heard these things. And the young men arose, wound him up, and carried him out, and buried him. And it was about the space of three hours after, when his wife, not knowing what was done, came in.

And Peter answered unto her, "Tell me whether ye sold the land for so much?"

And she said, "Yea, for so much."

Then Peter said unto her, "How is it that ye have agreed together to tempt the Spirit of the LORD? Behold, the feet of them which have buried thy husband are at the door, and shall carry thee out."

Then fell she down straightway at his feet, and yielded up the ghost: and the young men came in, and found her

LYDDA

*Photograph by W. A. Pottenger expressly for The Book of Life*

Lydda is an old town ten miles from Joppa on the plain which was in ancient days the plain of Sharon.

"And it came to pass, as Peter passed throughout all quarters, he came down also to the saints which dwelt at Lydda."—*Acts 9:32.*

dead, and, carrying her forth, buried her by her husband. And great fear came upon all the church, and upon as many as heard these things. — Acts 5:1–11.

## The Sick Are Brought Forth That at Least the Shadow of Peter May Fall on Them

And by the hands of the apostles were many signs and wonders wrought among the people; (and they were all with one accord in Solomon's porch. And of the rest durst no man join himself to them: but the people magnified them. And believers were the more added to the Lord, multitudes both of men and women.) Insomuch that they brought forth the sick into the streets, and laid them on beds and couches, that at the least the shadow of Peter passing by might overshadow some of them. There came also a multitude out of the cities round about unto Jerusalem, bringing sick folks, and them which were vexed with unclean spirits: and they were healed every one. — Acts 5:12–16.

## The First Imprisonment

The authorities were now determined to suppress those who were found proclaiming the new faith. Speaking boldly before the council, Peter charged the rulers with the death of Jesus. An unexpected defender was found in Gamaliel, the great rabbi, who counseled prudence and an honest examination of the new faith.

## The Disciples Continue to Preach in Spite of Threats

Then the high priest rose up, and all they that were with him, (which is the sect of the Sadducees,) and were filled with indignation, and laid their hands on the apostles, and put them in the common prison. But the angel of the Lord by night opened the prison doors, and brought them forth, and said, "Go, stand and speak in the temple to the people all the words of this life." And when they heard that, they entered into the temple early in the morning, and taught. But the high priest came, and they that were with him, and called the council together, and all the senate of the children of Israel, and sent to the prison to have them brought.

But when the officers came, and found them not in the prison, they returned, and told, saying, "The prison truly found we shut with all safety, and the keepers standing without before the doors: but when we had opened, we found no man within."

Now when the high priest and the captain of the temple and the chief priests heard these things, they doubted of them whereunto this would grow.

Then came one and told them, saying, "Behold, the men whom ye put in prison are standing in the temple, and teaching the people."

Then went the captain with the officers, and brought them without violence: for they feared the people, lest they should have been stoned. And when they had brought them, they set them before the council: and the high priest asked them, saying, "Did not we straitly command you that ye should not teach in this name? And, behold, ye have filled Jerusalem with your doctrine, and intend to bring this man's blood upon us."

Then Peter and the other apostles answered and said, "We ought to obey God rather than men. The God of our fathers raised up Jesus, whom ye slew and hanged on a tree. Him hath God exalted with his right hand to be a Prince and a Saviour, for to give repentance to Israel, and forgiveness of sins. And we are his witnesses of these things; and so is also the Holy Ghost, whom God hath given to them that obey him."

When they heard that, they were cut to the heart, and took counsel to slay them.

GATE OF SAINT STEPHEN—JERUSALEM

Photograph by W. A. Pottenger
expressly for The Book of Life

THIS is situated on the east side of the
city on the way to Mount Olive and it is
said to be the gate through which Saint
Stephen was taken on the way to be stoned.

Then stood there up one in the council, a Pharisee, named Gamaliel, a doctor of the law, had in reputation among all the people, and commanded to put the apostles forth a little space; and said unto them, "Ye men of Israel, take heed to yourselves what ye intend to do as touching these men. For before these days rose up Theudas, boasting himself to be somebody; to whom a number of men, about four hundred, joined themselves: who was slain; and all, as many as obeyed him, were scattered, and brought to naught. After this man rose up Judas of Galilee in the days of the taxing, and drew away much people after him: he also perished; and all, even as many as obeyed him, were dispersed. And now I say unto you, refrain from these men, and let them alone: for if this counsel or this work be of men, it will come to naught: but if it be of God, ye cannot overthrow it; lest haply ye be found even to fight against God."

And to him they agreed: and when they had called the apostles, and beaten them, they commanded that they should not speak in the name of Jesus, and let them go.

And they departed from the presence of the council, rejoicing that they were counted worthy to suffer shame for his name. And daily in the temple, and in every house, they ceased not to teach and preach Jesus Christ.

— Acts 5:17–42.

## The First Martyr

For a little space, two or three years perhaps, the new church at Jerusalem grew quietly, without much notice and without persecution. Then suddenly the hostility of the Jews broke out and the Age of Martyrdom began. This age was to last in its intensity for three centuries, but the "blood of the martyrs was the seed of the church," and it thrived upon persecution.

Stephen, one of the seven deacons of the first Christian Church at Jerusalem, led that noble army of martyrs. Paul had come back to Jerusalem after his graduation from college and an absence of some years.  He saw the stoning of Stephen.  The men of the mob, who did the deadly work, laid down their garments at the feet of the respectable young rabbi who watched with indifference.  How often that scene must have come back to him in later years!   The young man with the fine face, kneeling to receive the murderous rain of stones and crying, "Lord, lay not this sin to their charge!"

And in those days, when the number of the disciples was multiplied, there arose a murmuring of the Grecians against the Hebrews, because their widows were neglected in the daily ministration.  Then the twelve called the multitude of the disciples unto them, and said, "It is not reason that we should leave the word of God, and serve tables.  Wherefore, brethren, look ye out among you seven men of honest report, full of the Holy Ghost and wisdom, whom we may appoint over this business.  But we will give ourselves continually to prayer, and to the ministry of the word."

### STEPHEN, A MAN "FULL OF FAITH AND POWER," INCURS THE ENMITY OF THE JEWS

And the saying pleased the whole multitude: and they chose Stephen, a man full of faith and of the Holy Ghost, and Philip, and Prochorus, and Nicanor, and Timon, and Parmenas, and Nicolas, a proselyte of Antioch: whom they set before the apostles: and when they had prayed, they laid their hands on them.  And the word of God increased; and the number of the disciples multiplied in Jerusalem greatly; and a great company of the priests were obedient to the faith.  And Stephen, full of faith and power, did great wonders and miracles among the people.

Then there arose certain of the synagogue, which is called the synagogue of the Libertines, and Cyrenians, and Alexandrians, and of them of Cilicia and of Asia, disputing with Stephen. And they were not able to resist the wisdom and the spirit by which he spake. Then they suborned men, which said, "We have heard him speak blasphemous words against Moses, and against God."

### BEFORE THE COUNCIL — AN UNFAIR TRIAL

And they stirred up the people, and the elders, and the scribes, and came upon him, and caught him, and brought him to the council, and set up false witnesses, which said, "This man ceaseth not to speak blasphemous words against this holy place, and the law: for we have heard him say that this Jesus of Nazareth shall destroy this place, and shall change the customs which Moses delivered us." And all that sat in the council, looking steadfastly on him, saw his face as it had been the face of an angel.

Then said the high priest, "Are these things so?"

—Acts 6; 7:1.

### STEPHEN SPEAKS IN HIS OWN DEFENSE

And he said, "Men, brethren, and fathers, hearken. The God of glory appeared unto our father Abraham, when he was in Mesopotamia, before he dwelt in Charran, and said unto him, 'Get thee out of thy country, and from thy kindred, and come into the land which I shall show thee.' Then came he out of the land of the Chaldæans, and dwelt in Charran: and from thence, when his father was dead, he removed him into this land, wherein ye now dwell. And he gave him none inheritance in it, no, not so much as to set his foot on: yet he promised that he would give it to him for a possession, and to his seed after him, when as yet he had no child. And God spake on this wise, that his seed should sojourn in a strange land; and that they should bring them into bondage, and entreat them evil four hundred years. 'And the nation to whom they shall be in bondage will I judge,' said God: 'and after that shall they come forth, and serve me in this place.' And he gave him the covenant of circumcision: and so Abraham begat Isaac, and circumcised him the eighth day; and Isaac begat Jacob; and Jacob begat the twelve patriarchs. And the patriarchs, moved with envy, sold Joseph into Egypt: but God was with him, and delivered him out of all his afflictions, and gave him favour and wisdom in the sight of Pharaoh, King of Egypt; and he made him governor over Egypt and all his house. Now there came a dearth over all the land of Egypt and Chanaan, and great affliction: and our fathers found no sustenance. But when Jacob heard that there was corn in Egypt, he sent out our fathers first. And at the second time Joseph was made known to his brethren; and Joseph's kindred was made known unto Pharaoh. Then sent Joseph, and called his father Jacob to him, and all his kindred, threescore and fifteen souls. So Jacob went down into Egypt, and died, he and our fathers, and were carried over into Sychem, and laid in the sepulcher that Abraham bought for a sum of money of the sons of Emmor, the father of Sychem.

"But when the time of the promise drew nigh, which God had sworn to Abraham, the people grew and multiplied in Egypt, till another king arose, which knew not Joseph. The same dealt subtilly with our kindred, and evil entreated our fathers, so that they cast out their young children, to the end they might not live. In which time Moses was born, and was exceeding fair, and nourished up in his father's house three months: and when he was cast out, Pharaoh's daughter took him up, and nourished him for her own son. And Moses was learned in all the wisdom of the Egyptians, and was mighty in words and in

ROMAN FORUM

Photograph by W. A. Pottenger
expressly for The Book of Life

THIS fine picture shows the ancient columns of the Roman Forum and gives a
view of the city in the distance.

deeds. And when he was full forty years old, it came into his heart to visit his brethren, the children of Israel. And seeing one of them suffer wrong, he defended him, and avenged him that was oppressed, and smote the Egyptian: for he supposed his brethren would have understood how that God by his hand would deliver them: but they understood not. And the next day he showed himself unto them as they strove, and would have set them at one again, saying, 'Sirs, ye are brethren; why do ye wrong one to another?'

"But he that did his neighbour wrong thrust him away, saying, 'Who made thee a ruler and a judge over us? Wilt thou kill me, as thou diddest the Egyptian yesterday?'

"Then fled Moses at this saying, and was a stranger in the land of Midian, where he begat two sons. And when forty years were expired, there appeared to him in the wilderness of Mount Sinai an angel of the LORD in a flame of fire in a bush. When Moses saw it, he wondered at the sight: and as he drew near to behold it, the voice of the LORD came unto him, saying, 'I am the God of thy fathers, the God of Abraham, and the God of Isaac, and the God of Jacob.'

"Then Moses trembled, and durst not behold. Then said the LORD to him, 'Put off thy shoes from thy feet: for the place where thou standest is holy ground. I have seen, I have seen the affliction of my people which is in Egypt, and I have heard their groaning, and am come down to deliver them. And now come, I will send thee into Egypt.'

"This Moses whom they refused, saying, 'Who made thee a ruler and a judge?' The same did God send to be a ruler and a deliverer by the hand of the angel which appeared to him in the bush. He brought them out, after that he had showed wonders and signs in the land of Egypt, and in the Red Sea, and in the wilderness forty years.

"This is that Moses, which said unto the children of Israel, 'A prophet shall the LORD your God raise up unto you of your brethren, like unto me; him shall ye hear.' This is he, that was in the church in the wilderness with the angel which spake to him in the Mount Sinai, and with our fathers: who received the lively oracles to give unto us: to whom our fathers would not obey, but thrust him from them, and in their hearts turned back again into Egypt, saying unto Aaron, 'Make us gods to go before us: for as for this Moses, which brought us out of the land of Egypt, we wot not what is become of him.' And they made a calf in those days, and offered sacrifice unto the idol, and rejoiced in the works of their own hands. Then God turned, and gave them up to worship the host of heaven; as it is written in the book of the prophets,

'O ye house of Israel, have ye offered to me
    slain beasts and sacrifices
By the space of forty years in the wilderness?
Yea, ye took up the tabernacle of Moloch,
And the star of your god Rephan,
Figures which ye made to worship them:
And I will carry you away beyond Babylon.'

"Our fathers had the tabernacle of witness in the wilderness, as he had appointed, speaking unto Moses, that he should make it according to the fashion that he had seen. Which also our fathers that came after brought in with Jesus into the possession of the Gentiles, whom God drave out before the face of our fathers, unto the days of David; who found favour before God, and desired to find a tabernacle for the God of Jacob. But Solomon built him an

### THE APPIAN WAY, ROME

Photograph by Anderson, Rome, Italy

WE MAY be sure that Paul walked upon this very road, which is perhaps the most famous road in history. It was called the "Queen of Roads." It was begun by the blind Censor, Appius Claudius, 312 B.C. It was paved throughout. It was the main artery of travel from the imperial city to the sea. Along its course came and went the great tides of travel: emperors returning in triumph from their conquests; merchants, prisoners, slaves; Horatius, Nero, Cicero; and greatest men of all, the apostle Paul, and if tradition is to be believed, Peter also.

house.  Howbeit the most High dwelleth not in temples made with hands; as saith the prophet,

'Heaven is my throne,
And earth is my footstool:
What house will ye build me? saith the LORD:
Or what is the place of my rest?
Hath not my hand made all these things?'

"Ye stiffnecked and uncircumcised in heart and ears, ye do always resist the Holy Ghost: as your fathers did, so do ye.  Which of the prophets have not your fathers persecuted?  And they have slain them which showed before of the coming of the Just One;  of whom ye have been now the betrayers and murderers: who have received the law by the disposition of angels, and have not kept it."

### HIS ENEMIES ARE CUT TO THE HEART, BUT RELENTLESS

When they heard these things, they were cut to the heart, and they gnashed on him with their teeth.

But he, being full of the Holy Ghost, looked up steadfastly into heaven, and saw the glory of God, and Jesus standing on the right hand of God, and said, "Behold, I see the heavens opened, and the Son of man standing on the right hand of God."

### "AND THEY STONED STEPHEN"

Then they cried out with a loud voice, and stopped their ears, and ran upon him with one accord, and cast him out of the city, and stoned him: and the witnesses laid down their clothes at a young man's feet, whose name was Saul.  And they stoned Stephen, calling upon God, and saying, "Lord Jesus, receive my spirit."

And he kneeled down, and cried with a loud voice, "Lord, lay not this sin to their charge." And when he had said this, he fell asleep. And Saul was consenting unto his death.                                                                — Acts 6; 7; 8:1a.

## The First Great Persecution

The persecution, under the direction of Saul, scattered the disciples all over Syria.

And at that time there was a great persecution against the church which was at Jerusalem; and they were all scattered abroad throughout the regions of Judæa and Samaria, except the apostles. And devout men carried Stephen to his burial, and made great lamentation over him. As for Saul, he made havoc of the church, entering into every house, and haling men and women, committed them to prison. Therefore they that were scattered abroad went everywhere preaching the word.

## The Gospel Is Taken to Samaria

Then Philip went down to the city of Samaria, and preached Christ unto them. And the people with one accord gave heed unto those things which Philip spake, hearing and seeing the miracles which he did. For unclean spirits, crying with loud voice, came out of many that were possessed with them: and many taken with palsies, and that were lame, were healed. And there was great joy in that city.

But there was a certain man, called Simon, which beforetime in the same city used sorcery, and bewitched the people of Samaria, giving out that himself was some great one: to whom they all gave heed, from the least to the greatest, saying, "This man is the great power of God." And to him they had regard, because that of long

### THE CHURCH OF SAINT PETER IN
### CHAINS, ROME

Photograph by Anderson, Rome, Italy

THIS is one of the famous churches connected by tradition with the life of the Apostle Peter in Rome.

"The chains, left in the Mamertine Prisons after S. Peter's confinement there, are said to have been found by the martyr, S. Balbina, in 126, and by her given to Theodora, another sainted martyr, sister to Hermes, Prefect of Rome, from whom they passed into the hands of Alexander, then the bishop of Rome, and were finally deposited by him in the church erected by Theodora, where they have since remained. Such is the legend, but the historic origin of this basilica cannot be traced earlier than about the middle of the fifth century, subsequent to the year 439, when Juvenal, bishop of Jerusalem, presented to the Empress Eudoxia, wife of Theodosius the Younger, two chains, believed to be those of S. Peter, one of which was placed by her in the Basilica of the Apostles at Constantinople, and the other sent to Rome for her daughter Eudoxia, wife of Valentinian III, who caused this church, hence called Eudoxian, to be erected, as the special shrine of S. Peter's chains."—*Hemans.*

time he had bewitched them with sorceries. But when they believed Philip preaching the things concerning the kingdom of God, and the name of Jesus Christ, they were baptized, both men and women. Then Simon himself believed also: and when he was baptized, he continued with Philip, and wondered, beholding the miracles and signs which were done.

Now when the apostles which were at Jerusalem heard that Samaria had received the word of God, they sent unto them Peter and John: who, when they were come down, prayed for them, that they might receive the Holy Ghost: (for as yet he was fallen upon none of them: only they were baptized in the name of the Lord Jesus.) Then laid they their hands on them, and they received the Holy Ghost. And when Simon saw that through laying on of the apostles' hands the Holy Ghost was given, he offered them money, saying, "Give me also this power, that on whomsoever I lay hands, he may receive the Holy Ghost."

But Peter said unto him, "Thy money perish with thee, because thou hast thought that the gift of God may be purchased with money. Thou hast neither part nor lot in this matter: for thy heart is not right in the sight of God. Repent therefore of this thy wickedness, and pray God, if perhaps the thought of thine heart may be forgiven thee. For I perceive that thou art in the gall of bitterness, and in the bond of iniquity."

Then answered Simon, and said, "Pray ye to the Lord for me, that none of these things which ye have spoken come upon me."

And they, when they had testified and preached the word of the Lord, returned to Jerusalem, and preached the gospel in many villages of the Samaritans.

— Acts 8:1b—25.

## Philip and the Officer of Queen Candace

Far and wide the disciples were scattered, but wherever they went, they carried the good news with them. The rulers at Jerusalem were not shrewd; by driving the disciples from the city, they were simply scattering broadcast the seed of the new teaching. Everywhere the disciples went, they became little candle flames of light which would, in time, become the light of the world. One of the most interesting of all the stories of the victories of the new faith is that of Philip and the high officer of Candace, queen of the Ethiopians: how the apostle, walking along the road, met the officer in his chariot reading the book of Isaiah; how Philip accepted the gracious invitation to ride with him, made him a convert to "The Way," and baptized him in the water which was near at hand.

And the angel of the Lord spake unto Philip, saying, "Arise, and go toward the south unto the way that goeth down from Jerusalem unto Gaza, which is desert."

And he arose and went: and, behold, a man of Ethiopia, an eunuch of great authority under Candace, queen of the Ethiopians, who had the charge of all her

LUD—THE ANCIENT LYDDA
*Photograph by W. A. Pottenger expressly for The Book of Life*

This ancient town was the scene of a very early Christian community. It was here that Peter healed Æneas.

# The Liberation of Peter from Prison

By Raphael Sanzio (1483-1520)
In the Stanza d' Eliodoro of the Vatican, Rome
Photograph by Anderson, Rome, Italy

THIS famous wall decoration represents Peter's
escape from prison as given on pages 445-449. The
story is told here in three separate scenes. In the central space, above a window of the room, a radiant angel
is seen through prison bars, stooping down to wake the
apostle who is chained to two soldiers asleep at their
post. On the right, the same white-robed angel is shown
leading Peter, who follows as if in a dream, past the
sleeping guards. On the left, a warder, bearing a lighted
torch, rushes up the opposite flight of steps to give the
alarm. The Bible mentions that the alarm was given in
the morning. Here we see a crescent moon riding high
in the clouds while the dawn is breaking in the far east.
Never before or since has the story been told so simply
and so impressively. The beautiful light effects, uncom-
mon in Raphael's day, add much to the beauty of the
conception. A detail of this fresco is given in Volume I,
page 374.

Raphael Sanzio was born in Urbino in 1483. He won
distinction as an apprentice in the school of Pietro
Perugino at Perugia where he completely assimilated
the gentle style of that master. In 1504 he went to
Florence and was profoundly impressed by the newer
art of Leonardo and Michelangelo. In a brief four years
he mastered the Florentine realism of movement and
anatomy, and was called to Rome. By 1511 he was
acknowledged to have but one possible rival in Italy —
Michelangelo. The hall which contains this picture of
Peter was painted between 1511 and 1514. The remaining six years of Raphael's life were devoted to many
artistic pursuits and filled with success and honors.

Other pictures by Raphael are on pages 243, 246
and 360.

treasure, and had come to Jerusalem for to worship, was returning, and sitting in his chariot read Esaias the prophet.

Then the Spirit said unto Philip, "Go near, and join thyself to this chariot."

And Philip ran thither to him, and heard him read the prophet Esaias, and said, "Understandest thou what thou readest?"

And he said, "How can I, except some man should guide me?" And he desired Philip that he would come up and sit with him.

The place of the scripture which he read was this,

"He was led as a sheep to the slaughter;
And like a lamb dumb before his shearer,
So opened he not his mouth:
In his humiliation his judgment was taken away:
And who shall declare his generation?
For his life is taken from the earth."

And the eunuch answered Philip, and said, "I pray thee, of whom speaketh the prophet this? Of himself, or of some other man?"

Then Philip opened his mouth, and began at the same scripture, and preached unto him Jesus. And as they went on their way, they came unto a certain water: and the eunuch said, "See, here is water; what doth hinder me to be baptized?"

And Philip said, "If thou believest with all thine heart, thou mayest."

And he answered and said, "I believe that Jesus Christ is the Son of God."

And he commanded the chariot to stand still: and they went down both into the water, both Philip and the eunuch; and he baptized him. And when they were come up out of the water, the Spirit of the Lord caught away Philip, that the eunuch saw him no more: and he went on his way rejoicing. But Philip was found at Azotus: and passing through he preached in all the cities, till he came to Cæsarea. — Acts 8:26–40.

## Peter the Healer

Here Peter is at his very best. It makes us wish that we had more such stories and knew more of Peter's life. We think of Paul as the great apostle to the Gentiles, but Peter was also a great apostle to the Gentiles. This lesson which was taught him in such a striking way was never forgotten. It is not the cautious, cowardly Peter of the denial and the cock-crow of the morning of the crucifixion whom we have here, but a valiant and obedient Peter, who hurries to Cæsarea and baptizes the household of a Roman centurion, contrary to all the traditions and precedents of the church.

Then had the churches rest throughout all Judæa and Galilee and Samaria, and were edified; and walking in the fear of the Lord, and in the comfort of the Holy Ghost, were multiplied.

And it came to pass, as Peter passed throughout all quarters, he came down also to the saints which dwelt at Lydda. And there he found a certain man named Æneas, which had kept his bed eight years, and was sick of the palsy. And Peter said unto him, "Æneas, Jesus Christ maketh thee whole: arise, and make thy bed." And he arose immediately. And all that dwelt at Lydda and Saron saw him, and turned to the Lord.

Now there was at Joppa a certain disciple named Tabitha, which by interpretation is called Dorcas: this woman was full of good works and almsdeeds which she did. And it came to pass in those days that she was sick and died: whom when they had washed, they laid her in an upper chamber. And forasmuch as Lydda was nigh

### EMPEROR NERO

In the Vatican, Rome, Italy
Photograph by Anderson, Rome, Italy

THIS is a greatly idealized portrait of the emperor, who is characterized in history as a monster of cruelty. This is the emperor who condemned Paul to death.

Nero was born in 37 A.D. and died by his own hand 68 A.D. Rome was destroyed by fire 64 A.D. It is believed that Nero himself caused the fire to be started but the blame was placed upon the Christians, and the persecution of the new faith was begun.

MVN. PII. SEXTI

to Joppa, and the disciples had heard that Peter was there, they sent unto him two men, desiring him that he would not delay to come to them. Then Peter arose and went with them. When he was come, they brought him into the upper chamber: and all the widows stood by him weeping, and showing the coats and garments which Dorcas made, while she was with them. But Peter put them all forth, and kneeled down, and prayed; and turning him to the body said, "Tabitha, arise." And she opened her eyes: and when she saw Peter, she sat up. And he gave her his hand, and lifted her up, and when he had called the saints and widows, presented her alive. And it was known throughout all Joppa; and many believed in the Lord. And it came to pass that he tarried many days in Joppa with one Simon, a tanner.

— Acts 9:31–43.

## THE VISION OF PETER

### THE VISION OF CORNELIUS THE DEVOUT ROMAN CENTURION OF CÆSAREA

There was a certain man in Cæsarea called Cornelius, a centurion of the band called the Italian band, a devout man, and one that feared God with all his house, which gave much alms to the people, and prayed to God alway. He saw in a vision evidently about the ninth hour of the day an angel of God coming in to him, and saying unto him, "Cornelius."

And when he looked on him, he was afraid, and said, "What is it, Lord?"

And he said unto him, "Thy prayers and thine alms are come up for a memorial before God. And now send men to Joppa, and call for one Simon, whose surname is Peter: he lodgeth with one Simon, a tanner, whose house is by the seaside: he shall tell thee what thou oughtest to do."

And when the angel which spake unto Cornelius was departed, he called two of his household servants, and a devout soldier of them that waited on him continually; and when he had declared all these things unto them, he sent them to Joppa.

### HOW PETER SAW HEAVEN OPENED, AND THE CLEAN AND UNCLEAN BEASTS

On the morrow, as they went on their journey, and drew nigh unto the city, Peter went up upon the housetop to pray about the sixth hour: and he became very hungry, and would have eaten: but while they made ready, he fell into a trance, and saw heaven opened, and a certain vessel descending unto him, as it had been a great sheet knit at the four corners, and let down to the earth: wherein were all manner of four-footed beasts of the earth, and wild beasts, and creeping things, and fowls of the air.

### "WHAT GOD HATH CLEANSED, CALL NOT THOU COMMON"

And there came a voice to him, "Rise, Peter; kill, and eat."

But Peter said, "Not so, Lord; for I have never eaten anything that is common or unclean."

And the voice spake unto him again the second time, "What God hath cleansed, that call not thou common."

This was done thrice: and the vessel was received up again into heaven. Now while Peter doubted in himself what this vision which he had seen should mean, behold, the men which were sent from Cornelius had made enquiry for Simon's house, and stood before the gate, and called, and asked whether Simon, which was surnamed Peter, were lodged there.

TOMB OF CECILIA METELLA, APPIAN
WAY

Photograph by Anderson, Rome, Italy

OUT on the Appian Way beyond the cata-
combs of St. Calixtus and St. Sebastian
rises a round tower, the tomb of Cecilia
Metella, wife of Crassus. There is a wide
view here of the Campagna with the peaks
of the Sabine hills, snow-covered in winter,
in the distance.

## PETER GOES TO CÆSAREA

While Peter thought on the vision, the Spirit said unto him, "Behold, three men seek thee. Arise therefore, and get thee down, and go with them, doubting nothing: for I have sent them."

Then Peter went down to the men which were sent unto him from Cornelius; and said, "Behold, I am he whom ye seek: what is the cause wherefore ye are come?"

And they said, "Cornelius the centurion, a just man, and one that feareth God, and of good report among all the nation of the Jews, was warned from God by an holy angel to send for thee into his house, and to hear words of thee."

Then called he them in, and lodged them. And on the morrow Peter went away with them, and certain brethren from Joppa accompanied him. And the morrow after they entered into Cæsarea. And Cornelius waited for them, and had called together his kinsmen and near friends. And as Peter was coming in, Cornelius met him, and fell down at his feet, and worshiped him. But Peter took him up, saying. "Stand up; I myself also am a man."

## CORNELIUS TELLS PETER HIS STORY

And as he talked with him, he went in, and found many that were come together.

And he said unto them, "Ye know how that it is an unlawful thing for a man that is a Jew to keep company, or come unto one of another nation; but God hath showed me that I should not call any man common or unclean. Therefore came I unto you without gainsaying, as soon as I was sent for: I ask therefore for what intent ye have sent for me?"

And Cornelius said, "Four days ago I was fasting until this hour; and at the ninth hour I prayed in my house, and, behold, a man stood before me in bright clothing, and said, 'Cornelius, thy prayer is heard, and thine alms are had in remembrance in the sight of God. Send therefore to Joppa, and call hither Simon, whose surname is Peter; he is lodged in the house of one Simon, a tanner by the seaside: who, when he cometh, shall speak unto thee.'

"Immediately therefore I sent to thee; and thou hast well done that thou art come. Now therefore are we all here present before God, to hear all things that are commanded thee of God."

### "OF A TRUTH . . . GOD IS NO RESPECTER OF PERSONS"

Then Peter opened his mouth, and said, "Of a truth I perceive that God is no respecter of persons: but in every nation he that feareth him, and worketh righteousness, is accepted with him. The word which God sent unto the children of Israel, preaching peace by Jesus Christ: (he is Lord of all:) That word, I say, ye know, which was published throughout all Judæa, and began from Galilee, after the baptism which John preached; how God anointed Jesus of Nazareth with the Holy Ghost and with power: who went about doing good, and healing all that were oppressed of the devil; for God was with him. And we are witnesses of all things which he did both in the land of the Jews, and in Jerusalem; whom they slew and hanged on a tree: him God raised up the third day, and showed him openly; not to all the people, but unto witnesses chosen before of God, even to us, who did eat and drink with him after he rose from the dead. And he commanded us to preach unto the people, and to testify that it is he which was ordained of God to be the Judge of quick and dead. To him give all the prophets

## Symbolic Statue of the City of Antioch

In the Vatican Gallery, Rome, Italy
Photograph by Anderson, Rome, Italy

THE CITY of Antioch was a free city of the Roman Empire and this fine statue of the city, the figure with the civic crown, holding in its hand stalks of wheat, treading its enemy underfoot, was symbolic of the wealth and power of the city. At Antioch the early disciples were first called Christians. It was a center of influence in the early church.

witness, that through his name whosoever believeth in him shall receive remission of sins."

## "THE HOLY GHOST FELL ON ALL"

While Peter yet spake these words, the Holy Ghost fell on all them which heard the word. And they of the circumcision which believed were astonished, as many as came with Peter, because that on the Gentiles also was poured out the gift of the Holy Ghost. For they heard them speak with tongues, and magnify God. Then answered Peter, "Can any man forbid water, that these should not be baptized, which have received the Holy Ghost as well as we?" And he commanded them to be baptized in the name of the Lord. Then prayed they him to tarry certain days.　　　　　　　　　　—Acts 10.

## "THEN HATH GOD ALSO TO THE GENTILES GRANTED REPENTANCE UNTO LIFE"

And the apostles and brethren that were in Judæa heard that the Gentiles had also received the word of God. And when Peter was come up to Jerusalem, they that were of the circumcision contended with him, saying, "Thou wentest in to men uncircumcised, and didst eat with them."

But Peter rehearsed the matter from the beginning, and expounded it by order unto them, saying, "I was in the city of Joppa praying: and in a trance I saw a vision, a certain vessel descend, as it had been a great sheet, let down from heaven by four corners; and it came even to me: upon the which when I had fastened mine eyes, I considered, and saw four-footed beasts of the earth, and wild beasts, and creeping things, and fowls of the air. And I heard a voice saying unto me, 'Arise, Peter; slay and eat.'

"But I said, 'Not so, Lord: for nothing common or unclean hath at any time entered into my mouth.'

"But the voice answered me again from heaven, 'What God hath cleansed, that call not thou common.'

"And this was done three times: and all were drawn up again into heaven. And, behold, immediately there were three men already come unto the house where I was, sent from Cæsarea unto me. And the Spirit bade me go with them, nothing doubting. Moreover these six brethren accompanied me, and we entered into the man's house: and he showed us how he had seen an angel in his house, which stood and said unto him, 'Send men to Joppa, and call for Simon, whose surname is Peter; who shall tell thee words, whereby thou and all thy house shall be saved.'

"And as I began to speak, the Holy Ghost fell on them, as on us at the beginning. Then remembered I the word of the Lord, how that he said, 'John indeed baptized with water; but ye shall be baptized with the Holy Ghost.' Forasmuch then as God gave them the like gift as he did unto us, who believed on the Lord Jesus Christ; what was I, that I could withstand God?"

When they heard these things, they held their peace, and glorified God, saying, "Then hath God also to the Gentiles granted repentance unto life."     — Acts 11:1–18.

## THE DISCIPLES WERE FIRST CALLED CHRISTIANS AT ANTIOCH

The disciples, traveling far and wide, made converts chiefly of the Jews wherever they went. Antioch became an important center of the new faith.

Now they which were scattered abroad upon the persecution that arose about Stephen traveled as far as Phœnicia, and Cyprus, and Antioch, preaching the word

THE CHURCH OF DOMINE QUO VADIS

Photograph by Anderson, Rome, Italy

THIS church, situated on the Appian Way
a short distance beyond the arch of Drusus,
is of interest, because of the legend that it
is built upon the spot of the meeting of
Christ and Peter during Neronian persecu-
tions.   The story is finely told in the novel
"Quo Vadis."

to none but unto the Jews only. And some of them were men of Cyprus and Cyrene, which, when they were come to Antioch, spake unto the Grecians, preaching the Lord Jesus. And the hand of the Lord was with them: and a great number believed, and turned unto the Lord.

Then tidings of these things came unto the ears of the church which was in Jerusalem: and they sent forth Barnabas, that he should go as far as Antioch. Who, when he came, and had seen the grace of God, was glad, and exhorted them all, that with purpose of heart they would cleave unto the Lord. For he was a good man, and full of the Holy Ghost and of faith: and much people was added unto the Lord. Then departed Barnabas to Tarsus, for to seek Saul: and when he had found him, he brought him unto Antioch. And it came to pass, that a whole year they assembled themselves with the church, and taught much people. And the disciples were called Christians first in Antioch. — Acts 11:19–26.

## The Christians of Antioch Send Relief to Their Brethren of Judæa

And in these days came prophets from Jerusalem unto Antioch. And there stood up one of them named Agabus, and signified by the Spirit that there should be great dearth throughout all the world: which came to pass in the days of Claudius Cæsar. Then the disciples, every man according to his ability, determined to send relief unto the brethren which dwelt in Judæa: which also they did, and sent it to the elders by the hands of Barnabas and Saul. — Acts 11:27–30.

## James Is Killed and Peter Imprisoned

The account of the seizing of Peter and his imprisonment is one of the vivid accounts of the early church, told with much detail. We even know that "Rhoda" was the name of the little maid who heard Peter knocking at the door after his release. Rhoda was so excited that she did not let Peter in, until she had told the others.

Now about that time Herod the king stretched forth his hands to vex certain of the church. And he killed James, the brother of John, with the sword. And because he saw it pleased the Jews, he proceeded further to take Peter also. (Then were the days of unleavened bread.) And when he had apprehended him, he put him in prison, and delivered him to four quaternions of soldiers to keep him; intending after Easter to bring him forth to the people. Peter therefore was kept in prison: but prayer was made without ceasing of the church unto God for him. And when Herod would have brought him forth, the same night Peter was sleeping between two soldiers, bound with two chains: and the keepers before the door kept the prison. And, behold, the angel of the LORD came upon him, and a light shined in the prison: and he smote Peter on the side, and raised him up, saying, "Arise up quickly." And his chains fell off from his hands.

And the angel said unto him, "Gird thyself, and bind on thy sandals." And so he did. And he saith unto him, "Cast thy garment about thee, and follow me."

And he went out, and followed him; and wist not that it was true which was done by the angel; but thought he saw a vision. When they were past the first and the second ward, they came unto the iron gate that leadeth unto the city; which opened to them of his own accord: and they went out, and passed on through one street; and forthwith the angel departed from him. And when Peter was come to himself, he said, "Now I know of a surety, that the LORD hath sent his angel, and hath delivered me out of the hand of Herod, and from all the expectation of the people of the Jews."

THIS great church of St. Peter's is the largest cathedral in the world. It faces a splendid square in the middle of which is an Egyptian obelisk, and great fountains send their columns of spray into the air. The semicircular colonnades on either side are very effective. Behind the church are the buildings of the Vatican, the residence of the Pope, beyond whose precincts he does not go. The church which is the Mecca of all those of the Catholic faith was founded by the Emperor Constantine over the reputed grave of Peter. The dome of the present church is the masterpiece of Michael Angelo. The church was completed in 1621 on the one thousand three hundreth anniversary of its foundation.

And when he had considered the thing, he came to the house of Mary, the mother of John, whose surname was Mark; where many were gathered together praying. And as Peter knocked at the door of the gate, a damsel came to hearken, named Rhoda. And when she knew Peter's voice, she opened not the gate for gladness, but ran in, and told how Peter stood before the gate. And they said unto her, "Thou art mad." But she constantly affirmed that it was even so. Then said they, "It is his angel." But Peter continued knocking: and when they had opened the door, and saw him, they were astonished. But he, beckoning unto them with the hand to hold their peace, declared unto them how the Lord had brought him out of the prison. And he said, "Go show these things unto James, and to the brethren." And he departed, and went into another place.

Now as soon as it was day, there was no small stir among the soldiers, what was become of Peter. And when Herod had sought for him, and found him not, he examined the keepers, and commanded that they should be put to death. And he went down from Judæa to Cæsarea, and there abode. — Acts 12:1-19.

## THE DEATH OF HEROD

Herod, the persecutor of the Christians, died a singular and terrible death, "but the Word of the Lord grew and multiplied."

And Herod was highly displeased with them of Tyre and Sidon: but they came with one accord to him, and, having made Blastus, the king's chamberlain, their friend, desired peace; because their country was nourished by the king's country. And upon a set day Herod, arrayed in royal apparel, sat upon his throne, and made an oration unto them. And the people gave a shout, saying, "It is the voice of a god, and not of a man." And immediately the angel of the Lord smote him, because he gave not God the glory: and he was eaten of worms, and gave up the ghost. But the word of God grew and multiplied. And Barnabas and Saul returned from Jerusalem, when they had fulfilled their ministry, and took with them John, whose surname was Mark. — Acts 12:20-25.

## NOTES ON EARLY DAYS OF THE CHURCH AS FOUND IN THE BOOK OF ACTS

**The former treatise.** The "treatise" is the Gospel of Luke, which is also dedicated to Theophilus.

**"His passion."** Literally, "after he had suffered."

**Restore the Kingdom of Israel.** The disciples could not lay aside the hope of a great Jewish empire as the Messiah's kingdom.

**Olivet.** Usually "the Mount of Olives."

**A Sabbath day's journey.** About a mile.

**Witnesses in Jerusalem, Judæa, Samaria, and to the uttermost parts of the earth.** The plan of Acts can be made from this passage. The writer follows the growth of the church from Jerusalem to Rome, in the geographical order here stated.

**Pentecost.** One of the three great feasts of the year, the others being the passover and the feast of the tabernacles, or booths. Pentecost is a Greek word, and means "the fiftieth," because it fell on the fiftieth day after the Passover Sabbath. In the Old Testament it is called the feast of the first fruits, or the feast of weeks.

**Ninth hour.** About three in the afternoon.

**I wot.** Old English for "know." "Wit" is from the same word.

**Heaven must receive.** Since "the times of restitution of all things" had not yet arrived, Jesus had been taken back to heaven. In the fulness of time he would return and set up his kingdom. Meanwhile, seated at God's right hand, "he ever liveth to make intercession" for us.

**In Solomon's porch.** When at the hour of prayer the people came to the temple, it was customary for the followers of Jesus to gather in that part of the temple called Solomon's porch.

**The Council, and all the Senate.** Senate, literally "the eldermen," which the word "senate" means. The gathering consisted of the

ROMAN FORUM

Photograph by Anderson, Rome, Italy

THIS is a part of the great Roman Forum
which now lies many feet below the modern
city. Here all the great characters of Roman history walked and talked.

sanhedrin with the influential men of Jerusalem. This new movement was considered an important matter.

**Gamaliel,** the teacher of Paul (Acts 22:3), the grandson of a great scholar, Hillel, and grandfather of another scholar, Gamaliel the Younger. He died eighteen years before the temple was destroyed and the Talmud says that when he died "the glory of the Law ceased." If in all things he was as wise and judicious as he showed himself here his reputation was rightly earned.

**Theudas and Judas of Galilee.** Leaders of revolt against the Romans, whose efforts came to naught. Both are mentioned in Josephus, a Jewish historian of the time, though what he says about Theudas is hard to reconcile with what Gamaliel is reported to have said.

**Grecians.** Greek-speaking Jews. The officers who distributed the charities of the church were charged with neglecting the poor who came from other countries.

**Serve tables.** The "tables" were counters from which the distribution of the funds was made to the needy. The great number of poor in the Jerusalem church was perhaps due to the experiment of a common fund.

**Synagogue of the Libertini.** Literally "freedmen" (libertini), probably families of Jews formerly made captive by the Romans and sold as slaves, but later freed. With other Jews from foreign parts they had built a synagogue. There were many synagogues in Jerusalem.

**Stephen's speech** is an attempt to show that God was ever leading Israel on toward higher truth, and Israel was ever rejecting God's message. He was not allowed to finish, or he would have shown them that the message of Jesus and their treatment of him was another instance of the same sort.

**Charran.** Old Testament, Haran.

**Samaria.** Already the broadening influence of Christ's kind treatment of the despised Samaritans was bearing fruit.

**Simon, which had . . . used sorcery.** From the Greek *Magos*, sorcerer; this man is known as Simon Magus. Later tradition said that he became a great enemy of the church.

**The way . . . unto Gaza, which is desert.** "Go by the desert road to Gaza." There was more than one road from Jerusalem to Gaza.

**Gaza,** an old Philistine town on the route to Egypt, important as a center of commerce and travel. In World War I it was for a long time the headquarters of the Allied army, and from there started the great drive which won Palestine.

**Ethiopia.** A general name for what is now Nubia and Abyssinia; the region of the upper Nile. At this time there was a kingdom in the northern part called Meroe, ruled by queens. These queens all had the title *Candace,* as Egyptian kings had the title Pharaoh.

**Esaias.** Old Testament, Isaiah.

**He was led as a sheep.** Quoted from Isaiah 53. The whole chapter is one of the clearest predictions of Christ in the Old Testament. It tells of the sufferings of the Messiah for the sins of us all.

**Azotus.** Ashdod, another city of old Philistia, farther north than Gaza.

**Lydda.** A town on the road from Jerusalem to Joppa.

**Saron.** Hebrew, Sharon. The name for the plain on which Lydda stood.

**Joppa.** The old seaport, still in use as the only port south of Mount Carmel. An important town in the first Christian century.

**Tabitha, Dorcas.** Both mean gazelle.

**Centurion of the band called Italian.** A centurion was, literally, the captain of a hundred. His name Cornelius was that of an honored family in Rome, and doubtless he was a Roman. A garrison of soldiers was kept at Cæsarea, up the coast, a day's journey or more from Joppa. The company of Cornelius was called Italian because it was first recruited in Italy. Cornelius was a Gentile who had been drawn to worship the God of Israel, but had not joined the Jewish church and did not keep the Jewish ceremonial law.

**Sixth hour.** About noon.

**Common or unclean.** The Jews ate the flesh of only certain animals, and these must be killed with proper ceremonial.

**An unlawful thing.** If Jews consorted with Gentiles they might be led to eat unclean food.

**On the Gentiles were poured out.** Thus God showed that Christianity was to go beyond the circle of the Jews.

**Speak with tongues.** In the story of Pentecost, Acts 2, this refers to foreign languages; in I Cor. 14, Paul describes speech unintelligible except by divine interpretation.

**Phenice.** Phœnicia, the region of Tyre and Sidon.

**Antioch.** About 16 miles from the sea, on the River Orontes, near the northeast corner of the Mediterranean. One of the great cities of the world of that time. It had long been the capital of the Syrian Empire and at this time was the residence of the Roman proconsul of Syria, the chief governor of that part of the Roman empire, including Palestine. It also became important in the church. As Jerusalem was the first center of Christian progress, so this became the second.

## QUESTIONS

Who wrote the Book of the Acts? For what purpose? Who was chosen to take the place of Judas? What happened on the day of Pentecost? What nationalities were represented? How many were converted? What man did Peter heal at the gate of The Temple? Before what ruler was Peter brought? What was the defense? What was the offense of Ananias and Sapphira? Which of the apostles were imprisoned? How were they released? How many deacons were chosen? Who was the first martyr? Who was a witness to his death? What sorcerer was baptized? What sin did he commit? Where did Philip go? Whom did he meet and convert?

Where was Peter living at this time? What did he do for Æneas? What woman did Peter bring to life? What good deeds did she do? What societies are named for her, and what is their work? Who sent his servants with a message to Peter? What was his office? What vision did Peter have? What did it lead him to do? Describe Peter's visit to Cæsarea. How far did the early disciples travel? To whom did they preach? Who went to Tarsus to find Saul? When were the early disciples first called Christians? Who was Agabus? Who was put to death by Herod? How was Peter released from prison? Who came to the door when Peter knocked? What was the fate of Herod?

## VALLEY OF GIANTS (REPHAIM)
*Photograph by Frances Jenkins Olcott*

The Bible tells that, in this Valley of Giants southwest of Jerusalem, the army of the Philistines spread themselves out and were defeated by King David. He burned their images that they left behind.

And today we see olive pickers in the Valley of Giants at breakfast after beating the olive trees so that ripe olives have showered down to the ground. Moses in old days commanded Israel, "When thou beatest thine olive tree, thou shalt not go over the boughs again. It shall be for the stranger, for the fatherless, and for the widow."

See how these Arab olive pickers eat from one dish in native fashion, illustrating the Saviour's words at the Last Supper, "He that dippeth his hand with me in the dish, the same shall betray me."

Read 2 Samuel 5:17-25, Volume 3:90-1; Deuteronomy 24:20, Volume 2:315; Matthew 26:23, page 207.